3 for 1^{00}

92

3 for 1^{00}

W. B. Goldsmith, Jr.

BASIC PROGRAMS FOR HOME FINANCIAL MANAGEMENT

A SPECTRUM BOOK

PRENTICE-HALL, INC., Englewood Cliffs, New Jersey 07632

Library of Congress Cataloging in Publication Data

GOLDSMITH, W. B.
    Basic programs for home financial management.

    "A Spectrum Book."
    1. Basic (Computer program language) 2. Finance,
Personal--Data processing. I. Title.
HF5548.5.B3G64   332.024'0028'5424   81-13970
                                  AACR2

ISBN 0-13-066522-3

ISBN 0-13-066514-2 (PBK.)

10 9 8 7 6 5 4 3 2 1

Editorial/production supervision and
interior design by Carol Smith
Part-opening art by Katrinka Armas
Manufacturing buyer: Cathie Lenard

This Spectrum Book is available to businesses
and organizations at a special discount when ordered
in large quantities. For information, contact
Prentice-Hall, Inc., General Book Marketing,
Special Sales Division, Englewood Cliffs, N.J. 07632.

PRENTICE-HALL INTERNATIONAL, INC., London
PRENTICE-HALL OF AUSTRALIA PTY. LIMITED, Sydney
PRENTICE-HALL OF CANADA, LTD., Toronto
PRENTICE-HALL OF INDIA PRIVATE LIMITED, New Delhi
PRENTICE-HALL OF JAPAN, Inc., Tokyo
PRENTICE-HALL OF SOUTHEAST ASIA PTE., LTD., Singapore
WHITEHALL BOOKS LIMITED, Wellington, New Zealand

CONTENTS

PREFACE

This is a book about using your personal computer. It provides a system of programs to help take some of the boredom out of running the household. The programs are ready to use: Type the BASIC instructions into your computer, and you will have a personal financial management system that will save you money today and for many tomorrows.

Each chapter includes a program description, a BASIC command listing, and a sample operation sequence. When we wander into the accounting arena, a down-to-earth description of various accounting terms and methods is included; so you'll find valuable information and develop an increased understanding of these terms even if you never type a line of code.

For those of you to whom the word "computer" conjures up an image of some large hairy monster, remember that even elephants can be eaten, a single bite at a time. Similarly, we develop a computer program a single byte at a time. Although our financial system is comprehensive, we'll build it step-by-step. At each stage, you'll find complete programs to make your life easier and prove that your computer is less than a monster and much more than an entertainment device.

Program flow and theory is described fully to help you modify each of the routines to fit your exact needs and desires. Once you have each program running, you will be able to change it when your financial situation changes. Your financial management system will be the integrated masterpiece that proves your mastery of the computer. Many of our routines are useful in a business office as well as in the home. You may also find the seeds of a new business idea in these pages.

Our personal financial management system covers four major areas: money management, credit control, major asset management, and investment factors. You can control the cash you spend, the loans you want, and the items you purchase with the first three. The investment programs will help you multiply your money.

A file-manager program is provided to streamline operations. Three appendixes round out our presentation. An indexed summary of the BASIC commands used in the routines includes an explanation of each instruction. A discussion of the hardware used to develop our financial management system concludes with recommendations for your personal computer complement. The mathematical derivations of the arithmetic functions used in the programs concludes our book.

You don't need previous programming experience or accounting skills to have a home computer financial management tool. Your computer and the ready-to-use programs will help you get more out of your hard-earned dollars, and keep more of those dollars in your bank account.

1
INTRODUCTION

Shortly after you mention your home computer, someone will ask, "But what do you do with a computer at home?" I have some smart answers to that, but the truth is I'd have a hard time without my personal computer. It solves electronics problems, prepares income tax statements for my clients, and keeps my personal finances organized. I have learned to depend on it because it has freed me of many repetitive tasks and allowed me to expand the scope of my personal and business activities. Its memory is more reliable than mine, and its typing is far more consistent and faster than mine. And, yes, I can play games with it. (And, I do! Everything is more fun with a computer.)

You've probably discovered the games, possibly through your children, and you may have begun to use your electronic assistant for some of the day-to-day jobs involved in running the household. You can do almost anything with your home computer--faster and more accurately. This book concentrates on personal finances. With these programs, you can let your personal computer handle some of the daily money management chores in your home.

The following pages describe a personal financial management system that you can implement. The programs included are a little like frozen dinner rolls that you must bake at home. When you want a program, just add a little of yourself to the program listings to get a finished product. You can type the BASIC commands without modification and use the routines as is, or you can modify and add to the programs if you require a fancier system. Whatever way, you'll have as complete a financial system as you want. In addition, you'll have expanded your personal horizons into some of the mysteries of computers and accounting.

There are thirty-three separate programs presented. Each includes a description of the accounting or mathematics behind the program, instructions for program operation, programming notes to help you modify the routing for your special needs, and a sample input and output, and the complete BASIC program listing. The programs are written in a

1

standard version of BASIC that should translate readily to
the dialect that your personal computer understands. No
fancy graphics, sound effects, or other hardware-dependent
features are included to confuse the issue. These are
straightforward dollars-and-cents programs. Of the thirty-
three, nine require a disk or minidisk storage capability;
the rest can run with a minimum system. (Some of the disk
routines can be altered to operate with a cassette tape
recorder while you wait for your disk drive to be delivered.)
The entire personal finance system (with its file manager)
fits on one side of a 5¼-inch minidiskette.

The programs are loosely grouped in four general
categories: money management, credit control, major asset
management, and investment factors. The final program in
the book is a file-manager routine that allows you to control the other programs with a few key strokes.

We open the money management section with a warmup
Checkbook Reconciliation routine that will help reconcile
your checkbook with the bank statement. Next, the Check-
Writer routine gives you the power to print checks on your
system. These two routines become part of the third program, Electronic Checkbook. The checkbook will handle all
of your checking transactions and build a data base that
will help your family budgeting and income tax preparation.
You can pull expense data from your checkbook with Bookkeeping Worksheet and obtain a budget or income tax deduction summary. The budgeting information is also used to
prepare a formal accounting statement by the Cash Flow
Analysis program. The cash flow statement can be handy
when you apply for a loan or restructure your investment
portfolio. The worksheet output is also used in the
Income Tax Estimator program to keep track of your tax
burden throughout the year and help prepare those pesky
quarterly estimated income tax forms. The final money
management program is Budget Analysis, which will aid your
family spending evaluation.

There are eight programs in the credit control section.
Credit Card Organizer will keep track of the plastic money
we all seem to carry, and prepare notices to the credit card
companies if something happens to any of the cards. Almost
every loan or credit application requires a personal statement of net worth; Net Worth Statement program will prepare
a professional quality statement for you. Auto Loan Analysis
will let you explore the options you have in selecting the
term, interest rate, and down-payment combinations for your
next automobile loan. Consumer Loan Analysis will tell you
the true annual percentage rate of interest on those "simple"
loans, and calculate the monthly payments before you sign
the dotted line. Next, Real Estate Loan Analysis will calculate the monthly payment, principal amount, total number
of payments, or interest rate for your mortgage. Real
Estate Loan Analysis will calculate the monthly payment,
principal amount, total number of payments, or interest
rate for your mortgage. Real Estate Loan Status will provide an estimate of the total interest paid during a year

2

and the year-end balance of a mortgage. The Loan Records routine is a disk program that will keep records of loan balances, payment dates, normal payment amount, and the interest rate. It serves as a bookkeeper, budget aid, and payment reminder. Finally, the Loan Payment program collects payment data on a month-by-month basis and reports the remaining balance and year-to-date interest paid on a trust-deed type loan. This is useful whether you are a borrower or lender.

The first program in the major asset management section is Auto Expense Records, a cost-and-maintenance record keeper for your automobile. If you've wondered about leasing instead of buying a car, boat, or airplane, Lease/Buy will provide an economic analysis of the decision for you. When you're deciding any course of action that depends on more than the financial aspects, you can mimic the large corporations and conduct a tradeoff study: Trade Study really lets you compare apples and oranges! Or, you may have decided to buy, but want another economic opinion: Life-Cycle-Costing borrows another page from the method guides of government and industry to let you evaluate the cost of a car, refrigerator, or typewriter over its entire useful life. Rounding out the major asset management section is a disk program called Home Insurance Inventory that will let you keep an electronic inventory of your possessions.

The twelve programs in the investment factors section will aid your search for wise investments. The first two, Savings Account Analysis and Savings Account Records, provide a key to the best savings account return and let you keep track of your savings. The Retirement Fund program is an annuity calculator that will tell you how much you must invest now to reap the retirement benefit you want later. If you're thinking of entering the bond market, the next routine may be just your cup of tea: Bond Investment Analysis can help unsnarl the confusing market terms and provide an idea of the true return you can expect from corporate bonds. The Return on Investment program provides a choice of the operator's or investor's methods of calculating the actual expected return on a limited partnership or real estate opportunity. Net Present Value provides a discounted cash flow analysis of a prospective venture and will evaluate the prospect against a predetermined effective yield. Stock Analysis is a homegrown tool for comparing factors of common stocks. You can evaluate stocks in terms of percentage return on investment, price/earnings ratios, and price volatility. Ten-Day Average mechanizes a favorite management tool of commodity and options investors. You may want to enter this exciting market arena when your computer can help you track as many commodities as you wish. If you subscribe to the cyclic theories of the market, Stock Plotter is for you. It will give a graphic representation of the high and low market transactions for a stock for any selected period. Stock Records is an electronic bookkeeping aid for your stock portfolio. You can enter dividend payments, buy and sell transactions, and get an annual summary that will keep your income tax problems in check. If your investment preferences run to real estate, the last two investment programs should interest you. The Rental Unit routine will collect your annual income and expense details, calculate depreciation, and provide a statement of profit or loss for your rental investment. Rental Bookkeeping is a disk-based bookkeeping system for multiple units. You can enter data all through the year and use the summary as an input sheet for the Rental Unit annual statement.

Since the preceding descriptions are too brief to present all of the features of the routines, read through the program descriptions before you decide on a favorite. (You may find just what you've been seeking with a different name than you expected.) Although each chapter stands alone, some program descriptions refer to information in a previous chapter.

Once you've selected a program, type the BASIC statements into your computer's keyboard ("keypunch" is the computerese term for that task), and you're ready to run. There may be some minor translations needed to accommodate your version of BASIC, but that should be fairly simple unless you've got a weird machine. By the time you have that first program running, you'll feel like a programming veteran. By the time you've worked with a few more, you'll have a useful financial management system tailored to your specific needs. It will serve you for years, and you can be proud of your part in developing it.

Your computer and the programs presented in this book are tools. The routines are intended to give you more than just a workable system of programs: I hope to give you ideas for modification and expansion of your computer capability. The programs illustrate ways to computerize decision-making. The stock market routines, for example, are not presented as the best or only way to pick an investment. Each of the programs was selected to implement the methods popular with acquaintances who are active in the stock market. Many of the other investment analysis routines are set up to compare alternatives. You may want to compare something besides investments with these, and that's a good example of your potential creativity showing through. Follow that urge, and you'll have as much fun modifying these routines as I had putting them together in the first place. Computers can be fun! Enjoy yours!

The best reference to use in adapting these programs to your system is the BASIC manual or guide that came with your computer. The BASIC functions used throughout are summarized in Appendix A. A quick comparison of Appendix A with your BASIC manual will reveal how little modification is necessary to get your financial management system working.

Appendix B is a short discussion of the hardware used to prepare the programs. You don't need much fancy equipment to use the programs; each will fit into the standard

program memory that comes with most popular home computers. A hard-copy printer is the only addition to a
standard off-the-shelf computer that you might find essen-
tial.

Appendix C should appeal to you mathematics wizards.
Derivations of all the equations used to finagle our
financial facts are included. (Let the children play with
the algebra while you work at the keyboard.)

2
PROGRAM CONSTRUCTION

There are many ways to design computer programs. (And, I'd rather argue religion or politics than debate the merits of the various computer program design philosophies.) Let's say that any way that results in a useful program is a good one. Some techniques produce programs that run faster than others, and some save program memory space. The speed revisions can cut whole seconds from a program run time. Personally, I can't get too excited about a speedup from 38 seconds to 37 seconds, particularly when the manual task that the computer is performing took 3 hours. Most of our financial programs run faster than the operator can keypunch data or read the output. Memory-saving techniques are all right, but few of our financial programs will tax the memory capacity of the average home computer. It's been my experience that special memory-saving programming efforts take up a lot of programmer time for a minimal (5 or 10 percent) saving. The method I have used with the programs in this book is neither the most memory efficient nor the most speed efficient, but it works.

I prefer programs that are readily modified and easy to read. One value in a program is its capability to be altered to adapt to a changing need. Also, many of the programs that I prepare end up in a magazine or book (like this one), so readability is crucial to me. Generally, my programs start at a beginning and plow through to the end. (Some computer purists call this "straight-line" programming; others call it a more colorful--but quite unprintable!--waste of computer capability.) I try to use subroutines only to pick up repeating tasks that are long or apt to be modified often.

PROGRAM DESIGN

In preparing programs, I follow some standard steps. You may wish to use these six steps as a starting point for development of your own personal programming philosophy.

6

IDEA OR NEED The more carefully we detail the objective of our program, the easier program preparation will be. What do we want the program to do? Is there a standard output format that we wish? Since most of my programs have an application in the accounting field, my first step is to decide on the output format. When I know the desired result, I can work backward to the start and define the input and arithmetic needed. A handwritten draft of the output desired is a big help at this stage. As you might guess, I also write the output part of the program first to see what information the routine will need to develop.

FLOW CHART If the program will jump around a bit, either to use subroutines or follow operator selections, a flow chart may be helpful. Usually, the flow chart is very informal ("written on the backs of used envelopes") and is a general guide to help outline my thinking. The eventual program flow may not resemble the flow chart too closely, but the chart serves its purpose by getting us to the final program code. A few routines in our personal finance system have flow charts, proving that flow charts are sometimes handy tools to document computer programs. Since I don't like to draw flow charts (and haven't taught my computer to do that job yet), I like to minimize this as a formal step.

MATHEMATICS Occasionally, a special mathematical formula or routine is needed. It goes into the program notes to insure that I understand the formula well enough to write a program around it. A few programs in this book include mathematical manipulation that is complex enough to deserve special attention, and we'll address these as we encounter them.

PRELIMINARY PROGRAM The first-draft BASIC program is working skeleton. I use it to check the logic flow and test the arithmetic routines. It also lets me get my line-numbering scheme started.

VALIDATION With the first flush of code in the computer, it's time to start running the routine. Somehow, even a program that has been designed perfectly doesn't always work perfectly the first time. "Debugging" is the computerese term for the validation step. (A friend claims that there are no bugs in programs, just "features." Some features prove that programmers are not infallible.) Validation is a trial-and-error process. Whenever possible, I attempt to debug short pieces of a program by themselves. When the short chunks all work, you're only a few steps away from having the entire program working. Plan to debug any program you keypunch; you'll need to do a little debugging when you enter your version of our personal financial management system. It's an educational process--and when you plan for it, it can provide all the fun of a mystery, with you as the detective.

FINISHED CODE With the skeleton working, it's time to add the comment statements and my embellishments (in computerese, the "bells and whistles") that make the routine more fun to run. It's also time to add routines to trap operator errors and simplify the input tasks. As you go along, you should make periodic recordings of your program to keep a power outage or strange BASIC error from wiping out your efforts. With the finished code, you can erase the interim versions and record (at least) two copies of the final version. Put one copy--your backup--in a safe place. It should be far enough away from your computer that any stray magnetic field (from a passing flying saucer, for example) that erases your prime copy from tape or disk won't affect your backup.

COMMENTS

Within the BASIC code, I like to include comments (BASIC calls these "REMARKS") that explain what a particular piece of code is doing. These comments seem unnecessary at the time you are keypunching your program, but 6 months later they can be invaluable when you need to modify the routine. (I have found that with no effort at all I can completely forget a program structure in 6 weeks!) The programs that follow are commented, but not as heavily as I usually like. With the opportunity for some "plain English" text along with the BASIC, I left many comments out to keep each listing as uncluttered as possible. You may wish to add comments as you put these programs into your personal library. Sometimes, a keyword or two will solve the problem; other routines may need a line or two of comment. It's your program; add the comments that will help you!

OPERATOR MESSAGES

It's embarrassing to discover you've forgotten how to run a program you've prepared. (I know, because it has happened to me more than once!) Now, I try to structure the entry-prompting messages so that the slowest witted chowderhead I can imagine (me) can successfully breeze through it on a bad day. It costs only a few memory cells to include some extra words in the operator messages, but these extra words can smooth the way when you are in a hurry. Now and then, the whole structure of a data input sequence can invite operator error. (For example, requesting the entry of three or four pieces of information with one question can lead to operator confusion. Separate questions for each data item take a little more memory, but allow the operator to make correct entries.) When an input sequence is confusing, it's worth the time to rewrite it.

I've also tried to standardize my input messages from program to program. If all input sequences are similar, the user can make a habit of a pattern of entry that will avoid many erroneous entries. You also may wish to include

8

some data-review stages now and then to provide a graceful recovery from keypunch-data entry errors. Real frustration is making an error on the forty-ninth entry and finding that you must start the program again to get a successful output.

CONFIGURATION MANAGEMENT

One problem you may encounter when customizing programs is the many different versions of the same routine that seem to breed on your diskettes. There is an unwritten law of computer usage that governs your choice of the wrong version. (And the famous "Murphy's law" dictates that the whole error pattern will happen at the worst possible time.) You can defeat this error syndrome by keeping a modification status record in the program. Use the latest change date, a letter, or numbers. You can keep this record in a PRINT statement so that it is displayed when the program runs, in a REMARK that is only visible when you inspect the listing, or on a label pasted to the tape cassette or diskette envelope. I use a two-digit code in a REMARK statement in the program. The first digit tells me which major revision I have, and the second number identifies a minor modification. ("Major" and "minor" are pretty loosely defined in my system.)

When you wish to keep multiple versions alive, some other technique may serve you better. I modify many programs for the specific needs of a client, and have many versions of each lurking somewhere on a diskette. To keep out of trouble, I put the client name or business name in a REMARK statement in the program instead of a version number. (I also try to assign a diskette to each client requiring more than one or two unique program versions.)

IMPLEMENTATION

Now that I've had my chance to preach about computer program design and construction, I'll admit that there are some inconsistencies in the programs shared in this book. Many routines use different methods of accomplishing a similar task. I did this to provide some variety of example. When you find a particular method that is comfortable, stick with it. Use the one you like in all similar programs. You'll gain twice by doing this. First, you may be able to save some keypunch time by modifying one program into another. If your computer has a BASIC editor with line renumbering, automatic statement duplication, and substitution of phrases, you can have your second program by editing the first. The second advantage to using similar routines in all of your programs is the ease with which you can modify any one. By configuring the similar codes into subroutines, you may be able to achieve a true modular BASIC programming system. To invent a new program, just assemble the subroutines into a calling order. You could produce instant code.

Of course, you don't need to do any program designing to have a diskette full of financial programs. They're all here ready for you to use and enjoy.

I
MONEY MANAGEMENT

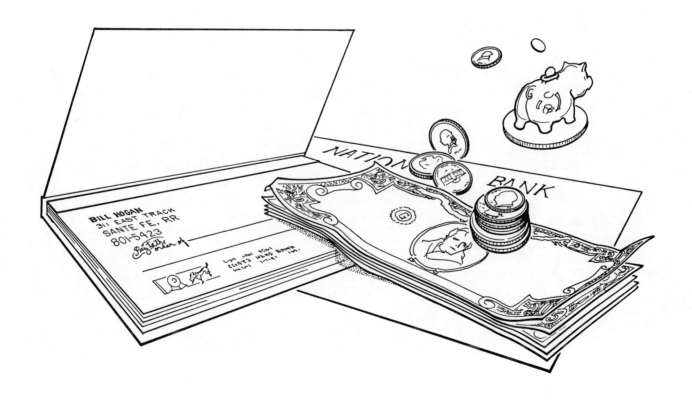

3
CHECKBOOK RECONCILIATION.

The first building block in our personal financial management system is a routine to help in the monthly task of reconciling the bank statement and our checkbook. The task itself is fairly simple. As a first step in our system, it's ideal. We can prepare a program that will be quick to keypunch, easy to validate, and useful.

BACKGROUND

Reconciliation is one of those necessary tasks that lends itself well to computer implementation. (I know some folks that just ignore it and take the bank's word for the checking-account balance.) Since you need to perform this chore every month for each checking account, the program will save you some time.

The whole idea behind reconciliation is a double-check of your version of your checking account balance with the bank's. Because you are writing checks and making deposits on a continuous basis, and the bank is clearing checks and deposits on a later time schedule, balances aren't always equal. You know what the balance in your account should be--if all the checks you've written and all the deposits you've made were to clear the bank. The bank knows what your account balance is--if you haven't issued a check or made a deposit since they closed the books on your monthly activity.

The problem is to put both statements (yours and the bank's) on the same basis. There are a number of acceptable ways of managing this. We're going to use the following:

Start with the checkbook balance, and add back the checks the bank hasn't seen. Subtract the deposits the bank hasn't cleared. Subtract bank charges that haven't been entered in your checkbook. The result is comparable to the bank statement and should agree with the bank bal-

13

ance. If it does, everything is rosy. If not, there is an error that must be found.

By reconciling each month, we put a time limit on the error—it must have happened between the most recent reconciliation and now. The amount of the disagreement will give us a valuable clue to the source of the error. If there is a check entered with the same amount as the difference, that check may have cleared or failed to clear while we recorded it incorrectly in the reconciliation. If there is a difference in one digit position (dollars, dimes, or pennies, for example), the error may be a simple addition or subtraction mistake in the checkbook. Because the error location requires some creative thinking, we're not going to address checkbook-error diagnosis in this program. (Later, when our entire system is on-line, we won't need to address the diagnostics. Any error will be a failure to indicate the clearing of a check, deposit, or bank charge—or an error at the bank.) Incidentally, a common reconciliation problem is caused by forgetting to enter the bank charges from _last_ _month_ after the reconciliation is complete. I know you won't do that often, but I have.

Our program goal is to do the proper arithmetic to determine whether our checkbook balance agrees with the bank's, and then to print a statement of reconciliation showing the agreement or error. No complicated mathematics, and the program isn't complex enough to justify a flow chart. An outline of the major subtasks includes:

Collect identification information.

Collect checking-account data.

Perform the reconciliation arithmetic.

Decide whether the balances agree.

Print the statement.

PROGRAMMING NOTES

Let's take a close look at the program listing before we discuss program operation. We'll go through it line by line to make sure there are no nasty surprises at keypunch time.

Line 10 through 40 are the header and configuration data. This is the spot for you to implement your favorite title block and configuration management scheme. The REM in each statement is short for REMARKS and tells the computer that these are not operating statements, but comments. Other REMs are used for titles of program segments (lines 100, 200, 300, 1300, and 1400). LINE = 0 in line 50 is a command to the BASIC interpreter to defeat an automatic carriage return/line feed sequence and let this program have complete control of the printing format. DIGITS=2 in line 60 instructs the computer to display all

14

numbers with two digits following the decimal point. Since all of our numerical entries are dollars and cents, this will put the numbers in a format that is familiar.

I decided to use a matrix variable for some of the check register information. Character string variable C$ (x,y) will store the check number in C$ (1,y), the payee in C$ (2,y), and the date of the check in (3,y). Since my version of BASIC automatically allocates a 10 by 10 matrix to variables like this, line 110 provides a DIMensioning command to limit the memory allocated. We're only using three columns of data, so we'll save the memory that might be assigned to the remaining seven. I seldom have as many as 10 checks outstanding at month end, so the remaining variables can be allocated 10 slots of memory. If you will need to store data on more than 10 checks at month end, DIMension all of the variables for the appropriate number. In addition to C$(x,y), you'll need to address C(x) for the check amount, D$(x) for the date of deposits or bank charges, and D(x) for the amount of deposits or bank charges. Lines 120 and 130 insure that variables C and D (which will be used to total outstanding checks and deposits) are set to zero when we start.

Two functions are defined in statements 210 and 220. These functions calculate numbers that will be used during the printing sequence to line up all of the decimal points. I chose to use the functions to save some keypunch in the print routine. We'll discuss this in a little more detail later.

Lines 300 through 350 collect the statement heading data. If this program will be used only for one checking account, you can omit the INPUT statements (except for the current date) and assign the variables to your name, address, and checking account number. For example:

    310 LET A$(1)="MY NAME"

    320 LET A$(2)="MY STREET ADDRESS"

The real business of collecting the checking-account data starts in line 1000. Lines 1010 and 1020 handle the input of the bank and checkbook balances. The PRINT in line 1030 is added to help keep the display terminal neat during the input sequence. The sequence from lines 1040 through 1120 requests the operator to enter the check number, payee, date, and amount of checks not cleared by the bank. Line 1110 totals the amounts of those uncleared items. We'll use this total later. If you typically have more than 10 checks outstanding, you'll want to change FOR X=1 TO 10 of line 1050 to reflect the total number you expect. Always put a higher number than you expect in the command; the statement of line 1070 will terminate the input sequence any time you do not enter a check number. Actually, there are two commands in line 1070. The colon following THEN X=10 is a separator. Because the first statement on the line is an IF..., the second statement will not be executed unless

15

the IF condition is satisfied. (Some BASICs will execute the second statement under all conditions, so if yours is one of these, you'll need to add a second IF...and put GOTO 1120 in that new statement.

Lines 1140 through 1200 echo the uncleared-check information-gathering sequence for deposits and bank charges. Deposits and bank charges are collected in the same routine because they are both subtracted from the checkbook balance to reconcile it. Most of the comments applicable to the earlier input sequence are also pertinent here. The major difference in the two routines is that we don't have a payee or check number for the deposits/charges entries. Since we're only reconciling the statement, we don't care whether an item is a deposit or a bank charge. It is treated the same in either case.

The arithmetic manipulation of reconciliation is contained in line 1310. The formula produces an adjusted checking account balance (B) by adding the check total (C) and subtracting the deposit/charge total (D) from the indicated checking account balance, which is B(2). Line 1320 determines that the adjusted checking account balance is or is not equal to the bank statement balance. If the two match, program flow continues on to line 1330, and you'll see the *** CONGRATULATIONS *** message at your terminal. Should there be a mismatch, program operation jumps to line 1370, and you are alerted that the reconciliation attempt has discovered an error.

Line 1400 starts the printing section of our program. The initial INPUT of line 1420 allows for output-device selection. My computer has the capability for eight output "ports", numbered from 0 to 7. If I inadvertently hit an input key twice, I don't want the computer to stumble on an impossible output selection, so line 1430 checks to see if the port selection is in the right range. This statement is an "Operator-Error Trapping" routine. We'll use more of these in other programs. You may wish to add some that I didn't think of.

Line 1500 starts the actual output of the reconciliation statement to the printer. The first PRINT #P commands are used to produce line feeds to provide an upper margin for the final document. The commands in lines 1530 through 1570 print the letterhead data on the form. The involved TAB functions center each line on the page. If you'll only use this for your own account, you may wish to change the letterhead statements to print your name and address directly. A routine like this will do it:

```
1530 PRINT #P,TAB(36); "MY NAME"

1540 PRINT #P,TAB(31); "MY STREET ADDRESS"

1550 PRINT #P,TAB(32); "CITY, STATE  ZIP"
```

The TABs are all calculated by subtracting the letter count in the message from the column width of the printer (in the example, the printer width is 80 columns), and dividing the result by 2. You can do the same thing in line 1600 to simplify the printing of the checking-account number. The date is printed by line 1620, and it will probably need to use an input variable and calculated centering TAB. (The TAB mimics the tabulator function of a standard typewriter by spacing a preset number of columns before beginning printing.)

In line 1710, we use the FNA function that was defined earlier. The purpose of the two functions is to line up the right margin of the numbers. (Since all of the numerics will be printed with two digits following the decimal point, this will line up the decimals in conventional accounting format.) The defined functions are keypunch shortcuts. Without the functions predefined, the TAB of line 1710 would look like:

    1710 PRINT #P, TAB((70-LEN(STR$(B(2))))-2); ...

instead of:

    1710 PRINT #P, TAB((FNA(B(2)))-2); ...

The listing of checks not yet cleared is handled by the FOR...NEXT loop of lines 1760 through 1820. If you've increased the maximum number of checks from 10 to a larger number, change the FOR X=1 TO 10 in line 1760 accordingly. Line 1770 cuts the printing short when a check without check number is detected. Mimic any modification you made to line 1070 here in 1770.

Lines 1880 through 1920 handle the printing of the deposits and charges not cleared. Again, you should echo any changes you made to lines 1140 through 1200 here. Lines 1930 through 2020 clean up all the sheet totals and complete the format.

Line 2030 issues a form-feed command to the system printer. My computer uses decimal representation for the CHR$ function; if yours likes hexadecimal (number base 16), send a hexadecimal "C" for the form feed.

The question in line 2050 will allow you to get another copy of the identical statement printed (with another choice of output port), while line 2070 permits a restart of the whole program.

The PRINT in line 2090 is included for the operator. Occasionally, I like to have someone say something pleasant to me--even if the "someone" is my computer. The END statement isn't required by all BASICs, but let's include it anyway. When we get into the file-manager routine, we'll want to change this to a different command. By including the END now, we'll know where to go to make the change.

OPERATING NOTES

The sample input/output illustrates just how easy this program is to run. You may enter a two-line name by separating the two elements with a comma. The computer will print the lines correctly. Two variables are also used for the CITY,

17

STATE ZIP entry, so you can enter the city, then a comma, then the state, and the ZIP code. This should match your established typing habit pattern. The one potential problem depends on your habit of typing dates: You must enter the date information without a comma. If you normally type "day month year" (for example, 23 September 1845), you'll have no trouble. If you normally type "month day, year" (for example, September 23, 1845), the comma will be a problem. A comma is used to terminate an entry in BASIC language, so the only date information input to the computer will be the month and day. Since this checkbook reconciliation is for your own use, the problem isn't too serious. If it really bugs you, add another variable to the date input and output commands to handle the part after the comma.

You'll notice that the program listing includes some upper-and lower-case messages, while the sample input is upper-case only. My video terminal and system printer handle both upper-and lower-case characters; my alternate terminal (an old printing terminal) is upper-case only. The terminal prints the upper-case equivalent of any lower-case letter sent to it. You can use all capitals if you like, and it won't affect anything but the appearance. I have spent so much time working with a capitals-only device that I like the change of pace. In all of our samples, operator input is underlined to distinguish it from computer prompting messages.

SAMPLE RUN

```
READY
# RUN
NAME? MIKE LIANT
STREET ADDRESS? 123 ANY STREET
CITY, STATE ZIP? UTOPIA, CALIFORNIA 99999
CHECKING ACCOUNT NUMBER? 123-456-789/0
TODAY'S DATE (DAY MONTH YEAR)? 31 JANUARY 1984
BALANCE PER BANK STATEMENT? 1001.21
BALANCE PER CHECKBOOK? 999.01

ENTER CHECKS NOT CLEARED BY BANK.
CHECK NUMBER? 101
PAYEE? MIAK KOUNTANT
DATE? 1/2/84
AMOUNT? 20.20
CHECK NUMBER? 104
PAYEE? CORNER GROCERY
DATE? 1/4/84
AMOUNT? 101.99
CHECK NUMBER? 108
PAYEE? DR. HEALER
DATE? 1/6/84
AMOUNT? 1000
CHECK NUMBER? 121
PAYEE? CANDY STORE
DATE? 28 JAN
AMOUNT? 1.01
CHECK NUMBER?

ENTER DEPOSITS NOT RECORDED AND BANK CHARGES.
DATE OF DEPOSIT/CHARGE? 1/3/84
AMOUNT OF DEPOSIT/CHARGE? 23
DATE OF DEPOSIT/CHARGE? 1/5/84
AMOUNT OF DEPOSIT/CHARGE? 1000
DATE OF DEPOSIT/CHARGE? 1/21
AMOUNT OF DEPOSIT/CHARGE? 98
DATE OF DEPOSIT/CHARGE?

*** CONGRATULATIONS ***
YOUR CHECKBOOK BALANCE RECONCILES WITH THE BANK STATEMENT.

WHAT OUTPUT PORT DO YOU WISH TO USE? 2

ANOTHER COPY? NO
ANOTHER RECONCILIATION? NO
THANK YOU.

READY
#
```

19

MIKE LIANT
123 ANY STREET
UTOPIA, CALIFORNIA 99999

CHECKBOOK RECONCILIATION
CHECKING ACCOUNT NUMBER 123-456-789/0

31 JANUARY 1984

BALANCE PER CHECK REGISTER $ 999.01

ADD CHECKS NOT CLEARED.

DATE	CHECK NR	PAYEE	AMOUNT
1/2/84	101	MIAK KOUNTANT	20.20
1/4/84	104	CORNER GROCERY	101.99
1/6/84	108	DR. HEALER	1000.00
28 JAN	121	CANDY STORE	1.01

TOTAL   + 1123.20

LESS DEPOSITS NOT CREDITED AND BANK CHARGES.

DATE	AMOUNT
1/3/84	23.00
1/5/84	1000.00
1/21	98.00

TOTAL   − 1121.00

TOTAL PER CHECK REGISTER $ 1001.21
                                                            ==========

BALANCE PER BANK STATEMENT $ 1001.21
                                                            ==========

```
0010 REM *********************************
0020 REM *    CHECKBOOK RECONCILIATION    *
0030 REM *********************************
0040 REM ********* VERSION 10 **********
0050 LINE= 0
0060 DIGITS= 2
0100 REM *** DIMENSION THE VARIABLES ****
0110 DIM C$(3,10)
0120  C=0
0130  D=0
0200 REM ****** DEFINE FUNCTIONS ********
0210 DEF FNA(X)=70-LEN(STR$(X))
0220 DEF FNB(X)=60-LEN(STR$(X))
0300 REM **** COLLECT HEADING INFO ******
0310 INPUT "Name",A$(1),A$(2)
0320 INPUT "Street Address",A$(3)
0330 INPUT "City, State ZIP",A$(4),A$(5)
0340 INPUT "Checking Account Number",A$(6)
0350 INPUT "Today's Date (Day Month Year)",A$(7)
1000 REM ** INPUT CHECKING ACCOUNT DATA *
1010 INPUT "Balance per Bank Statement",B(1)
1020 INPUT "Balance per Checkbook",B(2)
1030 PRINT
1040 PRINT "Enter checks not cleared by bank."
1050 FOR X=1 TO 10
1060 INPUT "Check Number",C$(1,X)
1070 IF C$(1,X)="" THEN X=10: GOTO 1120
1080 INPUT "Payee",C$(2,X)
1090 INPUT "Date",C$(3,X)
1100 INPUT "Amount",C(X)
1110  C=C+C(X)
1120 NEXT X
1130 PRINT
1140 PRINT "Enter deposits not recorded and bank charges."
1150 FOR X=1 TO 10
1160 INPUT "Date of Deposit/Charge",D$(X)
1170 IF D$(X)="" THEN X=10: GOTO 1200
1180 INPUT "Amount of Deposit/Charge",D(X)
1190  D=D+D(X)
1200 NEXT X
1210 PRINT
1300 REM *** RECONCILE THE BALANCE *****
1310  B=B(2)+C-D
1320 IF B(1)<>B THEN 1370
1330 PRINT "*** CONGRATULATIONS ***"
1340 PRINT "Your checkbook balance reconciles with the bank statement."
1350 PRINT
1360 GOTO 1400
1370 PRINT "******** OOPS! ********"
1380 PRINT "The bank report does not agree with your check register."
1400 REM ** PRINT THE RECONCILIATION ***
1410 PRINT
```

```
1420 INPUT "What output port do you wish to use",P
1430 IF P>7 PRINT"INVALID SELECTION";GOTO 1420
1500 PRINT #P
1510 PRINT #P
1520 PRINT #P
1530 PRINT #P,TAB((80-LEN(A$(1)))/2);A$(1)
1540 IF A$(2)="" THEN 1560
1550 PRINT #P,TAB((80-LEN(A$(2)))/2);A$(2)
1560 PRINT #P,TAB((80-LEN(A$(3)))/2);A$(3)
1570 PRINT #P,TAB((78-LEN(A$(4)+A$(5)))/2);A$(4);", ";A$(5)
1580 PRINT #P
1590 PRINT #P,TAB(28);"CHECKBOOK RECONCILIATION"
1600 PRINT #P,TAB((56-LEN(A$(6)))/2);"Checking Account Number ";A$(6)
1610 PRINT #P
1620 PRINT #P,TAB((80-LEN(A$(7)))/2);A$(7)
1630 PRINT #P
1640 PRINT #P
1700 PRINT #P,"BALANCE PER CHECK REGISTER";
1710 PRINT #P,TAB((FNA(B(2)))-2);"$ ";B(2)
1720 PRINT #P
1730 PRINT #P,"Add checks not cleared."
1735 PRINT #P
1740 PRINT #P,"Date    Check Nr           Payee";TAB(55);"Amount"
1750 PRINT #P
1760 FOR X=1 TO 10
1770 IF C$(1,X)="" THEN X=10: GOTO 1820
1780 PRINT #P,C$(3,X);
1790 PRINT #P,TAB(8);C$(1,X);
1800 PRINT #P,TAB(25);C$(2,X);
1810 PRINT #P,TAB(FNB(C(X)));C(X)
1820 NEXT X
1830 PRINT #P,TAB(50);"----------"
1840 PRINT #P,"Total";TAB((FNA(C))-2);"+ ";C
1850 PRINT #P
1860 PRINT #P,"Less deposits not credited and bank charges."
1865 PRINT #P
1870 PRINT #P,"Date";TAB(55);"Amount"
1875 PRINT #P
1880 FOR X=1 TO 10
1890 IF D$(X)="" THEN X=10: GOTO 1920
1900 PRINT #P,D$(X);
1910 PRINT #P,TAB(FNB(D(X)));D(X)
1920 NEXT X
1930 PRINT #P,TAB(50);"----------"
1940 PRINT #P,"Total";TAB((FNA(D))-2);"- ";D
1950 PRINT #P,TAB(60);"----------"
1960 PRINT #P,"TOTAL PER CHECK REGISTER";
1970 PRINT #P,TAB((FNA(B))-2);"$ ";B
1980 PRINT #P,TAB(60);"=========="
1990 PRINT #P
2000 PRINT #P,"BALANCE PER BANK STATEMENT";
2010 PRINT #P,TAB((FNA(B(1)))-2);"$ ";B(1)
```

```
2020 PRINT #P,TAB(60);"=========="
2030 PRINT #P,CHR$(12)
2040 PRINT
2050 INPUT "Another copy",Z$
2060 IF LEFT$(Z$,1)="Y" THEN 1400
2070 INPUT "Another reconciliation",Z$
2080 IF LEFT$(Z$,1)="Y" THEN 100
2090 PRINT "Thank you."
2100 END
```

4
CHECK-WRITER

How many checks do you write in a year? Are they all neat and legible? I write a lot of checks, and few are as readable as I'd like. Our home computers can write these money orders for us. (If you're in the habit of carrying your checkbook, you'll either have to change the habit or start towing a wagon with your personal computer. I recommend changing the habit.) Most of my checks are written at home, so I seldom carry a checkbook. With the whole process kept at my desk, I can keep my check-writing organized, relieve my worry that I might lose the checkbook, and cut down on impulse buying. All three advantages help my peace of mind, and the reduction in impulse buying helps my budget.

This is the second building block in our personal financial system. It's a short program that can be up and running in an easy evening of enjoyable keypunching and validation.

PROGRAMMING NOTES

The program listing should look familiar to you; a lot of it is identical to Checkbook Reconciliation. Since some of the programming notes would repeat those of the previous program, we'll concentrate on the different code.

Lines 10 through 60 are the same as the prior program (except for the name, of course). The sequences in lines 300 through 440 collect the identifying data of the account holder and bank. Since this is a personal program, you can make these inputs into a definition and reduce operator activity. Move the current date question from line 350 to 560, and define all the rest of the A\$(n) and B\$(n) variables with LET statements.

Lines 500 through 550 gather the data for the check. If you've altered the earlier input sequences, these questions will be the only ones the operator need see. Lines 1400 through 1430 will also look familiar. This output-port-selection routine will appear in many of our programs (with and without the error trap).

The real job of printing the check is covered in lines 1500 through 1700. The routine provides a complete check whether you use plain paper (as in the sample) or a commercial blank. A number of commercial firms offer blank checks in a continuous form style that will fit your computer's printer. Your bank will be happier if you use one of the commercial forms, since the supplier will print the account number in the special magnetic ink that the bank's sorting machinery can read. The TABs and spaces in the printing sequence are compatible with most of the commercial blanks, but plan on making an adjustment or two when you get your initial supply.

Line 1710 issues a form-feed command to the printer to set up for the next check. Lines 2000 through 2020 complete the program.

OPERATING NOTES

As you can see from the sample run, Check Writer is an operator's dream. If you include all your personal and bank information in the program definition section, there are just five entries per check. As before, be cautious about using commas in the date-entry field. Your checks are about to get that professional computer look!

SAMPLE INPUT

```
READY
# RUN
NAME? MIKE LIANT
STREET ADDRESS? 123 ANY STREET
CITY, STATE ZIP? UTOPIA, CALIFORNIA 99999
CHECKING ACCOUNT NUMBER? 123-456-789/0
TODAY'S DATE? 2 FEBRUARY 1984

NAME OF BANK? SUMMALESSA BANQUE
NAME OF BRANCH? NUMBER 110
STREET ADDRESS? 110 EASY STREET
CITY, STATE ZIP? UTOPIA, CA 99998

CHECK NUMBER? 128
PAY TO ORDER OF? JEAN'S USED CARS
AMOUNT (NUMERALS)? 123.45
ENTER THE DOLLAR AMOUNT IN WORDS, TYPE A COMMA, THEN ENTER
THE CENTS AMOUNT IN WORDS.? ONE HUNDRED TWENTY THREE, FORTY FIVE

WHAT OUTPUT PORT DO YOU WISH TO USE? 2
ANOTHER CHECK? NOPE

READY
#
```

SAMPLE OUTPUT

```
SUMMALESSA BANQUE
NUMBER 110
110 EASY STREET                           NUMBER 128
UTOPIA, CA 99998
                                          2 FEBRUARY 1984

PAY TO THE ORDER OF JEAN'S USED CARS      $ 123.45

ONE HUNDRED TWENTY THREE DOLLARS AND FORTY FIVE CENTS.


                            ------------------------------
                                      MIKE LIANT
```

26

```
0010 REM ******************************
0020 REM *     CHECKWRITER   PROGRAM      *
0030 REM ******************************
0040 REM ********* VERSION 10 **********
0050 LINE= 0
0060 DIGITS= 2
0300 REM **** COLLECT HEADING INFO ******
0310 INPUT "Name",A$(1),A$(2)
0320 INPUT "Street Address",A$(3)
0330 INPUT "City, State ZIP",A$(4),A$(5)
0340 INPUT "Checking Account Number",A$(6)
0350 INPUT "Today's Date",A$(7)
0360 PRINT
0400 INPUT "Name of Bank",B$(1)
0410 INPUT "Name of Branch",B$(2)
0420 INPUT "Street Address",B$(3)
0430 INPUT "City, State ZIP",B$(4),B$(5)
0440 PRINT
0500 REM ****** INPUT CHECK DATA ******
0510 INPUT "Check Number",C$(1)
0520 INPUT "Pay to order of",C$(2)
0530 INPUT "Amount (Numerals)",C
0540 PRINT "Enter the dollar amount in words, type a comma, then enter"
0550 INPUT "the cents amount in words.",C$(4),C$(5)
1400 REM ****** PRINT THE CHECK *******
1410 PRINT
1420 INPUT "What output port do you wish to use",P
1430 IF P>7 PRINT"INVALID SELECTION":GOTO 1420
1500 PRINT #P
1510 PRINT #P
1520 PRINT #P,TAB(5);B$(1)
1530 IF B$(2)="" THEN 1550
1540 PRINT #P,TAB(5);B$(2)
1550 PRINT #P,TAB(5);B$(3);
1560 PRINT #P,TAB(60);"Number ";C$(1)
1570 PRINT #P,TAB(5);B$(4);", ";B$(5)
1580 PRINT #P,TAB(60);A$(7)
1590 PRINT #P
1600 PRINT #P
1610 PRINT #P,"Pay to the order of ";C$(2);
1620 PRINT #P,TAB(60);"$ ";C
1625 PRINT #P
1630 PRINT #P,TAB(5);C$(4);" DOLLARS ";
1640 IF C$(5)="" THEN 1660
1650 PRINT #P,"and ";C$(5);" CENTS."
1660 PRINT #P
1670 PRINT #P
1680 PRINT #P
1690 PRINT #P,TAB(50);"----------------------------"
1700 PRINT #P,TAB(62-(LEN(A$(1))/2));A$(1)
1710 PRINT #P,CHR$(12)
2000 INPUT "Another check",Z$
2010 IF LEFT$(Z$,1)="Y" THEN 500
2020 END
```

5
ELECTRONIC CHECKBOOK

Now we'll use the two building blocks we've developed in a comprehensive money-control routine. This is the longest program in the book, and potentially the most useful. It's also the first to use a disk system. If you don't have disk-type storage ability just yet, I recommend that you bypass keypunching this routine until you acquire it. We're going to use the disk interactively throughout Electronic Checkbook, and trying to make the program work with a tape cassette could be slow and painful.

Our electronic version of the home checkbook is a complete account manager. It will write checks, record deposits and bank charges, reconcile the bank statement, provide a listing of all transactions in the file, and establish a data base that will be used by later programs. Since this is a personal checkbook, we include personal and bank information in the program to minimize operator keystrokes. Some of the once-a-year activities are hidden from the operator by the program displays. If you know how, you can exercise the initialization routine, but the casual operator won't accidently wipe out the data base. It is planned that a separate minidiskette will be used each year for the data record. Each account transaction requires 64 bytes of memory/disk space for storage; therefore, your diskette should hold 1,400 transactions. (There are 350 sectors of 256 bytes on most minidiskettes.)

This is a truly adaptable program, one that can be modified and added to (or cut) in many ways to serve your own needs. The disk-operating system (DOS) in my computer is a bit primitive, so my programs must take care of formatting and record keeping (the "housekeeping" functions) for the disk which another DOS might perform automatically. (While I like the primitive DOS because I feel it allows me more control, that is strictly a matter of personal preference. Some folks prefer automatic transmissions in automobiles, and others like manual shifting.) The bottom line is that your DOS won't be any more primitive than mine, and I suspect it will be a lot more automatic. When you modify Electronic Checkbook for your computer, you won't need to add anything to the disk routines; you can probably get by with a much simpler disk access.

Because it is composed of a number of subfunctions, the program seems to be complicated. Don't try to eat this elephant in one bite. Electronic Checkbook is just a collection of simple routines. The overview flow chart shown here illustrates just how simple the whole process is.

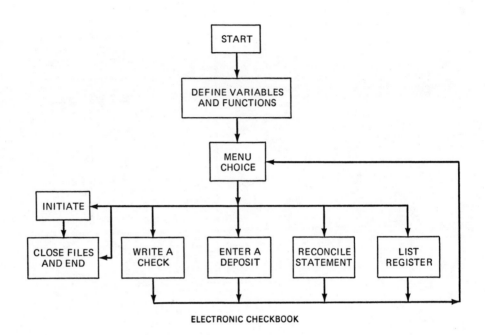

ELECTRONIC CHECKBOOK

The program has its own manager routine to present you a menu of choices and direct program operation to your choice. Each routine within the program returns control to the menu manager. (A side note on the flow chart is appropriate: If you are a computer purist, you'll cringe at the rectangles in my flow chart. Yes, I know that there are standard shapes for flow chart boxes to signify special functions of the box. I also believe that computer snobbery has no place in a family-oriented publication like this book. My flow charts use a lot of rectangles, and a few diamonds, and not much else. But my 10-year-old kid understands this flow chart, and understanding is what it's all about!)

The next flow chart is an example of one of the routines in the checkbook. It is more detailed than the previous one, but doesn't belabor detail. The BASIC listing is the next level of detail, and we'll discuss that shortly.

29

WRITE A CHECK

READ DISK TO LAST ENTRY

INPUT CHECK INFORMATION

VALID AMOUNT ? — NO

YES

BOOKKEEPING CODE INPUT SUBROUTINE

PRINT CHECK SUBROUTINE

STORE DATA ON DISK

YES — MORE? — NO — GOTO MENU

There's not much new accounting theory or higher mathematics used in Electronic Checkbook. When we write a check, we want to subtract the amount of the check from the account balance. We also want to subtract bank charges. Deposits are added to the bank balance as they are made. We discussed the accounting principles for reconciliation, and they don't change with this program.

PROGRAMMING NOTES

Don't let the program listing scare you. Yes, over 200 lines of code can be formidable. You are investing key-punch time now, and the return is a time saving every time you use Electronic Checkbook.

Let's look at the listing on a line-by-line basis again to make sure we don't skip anything important. You'll recognize the first few statements from previous programs--the title and configuration-management notation are lines 10 through 40. Line 50 will be common to most of our programs. Line=0 defeats a line feed/carriage return feature of BASIC to give our program full control of the output format.

Lines 100 through 240 define the account-holder personal information, the bank and branch information, and some constants. The REM statements on each line are pretty self-explanatory, so we won't dwell on those. Line 170 defines a constant that is needed by the DOS in my computer. The program must tell the DOS where to look for the disk data. In this case, the initial digit (2) indicates that the disk will be in drive 2. (I have a two-holer disk-drive system; drive 1 is normally used for program storage, and drive 2 is the data-manipulation slot.) The remaining three digits tell the system to start at sector number 001. You may not need this variable at all if your DOS assigns space on the diskette media. Line 240 is a planned annual change. It carries the identification of the current year. Each January, you'll have to modify your program to update Y$ to the proper year.

Lines 300 through 320 define the same functions we used in <u>Checkbook Reconciliation</u>. They serve the same purpose here, and we'll let these functions save us some key-punch time in the print routines.

Line 590 looks a little out of place. It's there because I put the initialization routine ahead of the menu. And the initialization routine is where it is because it will be changed periodically. Whenever a new disk is used, the system should be initialized to store the beginning balance and check number on disk. Line 620 defined the initial balance—you'll want to change this to the current account balance whenever you begin a new disk. Line 630 is the initial check number. When you start a new record, define C(1) as the last number used. The program will pick up this number and add one when the first transaction is encountered. Incidentally, although we've called this "check number," it really is a transaction number. Each check, deposit, and bank charge is assigned a unique number by the system. We are accustomed to numbering only checks in our manual checkbook, but the computer wants to keep track of all the transactions that affect our account balance.

This is probably a good spot to discuss the variables used by the routine for account information:

C(1) is the transaction number,

C$(2) defines the date (current year for the initial entry),

C$(3) is the payee of the check, or the words "Deposit" or "Bank Charge" as appropriate,

C(4) and C$(4) carry the amount of the transaction,

C$(5) is the bookkeeping code entry,

C$(6) indicates that the transaction has cleared the bank,

C$(1) combines C(1), C$(5), and C$(6) for recording,

B and B$ represent the current account balance.

All of the variables are configured to character string format for recording to allow the program control of the number of bytes allocated on the diskette. If yours is a more nearly automatic DOS, you may be able to dispense with some of the formatting in the program.

With the variables defined by the initialization routine, it's time to record. Line 690 calls the subroutine of lines 8100 through 8190 to format the data for disk writing. The first step in the subroutine, line 8110, defines X$ as 29 spaces. Next, C$(5) is redefined as the leftmost two characters in the variable made up of C$(5) and X$. Generally, the two characters will be the bookkeeping code entry. If we have the unusual situation where C$(5) has no entry, the addition of X$ insures that something will be in the variable when we record it. We must have a two-character entry in C$(5) when we record, or the disk packing will not be what the program expects, and the data base will become useless. Again, your DOS may make this playing unnecessary. If so, you can probably dispense with this entire subroutine. (If you're not sure about your DOS, leave room for the formatting.)

Line 8130 converts C(1) from a numerical to a character string variable. In the conversion, C(1) is limited to four digits. Next, line 8140 redefines C$(1) as the two digits of C$(5) and the four digits of C(1)--now an interim C$(1)--plus one digit of C$(6). When this variable is recorded, it will take up the 7 bytes we've defined and an additional byte for the record separator (a semicolon in the print statement). By the time this routine reaches the RETURN statement of line 8190, it will have formatted the variables to use up (with separators) exactly 64 bytes of real estate on the disk. With that assurance, we can return to the initialization routine.

Line 700 is the next statement execution, and it is the command to write the formatted data to the disk. The DOS in my computer knows that there are only eight output ports (numbered 0 to 7), and uses "ports" numbered 10, 11, 12, and 13 to address memory buffers that can be written to disk. Line 710 steers the program to the end sequence to insure that the initialization information is on the disk before we try to write a check and access that data.

The program start is at line 1000. The first command executed at program start is OPEN#10,S in line 1010. Before we can read or write a disk, we must alert the DOS that we intend to use it: OPEN is our DOS alarm clock, and S is the starting drive and sector that we defined in line 170.

The menu of operations is printed by lines 1020 through 1060, and line 1070 allows the operator to input a choice. While initialization is not one of the menu choices, you can select that option by typing a zero. Line 1100 will respond and steer the program to the disk initialization routine we discussed.

Lines 1110 and 1120 make sure that the number entered is between 1 and 5; otherwise, the menu is reprinted and the option asked again. Line 1130 is the traffic director. The INT(Z) takes only the integer part of the response to provide more operator-error trapping, and points the program to the selected routine.

Line 1200 is the beginning of the end. Before we just shut things off, we must clean up our disk operations. Line 1210 sets flag variable F to zero. The disk READ subroutine of lines 8000 to 8090 is called out by line 1220. The subroutine at 8100, which we discussed previously, formats and packs data for recording. The READ subroutine must now unpack the data so the program can operate on the information.

The actual READ disk operation is performed in line 8010. Note that with the DOS I'm using, we must read the variables in the same order in which we recorded them. When the READ statement encounters an end-of-data mark on the disk, it will transfer program control to line 8080, which resets flag F to a one. Before the end-of-data mark is read, each record is massaged to separate C(1), C$(5), and C$(6) from variable C$(1). C(4) is also recovered from C$(4) and B from B$. After each record, the subroutine returns control to the calling routine--in this case back to line 1230. For the end routine, we want to move the disk pointer to the actual end of recorded data. When we send the CLOSE command, the DOS will flush the memory buffer to the disk and write an end-of-data mark. We don't want this mark to be written over live data, so we ask the system to read the entire file before we try to CLOSE. As long as flag F is zero, the end-of-data point hasn't been reached, and line 1230 will send the program back to the subroutine call.

When the end-of-data point is sensed and the flag is set to one, it's safe to move on to line 1240 and CLOSE the disk files. The printed message in line 1250 lets us know that all is correct in DOS country. Line 1260 is the final statement in the program; we'll change it later when we implement our file manager.

The Write-a-Check routine extends from line 2000 to line 2280. The RESTORE command in line 2010 is peculiar to the DOS I'm using. Its function is to reset the DOS pointer to the beginning of the disk file (so we know where we are). Lines 2020 through 2050 echo the sequence in the final segment that moves the DOS pointer to the end-of-the-data file. (When this activity is complete, the current data in the check variables describe the last transaction.)

Line 2060 collects the current day and month information from the operator. The transaction number is updated by line 2070. Operator input for the payee and amount is handled by lines 2090, 2100, and 2110. Line 2120 checks to

see if we will overdraw the account with this check. If the
check exceeds the account balance, line 2140 gives the
operator a slap on the wrist, and line 2150 sends us back to
the menu. (Better enter that deposit first!)

If the check will be covered by the account balance,
the program asks for the bookkeeping code by calling the
subroutine located between lines 2500 and 2630. The subroutine provides a menu of bookkeeping codes that will tag
the transaction entries for later processing by our Bookkeeping Worksheet. This is a good time to review the bookkeeping categories. You may wish to combine some categories
or add new ones. This is going to be your program, so
modify it to suit your needs. (Just remember that any
changes you make to the codes now should be picked up when
you keypunch the worksheet program.) The checkbook data
base will faithfully record and store any two-character code
you wish to use.

The code input is handled by line 2170, while line 2180
enters an X in the flag to indicate whether the transaction
has cleared the bank. The check-writer subroutine is called
next to print the check. This subroutine (lines 2700
through 2920) is essentially the print routine from the
Check-writer program. In the present case, we don't print
the words for the dollars-and-cents amounts.

Finally, we call the subroutine at line 8100 which
will format the data prior to writing to disk in line 2210.
Line 2230 tells us what the account balance is after the
current check has been subtracted. Line 2260 will steer
the routine back to the payee-data-entry prompting point if
we wish to write another check immediately. This re-entry
position saves the current date entry from the first check
of the day to relieve a little operator keypunch. Line
2270 resets the DOS pointer before line 2280 sends us back
to the menu and program traffic manager.

Lines 3000 through 3300 allow us to enter deposits and
bank charges into the check register. Lines 3010 through
3040 should look familiar to you: They provide the same
"run-the-pointer-to-the-end" routine we used before. The
date input and transaction number increment of lines 3050
and 3060 mimic the check-writer segment. After the operator inputs of transaction type and amount, an error trap
is encountered in lines 3130 through 3150.

Line 3160 sets "Payee" equal to "Deposit", line 3170
puts a "DE" in the bookkeeping transaction code, and line
3180 adds the deposit amount to the account balance. Bank
charges are formatted (and the balance decremented) by
lines 3200, 3210, and 3230. The format-for-disk-write subroutine is used to configure the data prior to the disk
print statement of line 3250. Line 3270 presents the current balance to the operator, and line 3300 sends program
flow back to the menu.

Reconciliation of the bank statement is a little
different than in our earlier program. The accounting and
arithmetic treatment is the same, but now we're reading data
from the disk instead of asking for operator input. The

34

initial code in this segment will read the disk file, ask the operator to tag items that have cleared, then re-record each file to disk. If an item has previously been tagged as "cleared," the re-recording will be automatic and the operator will not be asked.

Line 4010 resets the file pointer for disk memory buffer #10 and opens a second buffer. We'll read with buffer #10 and re-record with #11. Since they both start at the same beginning (drive 2, sector 001) and since all transaction records are the same length, buffer #11 will print data onto the same disk space from which it was read by buffer #10. If any transaction has cleared the bank, C$(6) will be changed from the X that was recorded when the transaction was initially handled to a C. On subsequent reconciliations, the C will be sensed by line 4060, and the transaction will be quietly re-recorded.

The routine in lines 4200 through 4300 is used to count the number of transactions that have not cleared, and to separate the count by "Deposit" and "Other." We'll later use this count to configure a couple of FOR...NEXT loops to print the reconciliation statement.

After the operator input of the bank statement account balance, the statement printing is called through the subroutine at line 8400. There's nothing new in the print segment. The explanation given for the <u>Checkbook Reconciliation</u> printing code is still valid. The primary difference in this reconciliation statement is found in lines 8920 through 9090. Before, we printed the statement with no indication that the check register and bank statement agreed or disagreed. Now that the check register is under the control of the computer, a value is printed. If the two balances do not agree, a diagnostic message is appended to the statement to aid your troubleshooting. When the statement has been printed, line 4390 resets the disk pointer, and line 4400 directs us back to the menu and traffic manager.

The final segment of <u>Electronic Checkbook</u> is a short piece of BASIC code (lines 8200 through 8380) that will produce the largest output. The listing is a brute-force "read-the-data-and-print-it" routine. It will list every transaction (including the initialization entry) in the register. There's nothing you haven't seen in one of the previous descriptions, so I won't dwell on the listing code.

OPERATING NOTES

You will see from the sample input and output that the program is easy to run. Each segment of the operator input routine starts with the menu. All operator responses in our samples are underlined to distinguish them from the computer generated message.

35

The first sample is a check-writing exercise. The program requires only four inputs for a check: the date, payee, amount, and the bookkeeping code. (Subsequent checks on the same day need only three entries, since the previously entered date is used again.)

Any response to the ANOTHER CHECK? inquiry that begins with "Y" is taken as positive (yes), while anything beginning with "N" is negative. This lets me be a little sassy with my computer by answering "YEP" or "NOPE" at times. (Little things like that keep the fun in any computer operation.)

The next sample input is the entering of a deposit. No hard copy results from this transaction; and only the date, the word "Deposit," and the amount need to be keypunched. The system responds with the present account balance to let you know it has accepted the entry.

A listing of the complete check register is requested next. The listing shows all transactions entered on the disk--usually all transactions for the year. The listing of the register is a one-stroke request. Type the numeral five as your menu response and watch the printer go.

Reconciliation is another computer labor that the operator can watch. Type the numeral four to request the reconciliation routine, and answer "Y" or "N" as the program asks if transactions have cleared. Note that on the sample, transactions 1001 through 1020 were not presented for a clearing decision. These had been cleared on a previous bank reconciliation run. Only outstanding items are offered for an operator "cleared" choice during the reconciliation run. When the program asks for the balance from the bank statement, you know the input task is over. Sit back and watch the printer spew out that statement of account reconciliation.

Finally, we exercise the program end feature. Type a one and wait until the display indicates "DISK FILES CLOSED".

In summary, Electronic Checkbook is a powerful routine that will save you hours of manual checkbook frustration every month. The program is long, but the time you invest in keypunching it will be repaid many times when you use it.

SAMPLE INPUT - CHECKBOOK

```
READY
# RUN
ENTER A '1' TO END
        '2' TO WRITE A CHECK
        '3' TO ENTER A DEPOSIT OR BANK CHARGE
        '4' TO RECONCILE THE BANK STATEMENT
        '5' TO LIST THE CHECK REGISTER
? 2
TODAY'S DATE (2 DIGITS FOR DAY, 3 LETTERS FOR MONTH)? 23 FEB

PAYEE? SECOND TRUST DEED COMPANY

AMOUNT? 102.13

ENTER THE CODE FOR THIS CHECK FROM THE LIST:

MEDICINE/DRUGS          HEALTH INSURANCE
HOSPITALS/LABS          DOCTORS/DENTISTS/NURSES
TAXES                   CONTRIBUTIONS
INTEREST                EMPLOYEE BUSINESS EXPENSE
FOOD                    MISCELLANEOUS DEDUCTIBLES
SHELTER                 UTILITIES
TRANSPORTATION          ENTERTAINMENT
EDUCATION               CLOTHING
OTHER EXPENSES
? INTEREST
WHAT OUTPUT PORT DO YOU WISH TO USE? 2
***** PRESENT ACCOUNT BALANCE IS $291.08
ANOTHER CHECK? NOPE
ENTER A '1' TO END
        '2' TO WRITE A CHECK
        '3' TO ENTER A DEPOSIT OR BANK CHARGE
        '4' TO RECONCILE THE BANK STATEMENT
        '5' TO LIST THE CHECK REGISTER
? 3
TODAY'S DATE (2 DIGITS FOR DAY, 3 LETTERS FOR MONTH)? 25 FEB

DEPOSIT OR BANK CHARGE? DEPOSIT
AMOUNT? 420

***** PRESENT ACCOUNT BALANCE IS $711.08
ENTER A '1' TO END
        '2' TO WRITE A CHECK
        '3' TO ENTER A DEPOSIT OR BANK CHARGE
        '4' TO RECONCILE THE BANK STATEMENT
        '5' TO LIST THE CHECK REGISTER
? 5
WHAT OUTPUT PORT DO YOU WISH TO USE? 2
ENTER A '1' TO END
        '2' TO WRITE A CHECK
        '3' TO ENTER A DEPOSIT OR BANK CHARGE
        '4' TO RECONCILE THE BANK STATEMENT
        '5' TO LIST THE CHECK REGISTER
```

37

```
? 4
HAS TRANSACTION NUMBER 1021 , (DEPOSIT                     ,
FOR $420 ), CLEARED? YES
HAS TRANSACTION NUMBER 1022 , (STATE COLLEGE              ,
FOR $250 ), CLEARED? YUP
HAS TRANSACTION NUMBER 1023 , (COLLEGE BOOK STORE         ,
FOR $52.66 ), CLEARED? YES
HAS TRANSACTION NUMBER 1024 , (DEPOSIT                    ,
FOR $531 ), CLEARED? YOU BET
HAS TRANSACTION NUMBER 1025 , (BUSINESS CLUB              ,
FOR $125 ), CLEARED? YEAH
HAS TRANSACTION NUMBER 1026 , (FAST PRINTER SERVICE       ,
FOR $25 ), CLEARED? YES
HAS TRANSACTION NUMBER 1027 , (VALENTINE RESTAURANT       ,
FOR $36.25 ), CLEARED? YESSIREE
HAS TRANSACTION NUMBER 1028 , (BANK CHARGE                ,
FOR $12 ), CLEARED? YES
HAS TRANSACTION NUMBER 1029 , (LOCAL LAUNDRY              ,
FOR $23.05 ), CLEARED? NO
HAS TRANSACTION NUMBER 1030 , (CABLE TELEVISION SERVICE,
FOR $36.18 ), CLEARED? NOPE
HAS TRANSACTION NUMBER 1031 , (STATE BANK                 ,
FOR $10.50 ), CLEARED? NOT YET
HAS TRANSACTION NUMBER 1032 , (SECOND TRUST DEED COMPANY,
FOR $102.13 ), CLEARED? NOOOO
HAS TRANSACTION NUMBER 1033 , (DEPOSIT                    ,
FOR $420 ), CLEARED? NUP

ENTER THE BALANCE FROM THE BANK STATEMENT? 462.94

WHAT OUTPUT PORT DO YOU WISH TO USE? 2
ENTER A '1' TO END
        '2' TO WRITE A CHECK
        '3' TO ENTER A DEPOSIT OR BANK CHARGE
        '4' TO RECONCILE THE BANK STATEMENT
        '5' TO LIST THE CHECK REGISTER
? 1

DISK FILES CLOSED.

READY
#

SAMPLE OUTPUT - WRITE A CHECK

FIRST STATE BANK
LOCAL BRANCH
#1 GOLD AVENUE                               NUMBER 1032
GOLDRUSH, CA 99099

                                             23 FEB 1984


PAY TO THE ORDER OF SECOND TRUST DEED COMPANY      $ 102.13

102 DOLLARS AND 13 CENTS


                                    --------------------
                                    MIKE LIANT
```

CHECK REGISTER

DATE	NR.	PAYEE	AMOUNT	BALANCE
1984	1000	INITIAL ENTRY	0.00	1000.00
05 JAN	1001	CORNER BAKERY	25.47	974.53
05 JAN	1002	NEIGHBORHOOD ICE CREAM	32.19	942.34
05 JAN	1003	PARTY GIFT SHOP	12.98	929.36
08 JAN	1004	DEPOSIT	420.00	1349.36
11 JAN	1005	DR. HEALER	250.00	1099.36
11 JAN	1006	LOCAL PHARMACY	25.69	1073.67
13 JAN	1007	CITY FUEL	52.79	1020.88
13 JAN	1008	COUNTY GAS & WATER	22.08	998.80
15 JAN	1009	BANK CHARGE	12.00	986.80
18 JAN	1010	JEAN'S AUTO PARTS	122.27	864.53
18 JAN	1011	STATE GAS & OIL	25.33	839.20
20 JAN	1012	UNITED FUND	100.00	739.20
20 JAN	1013	FIRST MORTGAGE COMPANY	680.22	58.98
21 JAN	1014	DEPOSIT	420.00	478.98
22 JAN	1015	FRIENDLY GROCERS	53.18	425.80
22 JAN	1016	SMART CLOTHIERS	250.72	175.08
23 JAN	1017	SHALE OIL	72.07	103.01
25 JAN	1018	DEPOSIT	240.00	343.01
29 JAN	1019	STATE TAX AUTHORITY	300.21	42.80
29 JAN	1020	LOCAL TAX AUTHORITY	29.95	12.85
02 FEB	1021	DEPOSIT	420.00	432.85
04 FEB	1022	STATE COLLEGE	250.00	182.85
04 FEB	1023	COLLEGE BOOK STORE	52.66	130.19
05 FEB	1024	DEPOSIT	531.00	661.19
10 FEB	1025	BUSINESS CLUB	125.00	536.19
10 FEB	1026	FAST PRINTER SERVICE	25.00	511.19
14 FEB	1027	VALENTINE RESTAURANT	36.25	474.94
15 FEB	1028	BANK CHARGE	12.00	462.94
18 FEB	1029	LOCAL LAUNDRY	23.05	439.89
18 FEB	1030	CABLE TELEVISION SERVICE	36.18	403.71
18 FEB	1031	STATE BANK	10.50	393.21
23 FEB	1032	SECOND TRUST DEED COMPANY	102.13	291.08
25 FEB	1033	DEPOSIT	420.00	711.08

MIKE LIANT
AUTHOR AND HISTORIAN
123 EASY STREET
UTOPIA, CA 90999

CHECKBOOK RECONCILIATION
CHECKING ACCOUNT NUMBER 12-345678-90

BALANCE PER CHECK REGISTER $ 711.08

ADD CHECKS NOT CLEARED.

DATE	CHECK NR	PAYEE	AMOUNT
18 FEB	1029	LOCAL LAUNDRY	23.05
18 FEB	1030	CABLE TELEVISION SERVICE	36.18
18 FEB	1031	STATE BANK	10.50
23 FEB	1032	SECOND TRUST DEED COMPANY	102.13

TOTAL   + 171.86

LESS DEPOSITS NOT CREDITED.

DATE	AMOUNT
25 FEB	420.00

TOTAL   - 420.00

TOTAL PER CHECK REGISTER $ 462.94

BALANCE PER BANK STATEMENT   462.94
                                                              ==========

*** THE CHECK REGISTER AND BANK STATEMENT AGREE ***

40

```
0010 REM ********************************
0020 REM *       ELECTRONIC CHECKBOOK       *
0030 REM ********************************
0040 REM ********* VERSION 10 **********
0050 LINE= 0
0100 REM ****** DEFINE VARIABLES *******
0110   A$(1)="MIKE LIANT"
0120   A$(2)="Author and Historian"
0130   A$(3)="123 Easy Street": REM ** ADDRESS ***
0140   A$(4)="Utopia": REM ******** CITY *********
0150   A$(5)="CA 90999": REM **** STATE/ZIP ****
0160   A$(6)="12-345678-90": REM ** ACCOUNT NR ***
0170   S=2001: REM **** STARTING DRIVE/SECTOR ****
0190   B$(1)="FIRST STATE BANK": REM * BANK NAME *
0200   B$(2)="Local Branch": REM ** BRANCH NAME **
0210   B$(3)="#1 Gold Avenue": REM *** ADDRESS ***
0220   B$(4)="Goldrush": REM ****** CITY ********
0230   B$(5)="CA 99099": REM **** STATE/ZIP ****
0240   Y$="1984": REM ****** CURRENT YEAR ******
0300 REM ****** DEFINE FUNCTIONS *******
0310 DEF FNA(X)=70-LEN(STR$(X))
0320 DEF FNB(X)=55-LEN(STR$(X))
0590 GOTO 1000
0600 REM ***** INITIALIZE THE FILE ******
0620   B=1000.00: REM ***** INITIAL BALANCE ******
0630   C(1)=1000: REM **** INITIAL CHECK NR ****
0640   C$(2)=Y$
0650   C$(3)="INITIAL ENTRY"
0660   C(4)=0
0670   C$(5)="XX"
0680   C$(6)="C"
0690 GOSUB 8100
0700 PRINT #10,C$(1);C$(2);C$(3);C$(4);B$
0710 GOTO 1240
1000 REM ******** PROGRAM START *********
1010 OPEN #10,S
1020 PRINT "Enter a '1' to End"
1030 PRINT "         '2' to Write a Check"
1040 PRINT "         '3' to Enter a Deposit or Bank Charge"
1050 PRINT "         '4' to Reconcile the Bank Statement"
1060 PRINT "         '5' to List the Check Register"
1070 INPUT Z
1100 IF Z=0 GOTO 600: REM ** INITIALIZE DISK ***
1110 IF Z<1 THEN 1020
1120 IF Z>5 THEN 1020
1130 ON INT(Z) GOTO 1200,2000,3000,4000,8200
1200 REM **** CLOSE FILES AND END ******
1210   F=0: REM *********** SET FLAG ************
1220 GOSUB 8000
1230 IF F=0 THEN 1220
1240 CLOSE #10
1250 PRINT "Disk files closed."
1260 END
2000 REM ******** WRITE A CHECK *********
```

41

```
2010 RESTORE #10
2020   F=0: REM ********** SET FLAG **************
2040 GOSUB 8000
2050 IF F=0 THEN 2040
2060 INPUT "Today's date (2 digits for day, 3 letters for month)",C$(2)
2070   C(1)=C(1)+1
2080 PRINT
2090 INPUT "Payee",C$(3)
2100 PRINT
2110 INPUT "Amount: ",C(4)
2120   B=B-C(4)
2130 IF B>0 THEN 2160
2140 PRINT "OOPS! That's more than the remaining balance! Try Again."
2150 GOTO 1020
2160 GOSUB 2500
2170 INPUT C$(5)
2180   C$(6)="X"
2190 GOSUB 2700
2200 GOSUB 8100
2210 PRINT #10,C$(1);C$(2);C$(3);C$(4);B$
2220 DIGITS= 2
2230 PRINT "***** Present Account Balance is $";B
2240 DIGITS= 0
2250 INPUT "Another check",Z$
2260 IF LEFT$(Z$,1)="Y" THEN 2070
2270 RESTORE #10
2280 GOTO 1020
2500 REM ****** BOOKKEEPING CODE ******
2510 PRINT
2520 PRINT "Enter the code for this check from the list:"
2530 PRINT
2540 PRINT "MEdicine/Drugs            HEalth Insurance"
2550 PRINT "HOspitals/Labs            DOctors/Dentists/Nurses"
2560 PRINT "TAxes                     COntributions"
2570 PRINT "INterest                  EMployee Business Expense"
2580 PRINT "FOod                      MIscellaneous Deductibles"
2590 PRINT "SHelter                   UTilities"
2600 PRINT "TRansportation            ENtertainment"
2610 PRINT "EDucation                 CLothing"
2620 PRINT "OTher Expenses"
2630 RETURN
2700 REM ******** CHECKWRITER *********
2710 INPUT "What output port do you wish to use",P
2720 PRINT #P:PRINT#P
2730 PRINT #P,TAB(5);B$(1)
2740 IF B$(2)="" THEN 2760
2750 PRINT #P,TAB(5);B$(2)
2760 PRINT #P,TAB(5);B$(3);
2770 PRINT #P,TAB(60);"Number ";C(1)
2780 PRINT #P,TAB(5);B$(4);", ";B$(5)
2790 PRINT #P,TAB(60);C$(2);" ";Y$
2800 PRINT #P:PRINT#P
2810 PRINT #P,"Pay to the order of ";C$(3);
2820 DIGITS= 2
```

```
2830 PRINT #P,TAB(60);"$ ";C(4)
2840 PRINT #P
2850 DIGITS= 0
2860 PRINT #P,TAB(5);INT(C(4));" DOLLARS and ";
2870 PRINT #P,100*(C(4)-INT(C(4)));" CENTS"
2880 PRINT #P:PRINT#P:PRINT#P
2890 PRINT #P,TAB(50);"----------------------------"
2900 PRINT #P,TAB(62-LEN(A$(1))/2);A$(1)
2910 PRINT #P,CHR$(12)
2920 RETURN
3000 REM ***** ENTER DEPOSIT/CHARGE *****
3010 RESTORE #10
3020  F=0: REM ********** SET FLAG ************
3030 GOSUB 8000
3040 IF F=0 THEN 3030
3050 INPUT "Today's date (2 digits for day, 3 letters for month)",C$(2)
3060  C(1)=C(1)+1
3070 PRINT
3080 INPUT "Deposit or Bank Charge",Z$
3090 INPUT "Amount: ",C(4)
3100 PRINT
3110 IF LEFT$(Z$,1)="D" THEN 3160
3120 IF LEFT$(Z$,1)="B" THEN 3200
3130 PRINT "I'm sorry, I don't understand your transaction code entry"
3140 PRINT "of ";Z$;".  Please try again."
3150 GOTO 3080
3160  C$(3)="Deposit"
3170  C$(5)="DE"
3180  B=B+C(4)
3190 GOTO 3230
3200  C$(3)="Bank Charge"
3210  C$(5)="BC"
3220  B=B-C(4)
3230 PRINT
3240 GOSUB 8100
3250 PRINT #10,C$(1);C$(2);C$(3);C$(4);B$
3260 DIGITS= 2
3270 PRINT "***** Present Account Balance is $";B
3280 DIGITS= 0
3290 RESTORE #10
3300 GOTO 1020
4000 REM *** RECONCILE THE STATEMENT ****
4010 RESTORE #10: OPEN#11,S
4020  X=1: Y=1: REM ****** SET COUNTERS *******
4030  F=0: REM ********** SET FLAG **********
4040 GOSUB 8000 : REM *** READ A CHECK ENTRY ***
4050 IF F=1 THEN 4310: REM *** ALL DATA READ ***
4060 IF C$(6)="C" THEN 4130: REM ** WRITE IT ***
4070 PRINT "Has transaction number ";C(1);", (";C$(3);","
4080 PRINT "for $";C(4);"), cleared";
4090 INPUT Z$
4100 IF LEFT$(Z$,1)<>"Y" THEN 4200
4110  C$(6)="C"
4120 GOSUB 8100: REM ***** FORMAT FOR DISK *****
```

```
4130 PRINT #11,C$(1);C$(2);C$(3);C$(4);B$
4140 GOTO 4040
4200 IF C$(5)="DE" THEN 4270
4210   R(1,X)=C(1)
4220   R$(2,X)=C$(2)
4230   R$(3,X)=C$(3)
4240   R(4,X)=C(4)
4250   X=X+1
4260 GOTO 4120
4270   D$(1,Y)=C$(2)
4280   D(2,Y)=C(4)
4290   Y=Y+1
4300 GOTO 4120
4310 CLOSE #11
4320 PRINT
4330   B(2)=B
4340 INPUT "Enter the balance from the Bank Statement",B(1)
4350 PRINT
4360   C=0
4370   D=0
4380 GOSUB 8400
4390 RESTORE #10
4400 GOTO 1020
8000 REM **** READ/FORMAT CHECK DATA ****
8010 READ #10,C$(1),C$(2),C$(3),C$(4),B$\8080
8020   C(1)=VAL(MID$(C$(1),3,4)): REM * CHECK NR *
8030   C$(5)=LEFT$(C$(1),2): REM * EXPENSE CODE **
8040   C$(6)=RIGHT$(C$(1),1): REM *** CLEARED? ***
8050   C(4)=VAL(C$(4))
8060   B=VAL(B$): REM ***** ACCOUNT BALANCE *****
8070 RETURN
8080   F=1
8090 RETURN
8100 REM ***** FORMAT DATA TO WRITE *****
8110   X$="                        "
8120   C$(5)=LEFT$(C$(5)+X$,2)
8130   C$(1)=LEFT$(STR$(C(1)),4)
8140   C$(1)=LEFT$(C$(5)+C$(1)+C$(6),7)
8150   C$(2)=LEFT$(C$(2)+X$,6)
8160   C$(3)=LEFT$(C$(3)+X$,29)
8170   C$(4)=LEFT$(STR$(C(4))+X$,7)
8180   B$=LEFT$(STR$(B)+X$,10)
8190 RETURN
8200 REM **** LIST THE CHECK REGISTER ***
8210 INPUT "What output port do you wish to use",P
8220   F=0: REM ********** SET FLAG ************
8230 PRINT #P:PRINT#P:PRINT#P
8240 PRINT #P,TAB(33);"CHECK REGISTER"
8250 PRINT #P
8260 PRINT #P," DATE      NR.";
8270 PRINT #P,TAB(22);"PAYEE";TAB(49);"AMOUNT";TAB(63);"BALANCE"
8280 PRINT #P
8290 GOSUB 8000
8300 IF F=1 THEN 8370
```

```
8310 PRINT #P,C$(2);TAB(10);C(1);TAB(17);C$(3);
8320 DIGITS= 2
8330 PRINT #P,TAB(FNB(C(4)));C(4);
8340 PRINT #P,TAB(FNA(B));B
8350 DIGITS= 0
8360 IF F=0 THEN 8290
8370 PRINT #P,CHR$(12)
8380 GOTO 1020
8400 REM *** PRINT THE RECONCILIATION ***
8410 INPUT "What output port do you wish to use",P
8420 PRINT #P:PRINT#P:PRINT#P
8430 PRINT #P,TAB((80-LEN(A$(1)))/2);A$(1)
8440 IF A$(2)="" THEN 8460
8450 PRINT #P,TAB((80-LEN(A$(2)))/2);A$(2)
8460 PRINT #P,TAB((80-LEN(A$(3)))/2);A$(3)
8470 PRINT #P,TAB((78-LEN(A$(4)+A$(5)))/2);A$(4);", ";A$(5)
8480 PRINT #P
8490 PRINT #P,TAB(28);"CHECKBOOK RECONCILIATION"
8500 PRINT #P,TAB((56-LEN(A$(6)))/2);"Checking Account Number ";A$(6)
8510 PRINT #P:PRINT#P:PRINT#P
8520 PRINT #P,"BALANCE PER CHECK REGISTER";
8530 PRINT #P,TAB((FNA(B(2)))-2);"$ ";B(2)
8540 PRINT #P
8550 PRINT #P,"Add Checks Not Cleared."
8560 PRINT #P
8570 PRINT #P,"Date    Check Nr           Payee";
8580 PRINT #P,TAB(55);"Amount"
8590 PRINT #P
8600 FOR J=1 TO X-1
8610 PRINT #P,R$(2,J);TAB(8);R(1,J);
8620 PRINT #P,TAB(25);R$(3,J);
8630 DIGITS= 2
8640 PRINT #P,TAB(FNB(R(4,J)));R(4,J)
8650 DIGITS= 0
8660  C=C+R(4,J)
8670 NEXT J
8680 DIGITS= 2
8690 PRINT #P,TAB(55);"-----------"
8700 PRINT #P,"Total";TAB(FNA(C)-2);"+ ";C
8710 PRINT #P
8720 PRINT #P,"Less Deposits Not Credited."
8730 PRINT #P
8740 PRINT #P,"Date";TAB(55);"Amount"
8750 PRINT #P
8760 FOR J=1 TO Y-1
8770 PRINT #P,D$(1,J);
8780 PRINT #P,TAB(FNB(D(2,J)));D(2,J)
8790  D=D+D(2,J)
8800 NEXT J
8810 PRINT #P,TAB(55);"-----------"
8820 PRINT #P,"Total";TAB(FNA(D)-2);"- ";D
8830 PRINT #P,TAB(60);"-----------"
8840  B(3)=B(2)+C-D
8850 PRINT #P,"TOTAL PER CHECK REGISTER";
```

```
8860 PRINT #P,TAB(FNA(B(3))-2);"$ ";B(3)
8870 PRINT #P
8880 PRINT #P,"BALANCE PER BANK STATEMENT";
8890 PRINT #P,TAB(FNA(B(1)));B(1)
8900 PRINT #P,TAB(60);"==========="
8910   B(4)=B(3)-B(1)
8920 IF B(4)>0 THEN 8960
8930 IF B(4)<0 THEN 9010
8940 PRINT #P," *** The Check Register and Bank Statement Agree ***"
8950 GOTO 9070
8960 PRINT #P,"THE CHECK REGISTER SHOWS AN OVERAGE OF ";B(4)
8970 PRINT #P,"A check may have cleared without being entered,"
8980 PRINT #P,"a deposit may not have cleared that was entered as"
8990 PRINT #P,"cleared, or a bank charge may not have been entered."
9000 GOTO 9070
9010   B(4)=-B(4)
9020 PRINT #P,"THE CHECK REGISTER SHOWS A SHORTAGE OF ";B(4)
9030 PRINT #P,"A check may not have cleared that is recorded as"
9040 PRINT #P,"clearing, a deposit may have cleared that wasn't"
9050 PRINT #P,"recorded, or a bank charge may have been entered"
9060 PRINT #P,"more than once."
9070 PRINT #P,CHR$(12)
9080 DIGITS= 0
9090 RETURN
```

6
BOOKKEEPING WORKSHEET

Now we can use the data base we established with Electronic Checkbook to simplify more of our home accounting tasks. Once a year (at least), we'd like to extract income tax deduction data from the checkbook. Perhaps once each month, we want to see how well our home spending plan is going. Both jobs can take the better part of an evening when we have to go through the old paper check register manually. Now, our electronic version will be sorted in minutes. Bookkeeping Worksheet takes the work out of compiling expenditures and relieves that nagging worry that we may have missed something in going through the written records. Personal computers are masters at sorting through data lists, and we're going to take advantage of that talent here.

Obviously, the program requires disk capability. The routine will use the checkbook disk established previously as a source. No mathematics manipulation is involved, but you can add some if you wish. The program merely is a sort-and-print exercise. Before we discuss the BASIC listing, let's talk about a typical sample run to prove how few operator actions are required.

OPERATING NOTES

This program provides a successful bookkeeping summary with only three keyboard entries. (The sample run actually illustrates two program operation sequences.) At the beginning, the program will remind you to insert the Electronic Checkbook diskette in the proper disk-drive slot. The routine will wait for you to press "RETURN" to indicate you're ready. Your second keystroke will tell the computer which output device you wish to use. The third entry selects either an "Income Tax" or "Budget" output. Typing an "I" or a "B" is sufficient to tell your computer the choice. Now, sit back and let your digital helper do the work.

47

Bookkeeping Worksheet is a brute-force routine that seems to take forever, but everything is relative! With a full diskette, the sort-and-print routine might use 15 minutes of clock time. While that's a long time for your computer, it's less than the blink of an eye compared to the manual sorting exercise. (I'm spoiled by my computer. It does so many jobs in seconds that I am upset when a task takes minutes.) If the time bothers you, start the run then walk out to the kitchen for a cup of coffee. Your computer will be awaiting your further commands when you return.

The output is a printed sort of your check expenditures. Each category contains a listing of the checks written. As it is presented, the program does not total the amounts in each category. When you modify the program for your own needs, you can add that readily. You can also change the categories or category combinations to suit your personal situation. Now, let's look at the BASIC listing and begin that personalization.

PROGRAMMING NOTES

Bookkeeping Worksheet is a fairly simple routine--or series of routines. The main part of each sort sequence is a series of short comparison steps. You can cut your keypunch time considerably if your computer has a BASIC editor. Just punch one set of compares and duplicate them the necessary number of times. In any case, one evening of keyboard work will have the program in your computer's memory, up and running. Let's again go through the listing and see what each line does.

Lines 10 through 60 provide the same type of heading information that we've seen in previous programs. Line 100 prints a routine title on the terminal, while lines 120 and 130 remind the user to install the checkbook diskette in the disk drive.

Line 140 is our disk-operating system (DOS) alarm clock. It alerts the DOS that we'll be using disk capability with the program and tells the DOS where to start looking for data. Since this command is peculiar to the disk system on my computer, check the requirements of your DOS before keypunching. Line 160 asks which output device you wish to use. (If you have one output printer that is your favorite, you could omit the question and define that output always.)

Lines 180 through 210 put the heading on the output statement. Lines 220 through 240 let the user decide which type of sort is wanted and steer the program to the appropriate program segment. The routine in lines 250, 260, and 270 is another one of our operator-error traps. If you enter anything that doesn't begin with an "I" or "B" when responding to the type-of-sort query, you'll get the error message and be rerouted to the input statement.

The first major program segment is the Income Tax Deduction Sort (lines 300 through 960). The categories we'll use for the sort correspond to the categories of itemized deductions on IRS Form 1040, Schedule A. When this sort is complete, most of the bookkeeping needed for your annual income tax preparation is done.

The sorting is governed by a series of flags. The variable F is a flag used to count categories and steer the routine to the appropriate subsegment, according to the following key:

F	Category
0	Medicine/Drugs
1	Health Insurance
2	Doctors, Dentists, Nurses
3	Hospitals, Laboratories
4	Taxes
5	Interest
6	Contributions
7	Miscellaneous
8	End

Flag variable E is used to control the printing of the category title. If E=0, the title is printed (indicating the first check in the category); if E-1, the title is not printed (we've already printed it).

Variable D indicates that we've looked at everything on the diskette. If D=0, we haven't come to the end-of-data mark on the disk; if D=1, we've found the end-of-data mark and it's time to reset things for another pass.

Much of the BASIC code is involved with checking the flags and steering program flow accordingly. Line 310 initializes F=0. Three commands are included in line 320 (the colons separate the statements). First, the disk pointer is returned to the head of the data file; next, D is reset; and, finally, E is set to zero for the next category.

With the flags set, line 330 calls the subroutine of lines 2000 through 2080. The subroutine is borrowed from our Electronic Checkbook listing. It reads one complete register entry from the disk and unpacks variable C$(1). Line 2020 extracts the transaction number, line 2030 picks out the bookkeeping code, and line 2040 fetches the "check-cleared" code. When the READ statement in line 2010 detects the end-of-data mark on the diskette, program flow is transferred to line 2060, where F is incremented to indicate the completion of a category. Line 2070 sets flag D to a value of one to show completion of a data pass. Line 2080 sends us back to the RETURN statement and the main routine.

The IF statement in line 340 checks for the end-of-data flag indication. When a pass is complete, line 340 forces the program to return to the reset commands of line 320. From this point, the Income Tax Deduction Sort segment uses a repeating sequence.

Lines 350, 420, 490, etc. check the F flag. When the flag is appropriate, the compare sequence is entered. If the flag has been incremented, program flow is routed forward to the next set of compares. Initially, only the sequence from lines 350 to 410 will be used. When F=1, line 350 will direct the program to lines 420 through 480. An F=2 invokes the sequence in lines 490 to 550, and so forth.

Lines 360, 430, 500, etc. check the bookkeeping code of the register entry currently active. If the code matches the sequence key, the routine continues to print the entry. When the code does not match, the program returns to line 330 for another diskette read operation.

Lines 370, 440, 510, etc. check the E flag. E=1 tells the computer that we've already printed the category title, so program flow jumps over the code that would accomplish that task. If E=0, the next two lines set up E=1 and print the deduction category title. Whether or not the title is printed, line 400, 470, etc. print the register entry by calling the subroutine at lines 3000 to 3060.

The check-record printer subroutine is straightforward. Line 3010 sets the number of digits printed after the decimal to zero. (Actually, this command causes the computer to print whatever digits are necessary after the decimal. If an integer is encountered, no decimal is printed. Should the number have a repeating decimal fractional part, the digits after the decimal will be printed to the limit of the computer precision.) Since the check number is an integer, we don't want any decimal printed. Lines 3020 and 3030 print the check number and payee. Line 3040 resets DIGITS=2 to provide a proper dollars-and-cents display for the check amount, which is printed by line 3050.

The final line in each subsequence vectors the program back to the disk-read calling statement of line 330. When F=8, indicating that we've addressed all income tax deduction categories, line 840 sends program flow to the end routine. Line 940 forwards a form-feed command to the printer to ready it for another routine, line 950 tells the DOS that we're through for a while, and line 960 is the program END.

The Budget Sort segment from lines 1000 to 1700 echoes the flow and logic of Income Tax Deduction Sort. The only differences are in the categories--some categories are combined, and more transaction codes are addressed. The Internal Revenue Service helped specify our sorting categories for the Income Tax Deduction Sort segment, but you may pick any categories or combination of codes that you like for the Budget Sort. If you elected to add some transaction types when you keypunched Electronic Checkbook, this is the place to pick up those new codes.

You may wish to add a third type of sort to the program. If you have a samll business, this program makes a good basic bookkeeper for your firm. With the techniques outlined here, you can adapt each program to your heart's delight. Your imagination is the only limit on your computer accomplishments--and since your imagination is unlimited, you can make your computer do anything!

SAMPLE INPUT - BOOKKEEPING WORKSHEET

READY
<u>RUN</u>

BOOKKEEPER

PLEASE PUT THE ELECTRONIC CHECKBOOK DISK IN DRIVE#2,
AND PRESS 'RETURN' WHEN YOU'RE READY?
WHAT OUTPUT PORT? <u>2</u>

IS THIS AN INCOME TAX OR A BUDGET EXERCISE? <u>INCOME TAX</u>

READY
<u>RUN</u>

BOOKKEEPER

PLEASE PUT THE ELECTRONIC CHECKBOOK DISK IN DRIVE#2,
AND PRESS 'RETURN' WHEN YOU'RE READY?
WHAT OUTPUT PORT? <u>2</u>

IS THIS AN INCOME TAX OR A BUDGET EXERCISE? <u>BUDGET</u>

READY
#

SAMPLE OUTPUT - INCOME TAX EXERCISE

CHECK SUMMARY

CHECK NR   PAYEE   AMOUNT

MEDICINE/DRUGS
1006   LOCAL PHARMACY   25.69

DOCTORS, DENTISTS, NURSES
1005   DR. HEALER   250.00

TAXES
1019   STATE TAX AUTHORITY   300.21
1020   LOCAL TAX AUTHORITY   29.95

INTEREST
1032   SECOND TRUST DEED COMPANY   102.13

CONTRIBUTIONS
1012   UNITED FUND   100.00

MISCELLANEOUS
1022   STATE COLLEGE   250.00
1023   COLLEGE BOOK STORE   52.66
1025   BUSINESS CLUB   125.00
1026   FAST PRINTER SERVICE   25.00
1031   STATE BANK   10.50

SAMPLE OUTPUT - BUDGET EXERCISE

CHECK SUMMARY

CHECK NR	PAYEE	AMOUNT
MEDICAL EXPENSE		
1005	DR. HEALER	250.00
1006	LOCAL PHARMACY	25.69
SHELTER EXPENSE		
1007	CITY FUEL	52.79
1008	COUNTY GAS & WATER	22.08
1013	FIRST MORTGAGE COMPANY	680.22
TAXES AND INTEREST		
1019	STATE TAX AUTHORITY	300.21
1020	LOCAL TAX AUTHORITY	29.95
1032	SECOND TRUST DEED COMPANY	102.13
FOOD AND ENTERTAINMENT		
1001	CORNER BAKERY	25.47
1002	NEIGHBORHOOD ICE CREAM	32.19
1003	PARTY GIFT SHOP	12.98
1015	FRIENDLY GROCERS	53.18
1027	VALENTINE RESTAURANT	36.25
1030	CABLE TELEVISION SERVICE	36.18
TRANSPORTATION AND CLOTHING		
1010	JEAN'S AUTO PARTS	122.27
1011	STATE GAS & OIL	25.33
1016	SMART CLOTHIERS	250.72
1017	SHALE OIL	72.07
EDUCATION/CONTRIBUTIONS		
1012	UNITED FUND	100.00
1022	STATE COLLEGE	250.00
1023	COLLEGE BOOK STORE	52.66
MISCELLANEOUS		
1025	BUSINESS CLUB	125.00
1026	FAST PRINTER SERVICE	25.00
1029	LOCAL LAUNDRY	23.05
1031	STATE BANK	10.50

```
0010  REM ***********************************
0020  REM *    BOOKKEEPING  WORKSHEET    *
0030  REM ***********************************
0040  REM ********* VERSION 10 *********
0050  LINE= 0
0060  DIGITS= 2
0100  PRINT TAB(20);"BOOKKEEPER"
0110  PRINT
0120  PRINT "Please put the Electronic Checkbook disk in Drive#2,"
0130  INPUT "and press 'RETURN' when you're ready",Z$
0140  OPEN #10,2001
0150  PRINT
0160  INPUT "What output port",P
0170  PRINT
0180  PRINT #P:PRINT#P:PRINT#P
0190  PRINT #P,TAB(32);"CHECK SUMMARY"
0200  PRINT #P:PRINT#P
0210  PRINT #P,"Check Nr";TAB(15);"Payee";TAB(60);"Amount"
0220  INPUT "Is this an INCOME TAX or a BUDGET exercise",Z$
0230  IF LEFT$(Z$,1)="I"  THEN 300
0240  IF LEFT$(Z$,1)="B"  THEN 1000
0250  PRINT "OOPS!  Your answer of '";Z$;"' doesn't help me."
0260  PRINT "Let's do it again."
0270  GOTO 220
0300  REM ** INCOME TAX DEDUCTION SORT ***
0310   F=0
0320  RESTORE #10:D=0:E=0
0330  GOSUB 2000
0340  IF D>0 THEN 320
0350  IF F>0 THEN 420
0360  IF C$(5)<>"ME" THEN 330
0370  IF E>0 THEN 400
0380  PRINT #P:E=1
0390  PRINT #P,"Medicine/Drugs"
0400  GOSUB 3000
0410  GOTO 330
0420  IF F>1 THEN 490
0430  IF C$(5)<>"HE" THEN 330
0440  IF E>0 THEN 470
0450  PRINT #P:E=1
0460  PRINT #P,"Health Insurance"
0470  GOSUB 3000
0480  GOTO 330
0490  IF F>2 THEN 560
0500  IF C$(5)<>"DO" THEN 330
0510  IF E>0 THEN 540
0520  PRINT #P:E=1
0530  PRINT #P,"Doctors, Dentists, Nurses"
0540  GOSUB 3000
0550  GOTO 330
0560  IF F>3 THEN 630
0570  IF C$(5)<>"HO" THEN 330
0580  IF E>0 THEN 610
0590  PRINT #P:E=1
```

```
0600 PRINT #P,"Hospitals, Laboratories"
0610 GOSUB 3000
0620 GOTO 330
0630 IF F>4 THEN 700
0640 IF C$(5)<>"TA" THEN 330
0640 IF C$(5)<>"TA" THEN 330
0650 IF E>0 THEN 680
0660 PRINT #P:E=1
0670 PRINT #P,"Taxes"
0680 GOSUB 3000
0690 GOTO 330
0700 IF F>5 THEN 770
0710 IF C$(5)<>"IN" THEN 330
0720 IF E>0 THEN 750
0730 PRINT #P:E=1
0740 PRINT #P,"Interest"
0750 GOSUB 3000
0760 GOTO 330
0770 IF F>6 THEN 840
0780 IF C$(5)<>"CO" THEN 330
0790 IF E>0 THEN 820
0800 PRINT #P:E=1
0810 PRINT #P,"Contributions"
0820 GOSUB 3000
0830 GOTO 330
0840 IF F>7 THEN 940
0850 IF C$(5)="EM" THEN 890
0860 IF C$(5)="ED" THEN 890
0870 IF C$(5)="MI" THEN 890
0880 GOTO 330
0890 IF E>0 THEN 920
0900 PRINT #P:E=1
0910 PRINT #P,"Miscellaneous"
0920 GOSUB 3000
0930 GOTO 330
0940 PRINT #P,CHR$(12)
0950 CLOSE #10
0960 END
1000 REM ******** BUDGET SORT *********
1010  F=0
1020 RESTORE #10:D=0:E=0
1030 GOSUB 2000
1040 IF D>0 THEN 1020
1050 IF F>0 THEN 1160
1060 IF C$(5)="ME" THEN 1110
1070 IF C$(5)="HO" THEN 1110
1080 IF C$(5)="HE" THEN 1110
1090 IF C$(5)="DO" THEN 1110
1100 GOTO 1030
1110 IF E>0 THEN 1140
1120 PRINT #P:E=1
1130 PRINT #P,"Medical Expense"
1140 GOSUB 3000
1150 GOTO 1030
```

```
1160 IF F>1 THEN 1250
1170 IF C$(5)="SH" THEN 1200
1180 IF C$(5)="UT" THEN 1200
1190 GOTO 1030
1200 IF E>0 THEN 1230
1210 PRINT #P:E=1
1220 PRINT #P,"Shelter Expense"
1230 GOSUB 3000
1240 GOTO 1030
1250 IF F>2 THEN 1340
1260 IF C$(5)="TA" THEN 1290
1280 GOTO 1030
1290 IF E>0 THEN 1320
1300 PRINT #P:E=1
1310 PRINT #P,"Taxes and Interest"
1320 GOSUB 3000
1330 GOTO 1030
1340 IF F>3 THEN 1430
1350 IF C$(5)="FO" THEN 1380
1360 IF C$(5)="EN" THEN 1380
1370 GOTO 1030
1380 IF E>0 THEN 1410
1390 PRINT #P:E=1
1400 PRINT #P,"Food and Entertainment"
1410 GOSUB 3000
1420 GOTO 1030
1430 IF F>4 THEN 1520
1440 IF C$(5)="TR" THEN 1470
1450 IF C$(5)="CL" THEN 1470
1460 GOTO 1030
1470 IF E>0 THEN 1500
1480 PRINT #P:E=1
1490 PRINT #P,"Transportation and Clothing"
1500 GOSUB 3000
1510 GOTO 1030
1520 IF F>5 THEN 1610
1530 IF C$(5)="ED" THEN 1560
1540 IF C$(5)="CO" THEN 1560
1550 GOTO 1030
1560 IF E>0 THEN 1590
1570 PRINT #P:E=1
1580 PRINT #P,"Education/Contributions"
1590 GOSUB 3000
1600 GOTO 1030
1610 IF F>6 THEN 940
1620 IF C$(5)="OT" THEN 1660
1630 IF C$(5)="EM" THEN 1660
1640 IF C$(5)="MI" THEN 1660
1650 GOTO 1030
1660 IF E>0 THEN 1690
1670 PRINT #P:E=1
1680 PRINT #P,"Miscellaneous"
1690 GOSUB 3000
1700 GOTO 1030
```

```
2000 REM **** READ/FORMAT CHECK DATA ****
2010 READ #10,C$(1),C$(2),C$(3),C$(4),B$\2060
2020   C(1)=VAL(MID$(C$(1),3,4))
2030   C$(5)=LEFT$(C$(1),2)
2040   C(4)=VAL(C$(4))
2050 RETURN
2060   F=F+1
2070   D=1
2080 GOTO 2050
3000 REM ***** PRINT CHECK RECORD *****
3010 DIGITS= 0
3020 PRINT #P,C(1);
3030 PRINT #P,TAB(13);C$(3);
3040 DIGITS= 2
3050 PRINT #P,TAB(65-LEN(STR$(C(4))));C(4)
3060 RETURN
```

7
CASH FLOW ANALYSIS

"Where does the money go?" We all ask that at times.
When we apply for some loans, the lender will ask it, too.
Lenders usually phrase the question more formally: They
will ask for a "cash flow" statement or "source and application of funds" statement. Big business uses the cash
flow statement to inform owners and potential investors
what happened to the cash that came through the treasury
during any month, quarter, or year.

Now your home computer can generate this formal accounting statement. While the program version presented
here is configured to prepare personal statements, a few
changes will produce the formal business style.

BACKGROUND

As its name suggests, the <u>Cash Flow Analysis</u> is interested
only in the cash you have received and spent. We want to
look at net income (take-home pay), other cash received
(gifts, proceeds from an automobile sale, etc.), and cash
spent (total loan payments, for example, instead of just
the interest or principal). You can use the summary provided by the <u>Bookkeeping Worksheet</u> program as an input
document.

The arithmetic involved in <u>Cash Flow Analysis</u> is simple addition and subtraction. The accounting theory is
pretty basic, too. Add all the items that bring cash in;
subtract those that drain cash out; the difference is the
increase or decrease in your working capital. The increase
in your working capital or discretionary income is money
you can invest or enjoy. A decrease means you may need to
cut back your investing or pleasure spending a bit. Too
many periods of decrease may indicate the need for a change
in your lifestyle.

Before we start through the listing, let's discuss the user involvement with Cash Flow Analysis. This is another minimum-operator-work routine. Since I use this program frequently in my private practice, the program requests personal data (name and address) to identify each client. When you keypunch the routine for your private use, you can omit the personal data input and include the information as part of the program.

After the heading is entered, the financial questions begin. The program is structured to ask for net income, interest and dividends received, and proceeds from the sale of assets (such as the sale of an automobile). Seven unstructured possibilities follow to handle the reporting of gifts, inheritances, side business income, or some other source of money that doesn't fit the preset categories. Make up the categories as you enter them. Type the name of the category, a comma, then the dollar amount. When you have entered as much as you intend to, type a comma and a zero to terminate the input routine.

We handle disbursement data the same way. The three predefined areas are living expenses, payments on purchase of assets, and payments of long-term debt. Another seven user-defined inputs may be entered. You may wish to include, for example, investments, vacation costs, special donations, or some other cash outflow here.

After the initial entry sequence, the routine will ask if you wish to review the entries. If you answer "YES" your inputs will be displayed for checking. The review cycle will also show you the unstructured categories that had no input. These will be suppressed at print time. If you don't like the numbers, a "NO" response to the O.K.? question will recycle the input routine and give you another chance.

When the input is satisfactory, choose the output device you wish and relax. Your computer will prepare a professional-quality statement. The sample output illustrates a standard accounting treatment of the source and application of funds format. After each printing, the program will ask if you want another copy. You may change output device selections from one copy to the next. (I use this feature to run the first copy on my video terminal as another check of the data; then, subsequent copies are produced on the printer.)

PROGRAMMING NOTES

The first six lines (10 through 60) are the header. These should be pretty familiar to you by now. The data input routine occupies lines 100 through 380. The first personalization step you may want to take is to delete the INPUTs in lines 110, 120, and 130 and substitute variable definitions that include your name and address.

Categories are titled with a slightly different technique than we've used before. The FOR...NEXT loop of lines 160 to 200 collects the standard category income items. Line 170 reads the title of the category from the DATA list of lines 2000 through 2050. The variable loaded in line 170 will be used later for the printout of the form, so you need change only the DATA statements to alter the standard category titles. Line 180 prints the title as an operator prompt; then line 190 gathers the monetary data.

User-defined categories are collected in lines 210 through 250. Line 240 terminates the input sequence whenever a null is sensed in character string variable C$(X). This feature saves the user from having to enter bunches of zeroes when few new titles are desired.

Lines 270 to 310 echo the input sequence for pre-defined cash applications. Lines 320 through 360 allow the user-defined input. Note that lines 220 through 330 run the FOR...NEXT loops from 4 to 10. This provides consecutive numbers in the matrix variable designators and allows another FOR...NEXT to handle the output.

A preview of the printing sequence is available in the checking routine of lines 400 through 490. The program presents your inputs on the control terminal and asks if the numbers are O.K. If you answer "NO", line 490 prints a re-enter message, RESTOREs the data pointer, and steers the program to the input sequence at line 160.

Most of the remaining BASIC code is concerned with printing the form. Line 510 allows user selection of the output port. We've used a slightly different output technique in Cash Flow Analysis. Instead of our normal PRINT #P, we've defined the control port as P in line 520. If your printer doesn't have a terminal feature (keyboard), this can be a bit risky until the program is debugged. (Your computer may send an error message or an input command to the nonterminal and just wait for a response until the cows come home.) Before you request another INPUT, you'll need to redefine the control port as we've done in line 1190.

The print routine is also the "number cruncher" (mathematics processor) for Cash Flow Analysis. The cash receipts and disbursements are totalled in lines 710 and 850, respectively. The determination of net increase or decrease in working capital is made in lines 900 and 910. As you'll note in the sample run, the increase or decrease is printed below the disbursements column to achieve a balance with the receipts. The increase is reported by lines 920 through 940; the decrease is handled in lines 1000 through 1040. Line 1010 changes the negative value (indicating a decrease in working capital) to a positive number for printing. Line 1030 is needed to re-negate the number to keep the arithmetic of line 960 proper.

Lines 1170 through 1220 provide the finishing touches for Cash Flow Analysis. Incidentally, the odd numbering sequence at the end of the program results from a modification I made to remove the code that printed a signature block at the bottom of the form. If you wish to include your signature on the form, use something like this:

```
980 GOTO 1100
.
.
.
1100 PRINT
1110 PRINT
1120 PRINT
1130 PRINT TAB (50); "--------------------"
1140 PRINT TAB (50); "MY NAME"
1150 PRINT TAB (50); "ACCOUNTANT"
1160 PRINT
```

This is a personal program, but you could use it for business. Let your computer serve you in every way possible.

SAMPLE INPUT - CASH FLOW

READY
RUN

NAME? MS. ENNA CHIPTZ
STREET ADDRESS? #1 EASY STREET
CITY, STATE ZIP? UTOPIA,CA 99999
MONTH AND YEAR OF REPORT? DECEMBER,1984

NET INCOME? 42678.30
INTEREST AND DIVIDENDS? 2513.74
PROCEEDS FROM SALE OF ASSETS? 677.25
ENTER 'SOURCE'<COMMA>'AMOUNT' OF OTHER CASH.
? GARAGE SALE PROFIT,1214.18
? CONSULTING FEES,2243.50
? ,0

LIVING EXPENSES? 24312.89
PAYMENTS ON PURCHASE OF ASSETS? 6109.10
PAYMENTS ON LONG TERM DEBT? 5088.60
ENTER 'APPLICATION' <COMMA> 'AMOUNT' OF OTHER EXPENDITURES.
? STOCK INVESTMENT,4279.90
? SCHOOL FUND ENDOWMENT,9500.
? ,0
WANT TO REVIEW ENTRIES? YES

NET INCOME $ 42678.30
INTEREST AND DIVIDENDS $ 2513.74
PROCEEDS FROM SALE OF ASSETS $ 677.25
GARAGE SALE PROFIT $ 1214.18
CONSULTING FEES $ 2243.50
  $ 0.00
  $ 0.00
  $ 0.00
  $ 0.00
  $ 0.00
LIVING EXPENSES $ 24312.89
PAYMENTS ON PURCHASE OF ASSETS $ 6109.10
PAYMENTS ON LONG TERM DEBT $ 5088.60
STOCK INVESTMENT $ 4279.90
SCHOOL FUND ENDOWMENT $ 9500.00
  $ 0.00
  $ 0.00
  $ 0.00
  $ 0.00
  $ 0.00
O.K.? YUP
WHAT OUTPUT PORT? 2

ANOTHER COPY? NO THANKS

READY
#

SAMPLE OUTPUT - CASH FLOW

                    MS. ENNA CHIPTZ
                    #1 EASY STREET
                    UTOPIA, CA 99999

        SOURCE AND APPLICATION OF FUNDS FOR DECEMBER, 1984

SOURCE OF FUNDS

NET INCOME $ 42678.30
INTEREST AND DIVIDENDS   2513.74
PROCEEDS FROM SALE OF ASSETS   6775.25
GARAGE SALE PROFIT   1214.18
CONSULTING FEES   2243.50

TOTAL $ 55424.97

APPLICATION OF FUNDS

LIVING EXPENSES $ 24312.89
PAYMENTS ON PURCHASE OF ASSETS   6109.10
PAYMENTS ON LONG TERM DEBT   5088.60
STOCK INVESTMENT   4279.90
SCHOOL FUND ENDOWMENT   9500.00

INCREASE IN WORKING CAPITAL   6134.48

TOTAL $ 55424.97
                                                     ===========

64

```
0010 REM **********************************
0020 REM *              CASH FLOW             *
0030 REM **********************************
0040 REM ********* VERSION 20 *********
0050 LINE= 0
0060 DIGITS= 2
0100 REM ******* INPUT ROUTINE *********
0110 INPUT "Name",A$(1),A$(2)
0120 INPUT "Street Address",A$(3)
0130 INPUT "City, State ZIP",A$(4),A$(5)
0140 INPUT "Month and year of report",A$(6),A$(7)
0150 PRINT
0160 FOR X=1 TO 3
0170 READ C$(X)
0180 PRINT C$(X);
0190 INPUT C(X)
0200 NEXT X
0210 PRINT "Enter 'SOURCE'<COMMA>'AMOUNT' of other cash."
0220 FOR X=4 TO 10
0230 INPUT C$(X),C(X)
0240 IF C$(X)="" THEN X=10
0250 NEXT X
0260 PRINT
0270 FOR X=1TO3
0280 READ D$(X)
0290 PRINT D$(X);
0300 INPUT D(X)
0310 NEXT X
0320 PRINT "Enter 'APPLICATION' <COMMA> 'AMOUNT' of other expenditures."
0330 FOR X=4 TO 10
0340 INPUT D$(X),D(X)
0350 IF D$(X)="" THEN X=10
0360 NEXT X
0370 INPUT "Want to review entries",Z$
0380 IF LEFT$(Z$,1)="N" THEN 500
0400 REM *************CHECKING ROUTINE********************
0410 FOR X=1 TO 10
0420 PRINT C$(X);" $ ";C(X)
0430 NEXT X
0440 FOR X=1 TO 10
0450 PRINT D$(X);" $ ";D(X)
0460 NEXT X
0470 INPUT "O.K.",Z$
0480 IF LEFT$(Z$,1)<>"N" THEN 500
0490 PRINT "Please re-enter the data.":RESTORE:GOTO160
0500 REM ** PRINT ROUTINE*********************
0510 INPUT "What output port",P
0520 PORT= P
0530 PRINT
0540 PRINT
0550 PRINT
0560 PRINT TAB((80-LEN(A$(1)))/2);A$(1)
0570 IF A$(2)="" THEN 590
0580 PRINT TAB ((80-LEN(A$(2)))/2);A$(2)
0590 PRINT TAB ((80-LEN(A$(3)))/2);A$(3)
0600 PRINT TAB ((78-LEN(A$(4)+A$(5)))/2);A$(4);", ";A$(5)
```

```
0610 PRINT
0620 PRINT TAB((40-LEN(A$(6)+A$(7)))/2);
0630 PRINT "SOURCE AND APPLICATION OF FUNDS FOR ";A$(6);", ";A$(7)
0640 PRINT :PRINT
0650 PRINT "Source of Funds":PRINT
0655  C=0
0660 FOR X=1TO10
0670 PRINT C$(X);
0680 IF X>1 THEN 700
0690 PRINT TAB(38);"$";
0700 PRINT TAB(50-LEN(STR$(C(X))));C(X)
0710  C=C+C(X)
0720 IF C$(X+1)="" THEN X=10
0730 NEXT X
0740 PRINT TAB(38);"--------------"
0750 PRINT "Total";
0760 PRINT TAB(65-LEN(STR$(C)));"$ ";C
0770 PRINT
0780 PRINT "Application of Funds":PRINT
0790  D=0
0800 FOR X=1 TO 10
0805 IF D$(X)="" THEN X=10
0810 PRINT D$(X);
0820 IF X>1 THEN 840
0830 PRINT TAB(38);"$";
0840 PRINT TAB(50-LEN(STR$(D(X))));D(X)
0850  D=D+D(X)
0860 IF D$(X+1)="" THEN X=10
0870 NEXT X
0880 PRINT TAB(38);"--------------"
0900  F=C-D
0910 IF F<0 THEN 1000
0920 PRINT "Increase in Working Capital";
0930 PRINT TAB(50-LEN(STR$(F)));F
0940 PRINT TAB(38);"--------------"
0950 PRINT "Total";
0960 PRINT TAB(65-LEN(STR$(F+D)));"$ ";F+D
0970 PRINT TAB(55);"============"
0980 GOTO 1170
1000 PRINT "Decrease in Working Capital";
1010  F=-F
1020 PRINT TAB(49-LEN(STR$(F)));"(";F;" )"
1030  F=-F
1040 GOTO 950
1170 PRINT CHR$(12)
1190 PORT= 1
1200 INPUT "Another copy",Z$
1210 IF LEFT$(Z$,1)="Y" THEN 500
1220 END
2000 DATA "Net Income"
2010 DATA "Interest and Dividends"
2020 DATA "Proceeds from Sale of Assets"
2030 DATA "Living Expenses"
2040 DATA "Payments on Purchase of Assets"
2050 DATA "Payments on Long Term Debt"
```

66

8
INCOME TAX ESTIMATOR

This is the only money-management program that doesn't provide a formal statement of some kind. It is a fun routine that will help predict your annual tax tab during the year. While it isn't to-the-penny precise, Income Tax Estimator will provide a method for calculation of those pesky quarterly estimated payments to the Internal Revenue Service.

The program is about as straightforward as they come. There are no subroutines, matrix variables, or FOR...NEXT loops. The arithmetic used stays with the basic four functions (add, subtract, multiply, and divide).

Income Tax Estimator will project your wages and income tax withholding for part of the year to predict year-end amounts. It will offer a vehicle and check list for entry of your estimated tax adjustments and deductions. When your year-end "tax-table" income has been estimated, the program will allow you to enter the tax figures from the IRS tables. Finally, the routine will tell you whether to expect a refund next April or increase your withholding to avoid a penalty.

BACKGROUND

The accounting theory here is straight from the IRS forms. We'll estimate your gross income, subtract deductions and tax adjustments to arrive at tax-table income, then look up the tax in the IRS tables. It has been my experience that the time spent in keypunching the IRS tax tables is not repaid in convenience gained. Since the tax laws and regulations change frequently, you'll spend a terrible amount of time keypunching and changing for a small benefit. This is another adaptable program; you can add any features you want. Add the tax calculation if you want the convenience of an automatic look-up. You may want a formal form to present your quarterly or annual estimate; or, add more input stages to handle your unique tax problems.

OPERATING NOTES

The sample run illustrates the ease of running Income Tax Estimator. Input the total wage and withholding information from the (current) family paycheck stubs in the first two queries. Gross wages and income tax withholding totals will be projected for the whole year by the routine. The "annualization" is driven by your entry of the name of the current month. To increase estimate accuracy, use the month just ended or about to end (for example, enter "April" until about mid-May).

You can use the output from Bookkeeping Worksheet to help you estimate your itemized deductions. This program asks for yearly estimated totals for deductions, because many expenses that qualify come up sporadically during the year (property taxes in many areas, for example, are paid once or twice per year). Annualization of these sporadic payments would provide a false picture of your tax position. In recent years, the Internal Revenue Service has used a tax-table look-up method of calculating your just due. The table incorporates a standard deduction (known as the "zero-bracket amount") which must be subtracted from itemized deductions before the table reference means anything. The zero-bracket amount changes periodically, so look on your tax forms to see what the current number is. After you enter income adjustments, the program will tell you what your estimated tax-table income is. Get out last year's IRS booklet, and look up the appropriate tax. When you type in that figure, the routine will compare it with your projected year-end withholding to predict additional tax due or a refund. When you prepay less than 80 percent of your yearly tax bill (through withholding or quarterly estimates), you may be subject to a penalty for underpayment. Income Tax Estimator will check for the potential penalty situation and warn you.

PROGRAMMING NOTES

As an inspection of the listing reveals, we've added a line to the header in this program. Line 70 ensures that variable M starts at zero. (Most BASICs zero all variables at program start, but line 70 takes care of the minority that allows a random initialization.) The remainder of the heading commands are standard.

Lines 100 to 180 receive income information. The information on other income requested in line 150 includes interest and dividends, side business profits, and any other potentially taxable receipts. Note that we've used a slightly different technique for naming variables here. The income (and deductions) variables are in subscripted form rather than matrix notation. "I2" is not the same as "I (2)". If your BASIC won't accept this notation comfortably, change to a version that your computer and you agree on.

68

We allow user input of the name of the month in line
170 to reduce the confusion that could result from trying
to remember what number month we're in. Lines 190 through
340 are a brute-force conversion of the month name to a
number. If the user hasn't typed a three-letter sequence
that is recognized, the operator-error trap in lines 320,
330, and 340 will route the program back to the month-input
statement.

Lines 350 and 360 project year-end income and withholding amounts. The technique is to divide by the month
number to get a monthly average, then multiply by 12 to get
an annual estimate. We get the same effect when multiplying by 12 divided by the month number.

There's nothing exotic about the deduction sequence in
lines 400 through 490. The variable names may need some
attention, but the code is straightforward. Line 500 totals the estimated amounts, and lines 520 and 530 remove the
zero-bracket amount. (Line 530 keeps your deduction amount
from going negative if itemized deductions fail to exceed
the standard.)

After lines 550, 560, and 570 collect the adjustments
to income, the tax-table income is calculated and displayed
by lines 600 through 640. Your input of the tax amount is
handled by lines 650 through 680.

Line 690 repeats the tax you typed in, and line 710
presents your projected withholding. Line 740 determines
that you have a deficiency or refund and steers the program
flow to the appropriate output message. Line 840 checks
the 80 percent payment status (only for deficiency calculations) and routes the program around the warning message
if it is not appropriate.

Income Tax Estimator won't do all your tax work, but
it will help you know what ball park you're in during the
year.

SAMPLE RUN - INCOME TAX ESTIMATE

READY
RUN

GROSS FAMILY WAGES TO DATE? 11302

FEDERAL WITHHOLDING TO DATE? 1122.25

OTHER INCOME TO DATE? 355

WHAT MONTH IS IT NOW? APRIL

ENTER ESTIMATED ANNUAL TOTALS FOR:

DEDUCTIBLE MEDICAL EXPENSE? 500
STATE SALES, INCOME, AND PROPERTY TAXES? 2350
INTEREST EXPENSE? 5500
CHARITABLE CONTRIBUTIONS? 250
DEDUCTIBLE CASUALTY LOSSES? 0
MISCELLANEOUS DEDUCTIBLE EXPENSES? 500

WHAT IS YOUR 'ZERO BRACKET AMOUNT'? 4350

ENTER THE TOTAL 'ADJUSTMENTS' - (MOVING EXPENSE,
EMPLOYEE BUSINESS EXPENSES, ALIMONY, IRA PAYMENTS,
OR INTEREST PENALTY ON SAVINGS WITHDRAWAL)? 3200

YOUR ESTIMATED ANNUAL 'TAX TABLE' INCOME IS $27021.00

LOOK IN THE CURRENT TAX TABLE (LAST YEAR'S VERSION IS
CLOSE ENOUGH) UNDER YOUR FILING STATUS AND NUMBER OF
EXEMPTIONS, AND TYPE IN THE TAX YOU FIND? 3624

YOUR ESTIMATED ANNUAL TAX IS $ 3624.00
YOUR ESTIMATED WITHHOLDING IS   3366.75

THE ESTIMATED TAX DUE IS $ 257.25

READY
#

```
0010 REM ************************************
0020 REM *        INCOME TAX ESTIMATOR        *
0030 REM ************************************
0040 REM ********** VERSION 20 **********
0050 LINE= 0
0060 DIGITS= 2
0070  M=0
0100 REM ********** DATA INPUT **********
0110 INPUT "GROSS FAMILY WAGES TO DATE",I1
0120 PRINT
0130 INPUT "FEDERAL WITHHOLDING TO DATE",W
0140 PRINT
0150 INPUT "OTHER INCOME TO DATE",I2
0160 PRINT
0170 INPUT "WHAT MONTH IS IT NOW",M$
0180 PRINT
0190 REM **** CHANGE MONTH TO NUMBER ****
0200 IF LEFT$(M$,3)="JAN" M=1
0210 IF LEFT$(M$,3)="FEB" M=2
0220 IF LEFT$(M$,3)="MAR" M=3
0230 IF LEFT$(M$,3)="APR" M=4
0240 IF LEFT$(M$,3)="MAY" M=5
0250 IF LEFT$(M$,3)="JUN" M=6
0260 IF LEFT$(M$,3)="JUL" M=7
0270 IF LEFT$(M$,3)="AUG" M=8
0280 IF LEFT$(M$,3)="SEP" M=9
0290 IF LEFT$(M$,3)="OCT" M=10
0300 IF LEFT$(M$,3)="NOV" M=11
0310 IF LEFT$(M$,3)="DEC" M=12
0320 IF M<>0 THEN 350
0330 PRINT "PLEASE -- JUST TYPE THE NAME OF THE CURRENT MONTH."
0340 GOTO 170
0350  I=(I1+I2)*(12/M)
0360  W=W*12/M
0400 REM ********** DEDUCTIONS **********
0410 PRINT "ENTER ESTIMATED ANNUAL TOTALS FOR:"
0420 PRINT
0430 INPUT "DEDUCTIBLE MEDICAL EXPENSE",D1
0440 INPUT "STATE SALES, INCOME, AND PROPERTY TAXES",D2
0450 INPUT "INTEREST EXPENSE",D3
0460 INPUT "CHARITABLE CONTRIBUTIONS",D4
0470 INPUT "DEDUCTIBLE CASUALTY LOSSES",D5
0480 INPUT "MISCELLANEOUS DEDUCTIBLE EXPENSES",D6
0490 PRINT
0500  D=D1+D2+D3+D4+D5+D6
0510 INPUT "WHAT IS YOUR 'ZERO BRACKET AMOUNT'",Z
0520  D=D-Z
0530 IF D<0 THEN D=0
0540 PRINT
0550 PRINT "ENTER THE TOTAL 'ADJUSTMENTS' - (MOVING EXPENSE,"
0560 PRINT "EMPLOYEE BUSINESS EXPENSES, ALIMONY, IRA PAYMENTS,"
0570 INPUT "OR INTEREST PENALTY ON SAVINGS WITHDRAWAL)",A
0580 PRINT
0600 REM ******* TAX TABLE INCOME *******
```

```
0610  T=I-A-D
0620 PRINT
0630 PRINT "YOUR ESTIMATED ANNUAL 'TAX TABLE' INCOME IS $";T
0640 PRINT
0650 PRINT "LOOK IN THE CURRENT TAX TABLE (LAST YEAR'S VERSION IS"
0660 PRINT "CLOSE ENOUGH) UNDER YOUR FILING STATUS AND NUMBER OF"
0670 INPUT "EXEMPTIONS, AND TYPE IN THE TAX YOU FIND",X
0680 PRINT
0690 PRINT "YOUR ESTIMATED ANNUAL TAX IS ";
0700 PRINT TAB(63-LEN(STR$(X)));"$ ";X
0710 PRINT "YOUR ESTIMATED WITHHOLDING IS ";
0720 PRINT TAB(65-LEN(STR$(W)));W
0730 PRINT TAB(55);"-----------"
0740 IF (X-W)>0 THEN 800
0750 PRINT "YOUR ESTIMATED REFUND IS";
0760 PRINT TAB(63-LEN(STR$(W-X)));"$ ";(W-X)
0770 PRINT
0780 PRINT
0790 GOTO 900
0800 PRINT "THE ESTIMATED TAX DUE IS ";
0810 PRINT TAB(63-LEN(STR$(X-W)));"$ ";(X-W)
0820 PRINT
0830 PRINT
0840 IF W>(0.8*X) THEN 900
0850 PRINT "YOUR WITHHOLDING IS EXPECTED TO BE LESS THAN 80% OF YOUR"
0860 PRINT "TOTAL TAX, SO YOU SHOULD EITHER INCREASE YOUR WITHHOLDING"
0870 PRINT "OR MAKE QUARTERLY ESTIMATED PAYMENTS OF ABOUT $";
0880 PRINT INT((X-W)/4)
0890 PRINT
0900 END
```

9
BUDGET ANALYSIS

The final program in this section is a bit deceptive. More than half of the code is devoted to data input. The good news is the golden opportunity you have to modify the program to your personal preferences. The bad news is a feeling of disappointment when you input a page of numbers and get only half a page of output.

Budget Analysis is another program used in my private practice. I use the input as a key to discussion of budgeting areas with clients. The old "rules of thumb" for budget guidelines have pretty well gone out the window. Housing/shelter costs vary from community to community, transportation expenses escalate weekly, and food and entertainment prices change daily. The relative percentage of income that you allocate to the different categories should be set for your unique situation. When you purchase a home, for example, the mortgage payments will take a larger percentage of your income than what is normally recommended by "experts." After you've been there a few years, your income generally will have risen more than the mortgage payments, making the percentage less than the guideline. No one can know your financial situation better than you. Your home computer can help you know it better than ever.

The first step in a budgeting exercise is a look at your present spending pattern. Bookkeeping Worksheet will give you a start; Budget Analysis completes the story. Your budget is a spending plan; is is not a law. Your family must be comfortable with the guidelines if the budget is to be helpful. Get the whole family to participate in the budget design to insure family-wide understanding and use of the plan.

The theory of Budget Analysis is simple. Collect your income and expenses, put everything on a monthly basis, and see if the income exceeds the expenses. Again, mathematical manipulations are limited to addition, subtraction, multiplication, and division. Program flow is linear; start at the beginning and move through to the end.

73

The sample run illustrates a typical input/output sequence. After requesting personal data, the program addresses income. The initial questions are used to set up the income-information-gathering routine. You can fudge a little on the input and enter nonwage income items as "paychecks." (For example, a monthly interest check from an investment fund could be treated as a paycheck without destroying the program logic.)

Expense categories are collected on a monthly basis because most of the items demand monthly payments. Insurance and tax payments are usually quarterly or semiannual, but convert them to an average monthly amount. If the standard categories don't cover all of your expenses, don't fret. The final expense entries allow up to 10 user-defined categories. To terminate the user-defined area, type a comma and a zero.

Since some loan payments are on a weekly basis (credit union loans, for example), a short input segment allows for special setup of loan payment data. If you entered a mortgage payment earlier, naturally you don't enter it again.

With all the financial facts in, it's time to select the output port for printing, and time for another operator aid: After port selection, the PRESS 'RETURN' TO PRINT? request affords an opportunity to check that your printer is energized and on-line. (Too often, I've tried to output a form to a printer that hasn't been turned on.) When the first output is complete, you'll get a chance to make another copy. Along with the second copy is another output-port choice, so you can print the first version on the video terminal to see if a hard copy is appropriate.

PROGRAMMING NOTES

While the listing seems a trifle long, much of the code involves short segments that repeat. Your BASIC editor can have this program in memory in short order; you should be able to keypunch the whole thing manually in an evening. (Practice helps increase your speed. By the time you've assembled your personal financial system, you'll have increased your keypunch speed considerably.)

Lines 10 through 60 are the usual heading. Because we use a lot of variables in Budget Analysis, it takes two statements to provide the DIMensioning. Line 70 handles the character string variables, and line 80 takes care of the numerics.

The personal data input is covered in lines 100 through 150. When you adapt this program for your personal use, you can omit the questions and include the data as definitions.

Lines 1000 through 1700 gather income information. You can customize this code considerably by keypunching only those segments applicable to your situation. For example, if your household is solely on a weekly paycheck basis, you can ignore the code that collects other income sources.

Lines 1010 through 1090 are used to set limits for the later input routines. Line 1060 breaks a pattern by asking a yes-or-no question instead of one requiring a numeric response. Any answer that doesn't begin with either a "Y" or "N" will be trapped by lines 1070, 1080, and 1090. Lines 1100 through 1460 gather the take-home income amounts and total each category. The variables set in lines 1010 to 1050 become the upper boundary of the FOR...NEXT loops. You'll note that the segments repeat (except for the frequency of receipt and variable subscripts), so here is an opportunity for your BASIC editor to save your keypunch time.

Line 1500 allows you to bypass the request for information on other income if I5=0. Again, the code from lines 1500 to 1700 is a series of echoes. The first step of each pair asks for a category and an amount. If the amount is zero, the second step will steer program flow past the remaining questions.

Monthly expenses are collected by lines 2000 through 2495. You can save more keypunch time by ignoring those categories that are not applicable in your home. You may also wish to add some categories that I've forgotten. By adding other categories, you can probably dispense with the inputs for "other expenses" altogether. Just remember to change the variable DIMensioning back in lines 70 and 80 to match your new category numbers.

The collection routine for other expenses looks a lot like the segment on other income. The flow is similar; however, variable O1 is used a flag for the printout. The code from line 2500 to line 2690 is a parallel to the paycheck input. The program flow is nearly identical; only the purpose and variable subscripts differ.

At this point, another opportunity for modification is available. All of the expense data and income information is in computer memory--all sorted in the large number of variables we defined. You may wish to include an output-listing routine to provide a hard-copy record. Lines 2700 through 3999 are open for use.

Our standard output-port selection routine is housed in lines 4000 through 4040. The INPUT of line 4020 is used to allow the operator a final check of printer readiness. Printing of the output statement (and the final mathematical wizardry) take place in lines 5000 to 5700. There's not much new here, so we'll just hit the high points.

Line 5120 multiplies each paycheck total by its annual frequency to get a yearly total, then divides the sum by 12 to present an effective monthly amount. Line 5140 sums the annual income items and divides by 12 for the same reason. Regular monthly expenses are totalled in lines 5350, 5360, and 5370. This is brute-force summation, but having a FOR...NEXT loop do the same job would take four lines of code:

```
5350 LET E=0
5360 FOR J=1 TO 25
5365 E = E + E(J)
5370 NEXT J
```

and E would have to be set to zero for subsequent printing routines.

The determination that you have excess income or greater expenses than income is made in lines 5490 and 5500. (Your checkbook has probably already told you the answer to this question, but not as quantitatively as Budget Analysis.) Line 5490 subtracts expense and loan totals from income and once-a-year receipts. Line 5500 asks if the absolute value of N is equal to N. If so, N is a positive number, and there is a surplus of income over outgo. Program flow jumps to line 5600 to report the happy news. Line 5620 calculates the surplus as a percentage of total income to fill in the blank in the savings/investment message of line 5650. The 10-percent savings goal reported in line 5660 is reasonable to conservative financial people. I included it because I am financially conservative. Some advisors advocate a 10-percent shortfall in inflationary times. If you agree with this philosophy, you may wish to have your version of Budget Analysis calculate the shortfall percent.

Lines 5700 through 5740 finish the listing with the standard choice of another printed copy. The use of the subroutine at lines 6000 to 6020 is almost the height of laziness. It saves keypunching two whole lines in the program! (It also provides the opportunity for some "bells and whistles" at program close.)

Budget Analysis has the greatest modification opportunity of any program we've seen so far. By this time, you've mastered the art of adapting my BASIC to your computer. Now you can stretch your creative wings and personalize this program to your heart's content!

SAMPLE INPUT - BUDGET

ENTER FIRST NAME(S) & INITIAL(S)?   HARRY & INA
LAST NAME? DANTRIED
NUMBER & STREET? #10 TENTH AVENUE
APT OR BOX (SPECIFY) NUMBER?
CITY, STATE & ZIP? UTOPIA,CA 99999
AREA CODE AND TELEPHONE NUMBER? (000) 555-1212

INCOME

HOW MANY WEEKLY PAY CHECKS? 2
HOW MANY BI-WEEKLY PAY CHECKS? 0
HOW MANY MONTHLY PAY CHECKS? 1
HOW MANY SEMI-MONTHLY CHECKS? 0
ANY OTHERS? NO
ENTER THE USUAL AMOUNT FOR EACH
WEEKLY TAKE HOME CHECK
#1 ? 523,22
#2 ? 532,14
MONTHLY CHECK
#1 ? 1250

FIXED MONTHLY EXPENSES

LIST THE USUAL AMOUNTS FOR:
ALIMONY? 0
AUTO INSURANCE? 75
BANK ACCOUNT CHARGES? 15
BUS/TAXI FARES? 50
CHILD CARE? 0
CHILD SUPPORT? 0
CIGARETTES, TOBACCO, ETC.? 95
CLOTHING? 350
CONTRIBUTIONS/GIFTS? 25
DUES? 50
ELECTRICITY? 125
ENTERTAINMENT? 350
GAS/OIL/HEATING? 400
GASOLINE,OIL,AUTO REPAIRS? 550
GROCERIES/FOOD? 650
HEALTH INSURANCE/MEDICAL COSTS? 50
HOME MAINTENANCE? 75
LAUNDRY/CLEANING? 50
LIFE INSURANCE? 0
NEWSPAPERS/MAGAZINES? 50
PERSONAL ALLOWANCES? 300
RENT/HOUSE PAYMENT? 1525
TAXES? 250
TELEPHONE? 50
WATER/SEWER/GARBAGE? 20
OTHER REGULAR MONTHLY EXPENSES
LIST ITEM (COMMA) AMOUNT
? ,0

77

LOAN PAYMENTS (NOT LISTED ABOVE)

HOW MANY WEEKLY LOAN PAYMENTS? 0
HOW MANY MONTHLY LOAN PAYMENTS? 0
HOW MANY OTHER LOAN PAYMENTS? 0
WHAT PORT FOR OUTPUT? 2
PRESS 'RETURN' TO PRINT?

SAMPLE OUTPUT - BUDGET

BUDGET ANALYSIS

FOR

HARRY & INA DANTRIED

#10 TENTH AVENUE
UTOPIA, CA 99999

TELEPHONE (000) 555-1212

INCOME

PAYCHECKS PROVIDE AN EFFECTIVE MONTHLY INCOME OF $ 5823.22

FOR A TOTAL MONTHLY INCOME OF $ 5823.22

EXPENSES

FIXED EXPENSES

REGULAR MONTHLY EXPENSES ARE $ 5105.00

LEAVING A MONTHLY SURPLUS OF $ 718.22
                                                      =========

THIS SURPLUS ALLOWS A SAVINGS/INVESTMENT FUND TO BE
ESTABLISHED AT 12 % OF TAKE HOME INCOME,
(10% IS CONSIDERED A REASONABLE GOAL.)

```
0010 REM *********************************
0020 REM *         BUDGET    ANALYSIS        *
0030 REM *********************************
0040 REM ********* VERSION 20 *********
0050 LINE= 0
0060 DIGITS= 0
0070 DIM A$(7),I$(9),L$(10),M$(10),O$(10)
0080 DIM E(25),I(5),L(10),M(10),O(10),P(9)
0100 INPUT "ENTER FIRST NAME(S) & INITIAL(S)",A$(1)
0110 INPUT "LAST NAME",A$(2)
0120 INPUT "NUMBER & STREET",A$(3)
0130 INPUT "APT OR BOX (SPECIFY) NUMBER",A$(4)
0140 INPUT "CITY, STATE & ZIP",A$(5),A$(6)
0150 INPUT "AREA CODE AND TELEPHONE NUMBER",A$(7)
1000 REM *********** INCOME ***********
1005 PRINT
1010 PRINT :PRINT"INCOME":PRINT
1020 INPUT "HOW MANY WEEKLY PAY CHECKS",I1
1030 INPUT "HOW MANY BI-WEEKLY PAY CHECKS",I2
1040 INPUT "HOW MANY MONTHLY PAY CHECKS",I3
1050 INPUT "HOW MANY SEMI-MONTHLY CHECKS",I4
1060 INPUT "ANY OTHERS",I$
1070 IF LEFT$(I$,1)="N" I5=0: GOTO 1100
1080 IF LEFT$(I$,1)="Y" I5=1: GOTO 1100
1090 GOTO 1060
1100 PRINT "ENTER THE USUAL AMOUNT FOR EACH"
1110 IF I1=0THEN1200
1120 PRINT "WEEKLY TAKE HOME CHECK"
1130 FOR J=1 TO I1
1140 PRINT "#";J;:INPUTI(1)
1150   I(2)=I(2)+I(1)
1160 NEXT J
1200 IF I2=0THEN1300
1220 PRINT "BI-WEEKLY CHECK"
1230 FOR J=1TOI2
1240 PRINT "#";J;:INPUTI(1)
1250   I(3)=I(1)+I(3)
1260 NEXT J
1300 IF I3=0THEN1400
1320 PRINT "MONTHLY CHECK"
1330 FOR J=1TOI3
1340 PRINT "#";J;:INPUTI(1)
1350   I(4)=I(4)+I(1)
1360 NEXT J
1400 IF I4=0THEN1500
1420 PRINT "SEMI-MONTHLY CHECK"
1430 FOR J=1TOI4
1440 PRINT "#";J;:INPUTI(1)
1450   I(5)=I(5)+I(1)
1460 NEXT J
1500 IF I5=0THEN2000
1510 PRINT "LIST OTHER INCOME ON A YEARLY"
1520 PRINT "BASIS.  ENTER SOURCE (COMMA)"
1530 PRINT "AMOUNT."
```

```
1540 INPUT I$(1),P(1)
1550 IF P(1)=0 THEN 2000
1560 INPUT I$(2),P(2)
1570 IF P(2)=0 THEN 2000
1580 INPUT I$(3),P(3)
1590 IF P(3)=0 THEN 2000
1600 INPUT I$(4),P(4)
1610 IF P(4)=0 THEN 2000
1620 INPUT I$(5),P(5)
1630 IF P(5)=0 THEN 2000
1640 INPUT I$(6),P(6)
1650 IF P(6)=0 THEN 2000
1660 INPUT I$(7),P(7)
1670 IF P(7)=0 THEN 2000
1680 INPUT I$(8),P(8)
1690 IF P(8)=0 THEN 2000
1700 INPUT I$(9),P(9)
2000 REM ********** EXPENSES **********
2010 PRINT :PRINT"FIXED MONTHLY EXPENSES":PRINT
2020 PRINT "LIST THE USUAL AMOUNTS FOR:"
2030 INPUT "ALIMONY",E(1)
2040 INPUT "AUTO INSURANCE",E(2)
2050 INPUT "BANK ACCOUNT CHARGES",E(3)
2060 INPUT "BUS/TAXI FARES",E(4)
2070 INPUT "CHILD CARE",E(5)
2080 INPUT "CHILD SUPPORT",E(6)
2090 INPUT "CIGARETTES, TOBACCO, ETC.",E(7)
2100 INPUT "CLOTHING",E(8)
2110 INPUT "CONTRIBUTIONS/GIFTS",E(9)
2120 INPUT "DUES",E(10)
2130 INPUT "ELECTRICITY",E(11)
2140 INPUT "ENTERTAINMENT",E(12)
2150 INPUT "GAS/OIL/HEATING",E(13)
2160 INPUT "GASOLINE,OIL,AUTO REPAIRS",E(14)
2170 INPUT "GROCERIES/FOOD",E(15)
2180 INPUT "HEALTH INSURANCE/MEDICAL COSTS",E(16)
2190 INPUT "HOME MAINTENANCE",E(17)
2200 INPUT "LAUNDRY/CLEANING",E(18)
2210 INPUT "LIFE INSURANCE",E(19)
2220 INPUT "NEWSPAPERS/MAGAZINES",E(20)
2230 INPUT "PERSONAL ALLOWANCES",E(21)
2240 INPUT "RENT/HOUSE PAYMENT",E(22)
2250 INPUT "TAXES",E(23)
2260 INPUT "TELEPHONE",E(24)
2270 INPUT "WATER/SEWER/GARBAGE",E(25)
2280 PRINT "OTHER REGULAR MONTHLY EXPENSES"
2290 PRINT "LIST ITEM (COMMA) AMOUNT"
2300 INPUT O$(1),O(1)
2310 IF O(1)=0 O1=0:GOTO 2500
2320 INPUT O$(2),O(2)
2330 IF O(2)=0 O1=1:GOTO 2500
2340 INPUT O$(3),O(3)
2350 IF O(3)=0 O1=2:GOTO 2500
2360 INPUT O$(4),O(4)
```

```
2370 IF O(4)=0 O1=3:GOTO 2500
2380 INPUT O$(5),O(5)
2390 IF O(5)=0 O1=4:GOTO 2500
2400 INPUT O$(6),O(6)
2410 IF O(6)=0 O1=5:GOTO 2500
2420 INPUT O$(7),O(7)
2430 IF O(7)=0 O1=6:GOTO 2500
2440 INPUT O$(8),O(8)
2450 IF O(8)=0 O1=7:GOTO 2500
2460 INPUT O$(9),O(9)
2470 IF O(9)=0 O1=8:GOTO 2500
2480 INPUT O$(10),O(10)
2490 IF O(10)=0 O1=9:GOTO 2500
2495  O1=10
2500 PRINT :PRINT"LOAN PAYMENTS (NOT LISTED ABOVE)":PRINT
2510 INPUT "HOW MANY WEEKLY LOAN PAYMENTS",L1
2520 INPUT "HOW MANY MONTHLY LOAN PAYMENTS",L2
2530 INPUT "HOW MANY OTHER LOAN PAYMENTS",L3
2540 IF L1=0THEN2600
2550 PRINT "LIST WEEKLY LOAN PAYMENTS (ITEM, AMOUNT)"
2560 FOR J=1 TO L1
2570 INPUT L$(J),L(J)
2580  L4=L4+L(J)
2590 NEXT J
2600 IF L2=0 THEN 2660
2610 PRINT "LIST MONTHLY LOAN PAYMENTS (ITEM, AMOUNT)"
2620 FOR J=1 TO L2
2630 INPUT M$(J),M(J)
2640  L5=L5+M(J)
2650 NEXT J
2660 IF L3=0 THEN 4000
2670 PRINT "ENTER THE TOTAL OF OTHER LOAN"
2680 PRINT "PAYMENTS ON A MONTHLY BASIS."
2690 INPUT L6
4000 REM ******** PORT SELECTION ********
4010 INPUT "WHAT PORT FOR OUTPUT",P
4020 INPUT "PRESS 'RETURN' TO PRINT",Z$
4030 DIGITS= 2
4040 PORT= P
5000 REM ******** PRINT  ROUTINE ********
5010 PRINT TAB(29);"BUDGET ANALYSIS"
5020 PRINT :PRINTTAB(35);"FOR"
5030 PRINT :A=LEN(A$(1)+A$(2))
5040 PRINT TAB(INT((70-A)/2));A$(1);" ";A$(2)
5050 PRINT
5060 PRINT TAB(INT((70-LEN(A$(3)+A$(4)))/2));A$(3);" ";A$(4)
5070 PRINT TAB(INT((70-LEN(A$(5)+A$(6)))/2));A$(5);", ";A$(6)
5080 PRINT
5090 PRINT TAB(INT((63-LEN(A$(7)))/2));"TELEPHONE ";A$(7)
5100 PRINT :PRINT:PRINT TAB(33);"INCOME":PRINT
5110 PRINT "PAYCHECKS PROVIDE AN EFFECTIVE ";
5120  I=(52*I(2)+26*I(3)+12*I(4)+24*I(5))/12
5130 PRINT "MONTHLY INCOME OF";TAB(65-LEN(STR$(I)));"$ ";I
5140  P=(P(1)+P(2)+P(3)+P(4)+P(5)+P(6)+P(7)+P(8)+P(9))/12
```

```
5150 IF P=0 THEN 5180
5160 PRINT "OTHER SOURCES ADD A MONTHLY ";
5170 PRINT "INCOME OF";TAB(67-LEN(STR$(P)));P
5180 PRINT TAB(55);"-------------"
5190 PRINT "FOR A TOTAL MONTHLY INCOME OF";
5200 PRINT TAB(65-LEN(STR$(P+I)));"$ ";P+I
5210 PRINT :PRINT
5300 PRINT TAB(32);"EXPENSES"
5310 PRINT
5320 PRINT "FIXED EXPENSES"
5330 PRINT
5340 PRINT "REGULAR MONTHLY EXPENSES ARE";
5350   E=E(1)+E(2)+E(3)+E(4)+E(5)+E(6)+E(7)+E(8)+E(9)+E(10)+E(11)
5360   E=E+E(12)+E(13)+E(14)+E(15)+E(16)+E(17)+E(18)+E(19)+E(20)
5370   E=E+E(21)+E(22)+E(23)+E(24)+E(25)
5380 IF O1=0THEN5420
5390 FOR J=1TOO1
5400   E=E+O(J)
5410 NEXT J
5420 PRINT TAB(65-LEN(STR$(E)));"$ ";E
5430 IF L4+L5+L6=0THEN5470
5440 PRINT "LOAN PAYMENTS CAUSE A MONTHLY ";
5450   L=(52*L4+12*L5+12*L6)/12
5460 PRINT "OUTGO OF";TAB(67-LEN(STR$(L)));L
5470 PRINT TAB(55);"-------------"
5480 PRINT :PRINT"LEAVING A MONTHLY ";
5490   N=(I+P)-(E+L)
5500 IF ABS(N)=N THEN5600
5510 PRINT "SHORTFALL OR DEFICIT OF";
5520 GOSUB 6000
5530 GOTO 5700
5600 PRINT "SURPLUS OF";
5610 GOSUB 6000
5620   Z=INT(100*N/(I+P))
5630 DIGITS= 0
5640 PRINT "THIS SURPLUS ALLOWS A SAVINGS/INVESTMENT FUND TO BE"
5650 PRINT "ESTABLISHED AT ";Z;"% OF TAKE HOME INCOME."
5660 PRINT "(10% IS CONSIDERED A REASONABLE GOAL.)"
5670 DIGITS= 2
5700 PRINT :PRINT
5710 PORT= 1
5720 INPUT "ANOTHER COPY",Z$
5730 IF LEFT$(Z$,1)="Y" THEN 4000
5740 END
6000 PRINT TAB(65-LEN(STR$(N)));"$ ";N
6010 PRINT TAB(55);"============="
6020 RETURN
```

II
CREDIT CONTROL

10
CREDIT CARD ORGANIZER

There is little functional difference between cash, money orders, and credit. Each is a form of money. Each can be used to bring home food, clothing, and entertainment. It seems that cash is more <u>real</u> than checks; credit isn't <u>really</u> money. (And if you subscribe to that theory, you're well on your way to financial trouble!) The intelligent use of credit can help you enjoy life to the extent your income will allow. In this section, we're going to explore some of the ways your personal computer can help you manage credit.

Perhaps the most widely used (and abused!) form of delayed payment is the credit card. We all seem to collect these plastic money symbols. They multiply when we're not looking. Bank cards, gasoline cards, and department-store charge cards jam our wallets. The instructions that came with the cards probably are filed in as many different places at home as we have cards. If you've ever lost some credit cards or had a batch stolen, you'll appreciate <u>Credit Card Organizer</u>. This program takes the place of those nooks and crannies full of credit card company addresses. Let your home computer keep track of your credit cards, and you can throw the paper away. (Of course, remember to keep a backup program tape!)

BACKGROUND

This is a data-handling program, so no arithmetic or accounting theory is involved. You can implement the program with or without a disk capability. The sample doesn't use a disk, but we'll discuss how little effort is needed to make the change. You may like the ease with which <u>Credit Card Organizer</u> manipulates names and addresses. If so, you can alter it to store and recall Christmas card lists, favorite recipes, or old jokes.

A look at the sample run will reveal what little operator action is required by Credit Card Organizer. The basic purpose of the routine is notification to credit card companies (banks, oil companies, etc.) that something unplanned has happened to a card. As a byproduct, we've included a listing of all the family charge cards as an alternate output. If you wish the listing, simply answer "NO" to the question about notifying a company. The routine will ask for the cardholder name and your output-port selection. Sit back and watch the listing grow.

Should you desire a notification letter, you'll be asked to type the current date and cardholder's name. The program will then present each card name and ask if that card is affected. A "NO" response will cycle the next name until the list is exhausted. A positive answer will prod the routine to ask you what happened to the card in question and for your selection of an output port. The program will do everything but lick and stamp the envelopes (that feature is one of the "bells and whistles" you could add).

PROGRAMMING NOTES

As it stands, Credit Card Organizer is a data-search and print routine that you can have keypunched in one enjoyable evening. We'll touch lightly on the lines that are new--some of this code should be old hat to you by now. The heading and introductory question take us through line 150. Lines 160 and 170 receive the cardholder name. (You can fill your data base with the entire family's cards and list only those of a particular individual.) The name will be used a little later to sort the data base. If there's only one name in your credit card dictionary, you can omit the name-matching to save some keypunch time. Lines 200 through 250 print the heading on the output form. Line 260 READs the first data element, which specifies the number of credit cards on file. If you wish to incorporate disk memory in your version of Credit Card Organizer, add one line and change another as follows:

```
0255 OPEN #10, 2001 (ADDED LINE)
0260 READ #10, N\330 (CHANGED LINE)
```

Actually, I'd add a "Wrong disk, Dummy" message somewhere and use that line number instead of 330 in the new line 260. If you find the end-of-data mark on the disk when you read the first entry, you've got the wrong disk.

The number of entries picked up in line 260 is used to put a limit on the FOR...NEXT loop of lines 270 through 320. This program segment collects all of the data for one credit card, checks the cardholder name, and prints desired files on the output sheet. If you're adding disk capability, modify the READ statement of line 280. The end-of-data default could go to the NEXT X of line 320, the form-feed command of line 330, or the error message you added. The name-compare statment measures the number of letters you typed for the cardholder name and matches the same number of letters in each file name. If you type only one letter, for example, any name beginning with that letter will satisfy the IF and allow the credit card information to be printed.

Lines 330 to 380 provide the cleanup and finish for the program. At the operator discretion, you can end or run through the program again.

The "long pole in the tent" is the notification side of the program. Fortunately, the length is due to the printing format and not programming complications. The remaining main program is covered by lines 400 to 560. The letter-writing opus is handled by a subroutine.

The data-gathering statements (lines 460 and 480) are similar to those used in the earlier listing routine. Make the same changes to those lines that you incorporated in lines 260 and 280 to implement disk operation. The program will display the name of the credit card on the control terminal and ask if it is one of those affected. A negative operator response recycles the loop to fetch another credit card file. A positive answer summons the letter-printing subroutine. When the DATA file has been exhausted, line 560 routes program flow to the end-game at line 340.

The letter-writing code is pretty straightforward. You'll want to include your own name and address in the letterhead of lines 640, 650, and 660. To calculate the TABs, count the letters in the printed line, subtract from the column width of the printer, and divide by 2. (For example, "I. M. CARDHOLDER" is 16 spaces. The printer on my system has an 80-column capability. Since 80 minus 16 equals 64, and half of 64 is 32, the TAB should be 32.) Be sure to modify the signature block in line 940 to match the letterhead. You should also alter the letter wording to suit your personality and communication style.

The DATA statements start at line 1000. The first entry must be the number of credit cards listed in the dictionary. I've included five fictitious entries for sample purposes. You can keep as many entries in your file as you have credit cards. The routine will recognize the following DATA SEQUENCE:

XXXX DATA "Company Name", "Street Address", "City, State ZIP"

XXXX DATA "Cardholder Name", "Card Number", "Expiration Date"

The quotation marks aren't strictly necessary for each data entry, but they're a good habit. You must use the quotations if the data item contains a comma (as in City, State ZIP).

87

One more comment regarding disk operation. Remember to add a CLOSE #10 to the end routine, and you'll probably want to add a routine to write data to the disk. The following will work:

```
xx10 OPEN#10, 2001
xx20 INPUT "How Many Entries", N
xx30 PRINT #10, N
xx40 FOR X=1 TO N
xx50 INPUT "Card Company Name", C$(1)
xx60 INPUT "Street Address", C$(2)
xx70 INPUT "City, State ZIP", C$(3), C$
xx80 C$(3)=C$(3)+", "+C$
xx90 INPUT "Cardholder name", C$(4)
x100 INPUT "Card Account Number", C$(5)
x110 INPUT "Card Expiration Date", C$(6)
x120 PRINT#10, C$(1); C$(2); C$(3); C$(4); C$(5); C$(6)
x130 NEXT X
```

This routine is for initialization only. There are some later programs that carry suitable update segments. I won't spoil your fun by telling which I'd use. Go ahead and experiment. You'll have fun.

SAMPLE INPUTS - CREDIT CARDS

READY
RUN

          CREDIT CARDS

DO YOU WANT TO NOTIFY A CREDIT CARD COMPANY? NO

THEN I'LL LIST YOUR CARDS.
WHAT IS THE CARD HOLDER NAME? I. M. CARDHOLDER

WHAT OUTPUT PORT? 2

ANYMORE? YES

          CREDIT CARDS

DO YOU WANT TO NOTIFY A CREDIT CARD COMPANY? YES

TODAY'S DATE? 18 AUGUST 1984

WHAT IS CARD HOLDER'S NAME? I. M.

IS SHALE OIL ONE OF THE CARDS AFFECTED? N
IS NATIONAL EXPRESS ONE OF THE CARDS AFFECTED? Y
WHAT HAPPENED TO CARD (LOST, STOLEN, DESTROYED)? LOST
WHAT OUTPUT PORT? 2

IS CASHKARD ONE OF THE CARDS AFFECTED? N
IS XYZ DEPT STORE ONE OF THE CARDS AFFECTED? N
IS LUNAR OIL ONE OF THE CARDS AFFECTED? N

ANYMORE? NO THANKS

READY
#

SAMPLE OUTPUT #1

CREDIT CARDS

NAME OF CARD   ACCOUNT NUMBER   EXPIRATION
------------   --------------   ----------

SHALE OIL   123-32123-21   INDEFINITE

NATIONAL EXPRESS   90909-09090   JULY, 1988

CASHKARD   1/2345-67890**   INDEFINITE

XYZ DEPT STORE   102030405060/7   GOLD CARD

LUNAR OIL   1-111222-333   DECEMBER, 1986

I. M. CARDHOLDER
#1 EASY STREET
UTOPIA, CA 99999

18 AUGUST 1984

NATIONAL EXPRESS
P.O.BOX #123
BOSTON, MA 06999

RE: ACCOUNT NUMBER 90909-09090
EXPIRATION DATE JULY, 1988

THIS IS NOTIFICATION THAT MY CREDIT CARD WAS LOST ON THE INDICATED DATE. THE ACCOUNT NUMBER AND EXPIRATION OF THE CARD ARE SHOWN ABOVE.

PLEASE TAKE THE ACTION NECESSARY TO REPLACE MY CARD AND TO INSURE THAT NO UNAUTHORIZED CHARGES ACCRUE TO MY ACCOUNT. PLEASE ADVISE ME OF ANY ADDITIONAL INFORMATION I CAN FURNISH.

THANK YOU.

SINCERELY,

I. M. CARDHOLDER

```
0010 REM *********************************
0020 REM *       CREDIT CARD CONTROL       *
0030 REM *********************************
0040 REM ********* VERSION 10 *********
0050 LINE= 0
0100 PRINT :PRINT:PRINT
0110 PRINT TAB(10);"CREDIT CARDS"
0120 PRINT
0130 INPUT "Do you want to notify a Credit Card Company",Z$
0140 IF LEFT$(Z$,1)="Y" THEN 400
0150 PRINT
0160 PRINT "Then I'll list your cards."
0170 INPUT "What is the card holder name",N$
0180 PRINT
0190 INPUT "What output port",P
0200 PRINT #P
0210 PRINT #P,TAB(34);"CREDIT CARDS"
0220 PRINT #P
0230 PRINT #P,"Name of Card";TAB(40);"Account Number";TAB(60);"Expiration"
0240 PRINT #P,"--------------";TAB(40);"----------------";TAB(60);"----------
0250 PRINT #P
0260 READ N
0270 FOR X=1 TO N
0280 READ C$(1),C$(2),C$(3),C$(4),C$(5),C$(6)
0290 IF LEFT$(C$(4),LEN(N$))<>N$ THEN 320
0300 PRINT #P,C$(1);TAB(41);C$(5);TAB(61);C$(6)
0310 PRINT #P
0320 NEXT X
0330 PRINT #P,CHR$(12)
0340 PRINT
0350 INPUT "Anymore",Z$
0360 IF LEFT$(Z$,1)="N" THEN END
0370 RESTORE
0380 GOTO 100
0400 REM ******** NOTIFICATION ********
0410 PRINT
0420 INPUT "Today's Date",D$
0430 PRINT
0440 INPUT "What is card holder's name",N$
0450 PRINT
0460 READ N
0470 FOR Q=1 TO N
0480 READ C$(1),C$(2),C$(3),C$(4),C$(5),C$(6)
0490 IF LEFT$(C$(4),LEN(N$))<>N$ THEN 550
0500 PRINT "Is ";C$(1);" one of the cards affected";
0510 INPUT Z$
0520 IF LEFT$(Z$,1)="N" THEN 550
0530 GOSUB 600
0540 PRINT
0550 NEXT Q
0560 GOTO 340
0600 REM ******** PRINT LETTER ********
0610 INPUT "What happened to card (lost, stolen, destroyed)",Y$
0620 INPUT "What output port",P
```

```
0630 PRINT #P:PRINT#P:PRINT#P
0640 PRINT #P,TAB(32);"I. M. CARDHOLDER"
0650 PRINT #P,TAB(33);"#1 Easy Street"
0660 PRINT #P,TAB(32);"Utopia, CA 99999"
0670 PRINT #P
0680 PRINT #P,TAB((80-LEN(D$))/2);D$
0690 FOR X=1 TO 9
0700 PRINT #P
0710 NEXT X
0720 PRINT #P,C$(1)
0730 PRINT #P,C$(2)
0740 PRINT #P,C$(3)
0750 PRINT #P:PRINT#P
0760 PRINT #P,TAB(10);"RE: Account Number  ";C$(5)
0770 PRINT #P,TAB(10);"    Expiration Date ";C$(6)
0780 PRINT #P
0790 PRINT #P,TAB(5);"This is notification that my credit card was ";Y$;
0800 PRINT #P," on the indicated"
0810 PRINT #P,"date.  The account number and expiration of the card are ";
0820 PRINT #P,"shown above."
0830 PRINT #P
0840 PRINT #P,TAB(5);"Please take the action necessary to replace my ";
0850 PRINT #P,"card and to insure"
0860 PRINT #P,"that no unauthorized charges accrue to my account.  ";
0870 PRINT #P,"Please advise me of"
0880 PRINT #P,"any additional information I can furnish."
0890 PRINT #P
0900 PRINT #P,TAB(5);"Thank you."
0910 PRINT #P:PRINT#P
0920 PRINT #P,TAB(35);"Sincerely,"
0930 PRINT #P:PRINT#P:PRINT#P:PRINT#P
0940 PRINT #P,TAB(35);"I. M. CARDHOLDER"
0950 PRINT #P,CHR$(12)
0960 RETURN
1000 DATA 5
1010 DATA "SHALE OIL","#1 PETROLEUM PLAZA","EL PASO, TX 79999"
1020 DATA "I. M. CARDHOLDER","123-32123-21","INDEFINITE"
1030 DATA "NATIONAL EXPRESS","P.O.BOX #123","BOSTON, MA 06999"
1040 DATA "I. M. CARDHOLDER","90909-09090","JULY, 1988"
1050 DATA "CASHKARD","99 CEILING STREET","NEW YORK, NY 10999"
1060 DATA "I. M. CARDHOLDER","1/2345-67890**","INDEFINITE"
1070 DATA "XYZ DEPT STORE","#2 MAIN STREET","LOS ANGELES, CA 90000"
1080 DATA "I. M. CARDHOLDER","102030405060/7","GOLD CARD"
1090 DATA "LUNAR OIL","P.O.BOX 987","LAREDO, TX 78999"
1100 DATA "I. M. CARDHOLDER","1-111222-333","DECEMBER, 1986"
```

11
NET WORTH STATEMENT

Loans are an important aspect of credit management. You need to be able to obtain the right loan at the right time to reap the maximum benefit. Whether you're applying for an investment loan, a home mortgage, or a revolving charge account, you'll be asked to supply a statement of net worth. (Some lenders call the statement by other names, but it is still a statement of net worth.) It's a good idea to run a periodic net worth statement for yourself. If you know where you stand financially, you can plan your complete fiscal package more confidently.

Net Worth Statement is one of my most useful programs. Both clients (borrowers) and lenders appreciate the professional quality of the statement generated by the routine. The intimidation of a computer-generated statement can help get a loan approval, too.

The basic premise of a net worth calculation is simple--the details make the computation appear complex. Take the value of all that you own and subtract the total amounts of all that you owe. The difference is your net worth. You can generate two different values of net worth. A "liquidation" net worth assumes that all of your assets must be sold in a forced sale to pay your bills. A "normal" net worth allows valuation of your hard goods at normal market or replacement values. Unless you're making a bankruptcy calculation, use the "normal" method. If your net worth calculation results in a negative number you had better revalue your financial planning, fast! You may be borrowing too heavily for pleasure or investing unwisely.

The arithmetic involved here is limited to adding and subtracting. Program flow is straight-line, so this routine should be easy to modify.

OPERATING NOTES

The sample run demonstrates the operating sequence. The name, address, and date entries are the same we've used

94

before. Remember that only the CITY, STATE ZIP? entry can handle a comma. The routine is structured to separate "current" assets and liabilities from "other" items. Current assets are those that can be readily converted to cash (usually within 1 year); current liabilities are those debts that must be paid within 1 year. Many lenders are interested in the "Solvency Ratio" or "Current Ratio," which is a term borrowed from business to describe the ratio of current assets to current liabilities. As a bonus, Net Worth Statement will perform the calculation and display the ratio on the statement.

The input-prompt messages are self-explanatory. There is a set of inputs allowing user definition of category. LIST OTHER CASH VALUE ASSETS requests that you enter a one- or two-word description of the asset, then a comma, and the dollar value. There is provision for up to four user-defined current assets (and, later, four categories for other assets). If you finish your list of user-defined items before the program has finished its prompting, just enter a comma and a zero. The routine will sense the null entry and move along to the next input sequence. The long-term asset entries are geared to accept replacement rather than liquidation values. A minor programming change can make this a bankruptcy statement.

The current-liabilities input section is entirely made up of user-defined categories. The program has provision for nine entries, but you can shorten the sequence by entering a comma followed by a zero. If you want to accept more than nine entries, a quick change in the BASIC will expand the routine. Some common long-term loans are suggested in the data-gathering steps for other liabilities. Another user-defined input set is ready to accept nine more categories. Once you select the output port, the hard work is done. Sit back and let your home computer prepare a statement of net worth. When the statement is complete, the program will ask if you want another copy. You may select a different output device for each subsequent printing exercise.

PROGRAMMING NOTES

By now you're familiar with the general style of these programs, so we'll just hit the high points. The descriptions for previous routines are applicable to many of the features, so flip back a few pages if you want to refresh your memory.

When you alter any of the data sequences, remember to also change the DIMensioning of variables in lines 100 and 110 to match. Line 120 illustrates a keypunch time-saving feature. The program will call the same PRINT message a number of times, so we've defined variable Z$ with the message. Later, instead of typing the entire message in the listing, we can call PRINT Z$.

You should have no difficulty in expanding the input question areas. Just add the appropriate questions and variables. Include the variables in the steps that total the numbers, also. For example, include extra current asset variables in line 360. If your investing posture is fairly static, you could omit the user-defined sections and add input statements for your specific asset and liability items. Any change you make in the input area must be mirrored on the output.

Lines 280, 300, 320, and 340 serve a dual purpose. First, the condition checks for a zero input to the user-defined category. When a zero is sensed, variable Z is given a value that will later control a FOR...NEXT loop (line 1390) in the output routine. The input group is ended with the second statement on the line (a GOTO). In my version of BASIC, the second statement on any line that begins with an IF is not executed unless the IF is satisfied. Yours may be different, so debug this area carefully. These condition-checking commands are repeated for other assets in lines 480 through 560, current liabilities in lines 670 to 850, and other liabilities in lines 950 through 1130.

An obvious area for personalization of the program is the prompting sequence for other assets in lines 370 through 460. Leave out those that are not applicable to your situation and add any that you need. The corresponding output statements are in lines 1540 to 1660.

Change the message in lines 390 and 1520 to convert to a "liquidation" statement. Nothing else will be affected by this change, so you can keypunch the routine for normal statements and add the special liquidation messages for specific runs. (One "bells-and-whistles" change you could make is a feature that asks if a liquidation statement is desired. A positive response could set a flag that will print the proper message at run time.)

The printing routine starts at line 1170 with the output-port selection. We've used the PORT=P method here instead of PRINT #P. Pick the method your BASIC likes better and stick with it.

The TABs in lines 1220 through 1250 are used to center the name, address, and date information on the statement. A program for personal use only can have commands to print your name and address with precalculated TABs. You could then leave out the input steps of lines 130, 140, and 150.

Lines 1300, 1320, etc. suppress the printing of any category with a zero value. If you've tailored the program to include only those categories that always have entries, you can omit these steps to save even more keypunch time and program memory. The zero suppressers are included ahead of each fixed-category PRINT statement.

The segment that calculates and prints the Current Ratio is contained in lines 2060 to 2080. The Current Ratio is a measure of your ability to pay your bills--your solvency. A Current Ratio of 1.00 indicates that your liquid assets will pay your current bills. Less than 1.00 indicates that you are insolvent; under certain circumstances, you could be forced to declare bankruptcy. Many lenders have rules of thumb on loan applications. They will lend money to you only if your Current Ratio is 5.0 or higher. If you are really scratching to simplify your version of this program, you could omit the code that displays the Current/Solvency Ratio. (The lenders can calculate the ratio easily enough, so you wouldn't be hiding anything.)

Net Worth Statement is a keystone program for your financial management system. If you only adapt a few of the programs in this book to your own needs, this should be one of them!

```
READY
# RUN
NAME? M. I. KLYENT
STREET ADDRESS? 123 ANY STREET
CITY, STATE  ZIP? HOMETOWN, TX 79797

STATEMENT DATE? 1 JANUARY 1984

*** ASSETS ***
CASH ON HAND AND IN BANK(S)? 1023.17
CASH VALUE OF LIFE INSURANCE? 980.22
VALUE OF SAVINGS BONDS? 18.75
CASH VALUE IN RETIREMENT PLANS? 0
MARKET VALUE OF STOCKS? 0
LIST OTHER CASH VALUE ASSETS.
ITEM (COMMA) AMOUNT
? CASH FUND INVESTMENT,10000
? ,0
MARKET VALUE OF REAL ESTATE? 80000
VALUE OF CAR(S)? 13000
REPLACEMENT COST OF:
FURNITURE? 6050
MACHINERY & TOOLS? 0
CLOTHING & PERSONAL EFFECTS? 1200
HOBBY EQUIPMENT? 1205
JEWELRY, FURS? 0
COIN OR STAMP COLLECTIONS? 0
EQUITY IN BUSINESS VENTURES? 0
ENTER OTHER ASSETS
ITEM (COMMA) AMOUNT
? ,0
*** LIABILITIES ***
LIST SHORT TERM LOANS/DEBTS
(THOSE DUE IN LESS THAN A YEAR)
ITEM (COMMA) AMOUNT
? PERSONAL LOAN,2500
? UTILITY BILLS,425
? ,0
ENTER THE REMAINING BALANCE FOR
REAL ESTATE MORTGAGES? 62989.38
AUTOMOBILE LOANS? 0
FURNITURE & APPLIANCE LOANS? 0
LIST THE BALANCE OF OTHER LONG
TERM LOANS
ITEM (COMMA) AMOUNT
? COMPUTER LOAN,4238.21
? ,0
WHAT PORT FOR STATEMENT? 2

ANOTHER COPY? NO THANKS

READY
#
```

```
                        NET WORTH
                       STATEMENT FOR

                       M. I. KLYENT
                      123 ANY STREET
                     HOMETOWN, TX 79797

                   AS OF 1 JANUARY 1984

                          ASSETS
          CURRENT ASSETS
CASH ON HAND/IN BANK(S)                          $ 1023.17
CASH VALUE OF LIFE INSURANCE                        980.22
VALUE OF SAVINGS BONDS                               18.75
CASH FUND INVESTMENT                              10000.00
                                                 ----------
TOTAL CURRENT ASSETS                             $ 12022.14

          OTHER ASSETS
MARKET VALUE OF REAL ESTATE                       80000.00
VALUE OF CAR(S)                                   13000.00
REPLACEMENT COST OF:
     FURNITURE                                     6050.00
     PERSONAL EFFECTS                              1200.00
     HOBBY EQUIPMENT                               1205.00
                                                 ----------
TOTAL ASSETS                                    $ 113477.14
                                                 ==========

                        LIABILITIES
          CURRENT LIABILITIES
PERSONAL LOAN                                    $ 2500.00
UTILITY BILLS                                       425.00
                                                 ----------
TOTAL CURRENT LIABILITIES                        $ 2925.00

          OTHER LIABILITIES
REAL ESTATE MORTGAGES                             62989.38
COMPUTER LOAN                                      4238.21
                                                 ----------
TOTAL LIABILITIES                               $ 70152.59

NET WORTH                                         43324.55
                                                 ==========


(SOLVENCY/CURRENT RATIO IS 4.11 )
```

```
0010 REM ***********************************
0020 REM *     STATEMENT OF NET WORTH      *
0030 REM ***********************************
0040 REM ********** VERSION 40 **********
0050 LINE= 0
0060 DIGITS= 2
0100 DIM A(14),C$(5),C(5),G$(5),G(5)
0110 DIM L$(10),M$(10),L(10),M(10)
0120   Z$="ITEM (COMMA) AMOUNT"
0130 INPUT "Name",A$(1)
0140 INPUT "Street Address",A$(2)
0150 INPUT "City, State  ZIP",A$(3),A$(4)
0160 PRINT
0170 INPUT "Statement Date",A$(5)
0180 PRINT
0190 PRINT "*** ASSETS ***"
0200 INPUT "Cash on hand and in bank(s)",A(1)
0210 INPUT "Cash Value of life insurance",A(2)
0220 INPUT "Value of Savings Bonds",A(3)
0230 INPUT "Cash Value in retirement plans",A(4)
0240 INPUT "Market Value of stocks",A(5)
0250 PRINT "LIST OTHER CASH VALUE ASSETS."
0260 PRINT Z$
0270 INPUT C$(1),C(1)
0280 IF C(1)=0 THEN Z=0: GOTO 360
0290 INPUT C$(2),C(2)
0300 IF C(2)=0 THEN Z=1: GOTO 360
0310 INPUT C$(3),C(3)
0320 IF C(3)=0 THEN Z=2: GOTO 360
0330 INPUT C$(4),C(4)
0340 IF C(4)=0 THEN Z=3: GOTO 360
0350   Z=4
0360   C(5)=C(1)+C(2)+C(3)+C(4)
0370 INPUT "Market value of real estate",A(6)
0380 INPUT "Value of car(s)",A(7)
0390 PRINT "Replacement cost of:"
0400 INPUT "Furniture",A(8)
0410 INPUT "Machinery & Tools",A(9)
0420 INPUT "Clothing & Personal Effects",A(10)
0430 INPUT "Hobby Equipment",A(11)
0440 INPUT "Jewelry, Furs",A(12)
0450 INPUT "Coin or Stamp Collections",A(13)
0460 INPUT "Equity in business ventures",A(14)
0470 PRINT "Enter other assets":PRINT Z$
0480 INPUT G$(1),G(1)
0490 IF G(1)=0 Y=0:GOTO570
0500 INPUT G$(2),G(2)
0510 IF G(2)=0 Y=1:GOTO570
0520 INPUT G$(3),G(3)
0530 IF G(3)=0 Y=2:GOTO570
0540 INPUT G$(4),G(4)
0550 IF G(4)=0 Y=3:GOTO570
0560   Y=4
0570   G(5)=G(1)+G(2)+G(3)+G(4)
```

```
0580   A=A(1)+A(2)+A(3)+A(4)+A(5)+C(5)
0590   B=A(6)+A(7)+A(8)+A(9)+A(10)+A(11)+A(12)+A(13)+A(14)+G(5)
0600   C=A+B
0610 REM ****** A = CURRENT ASSETS ******
0620 REM ******* C = TOTAL ASSETS *******
0630 PRINT "*** LIABILITIES ***"
0640 PRINT "List short term loans/debts"
0650 PRINT "(Those due in less than a year)"
0660 PRINT Z$
0670 INPUT L$(1),L(1)
0680 IF L(1)=0 W=0:GOTO860
0690 INPUT L$(2),L(2)
0700 IF L(2)=0 W=1:GOTO860
0710 INPUT L$(3),L(3)
0720 IF L(3)=0 W=2:GOTO860
0730 INPUT L$(4),L(4)
0740 IF L(4)=0 W=3:GOTO860
0750 INPUT L$(5),L(5)
0760 IF L(5)=0 W=4:GOTO860
0770 INPUT L$(6),L(6)
0780 IF L(6)=0 W=5:GOTO860
0790 INPUT L$(7),L(7)
0800 IF L(7)=0 W=6:GOTO860
0810 INPUT L$(8),L(8)
0820 IF L(8)=0 W=7:GOTO860
0830 INPUT L$(9),L(9)
0840 IF L(9)=0 W=8:GOTO860
0850   W=9
0860   L(10)=L(1)+L(2)+L(3)+L(4)+L(5)+L(6)+L(7)+L(8)+L(9)
0870 REM *L(10)=CURRENT LIABILITIES*
0880 PRINT "Enter the remaining balance for"
0890 INPUT "Real Estate Mortgages",L1
0900 INPUT "Automobile Loans",L2
0910 INPUT "Furniture & Appliance Loans",L3
0920 PRINT "List the balance of other lons"
0930 PRINT "term loans"
0940 PRINT Z$
0950 INPUT M$(1),M(1)
0960 IF M(1)=0 V=0:GOTO1140
0970 INPUT M$(2),M(2)
0980 IF M(2)=0 V=1:GOTO1140
0990 INPUT M$(3),M(3)
1000 IF M(3)=0 V=2:GOTO1140
1010 INPUT M$(4),M(4)
1020 IF M(4)=0 V=3:GOTO1140
1030 INPUT M$(5),M(5)
1040 IF M(5)=0 V=4:GOTO1140
1050 INPUT M$(6),M(6)
1060 IF M(6)=0 V=5:GOTO1140
1070 INPUT M$(7),M(7)
1080 IF M(7)=0 V=6:GOTO1140
1090 INPUT M$(8),M(8)
1100 IF M(8)=0 V=7:GOTO1140
1110 INPUT M$(9),M(9)
```

```
1120 IF M(9)=0 V=8:GOTO1140
1130  V=9
1140  M(10)=M(1)+M(2)+M(3)+M(4)+M(5)+M(6)+M(7)+M(8)+M(9)
1150  L=L1+L2+L3+L(10)+M(10)
1160 REM *L=TOTAL LIABILITIES*
1170 INPUT "What Port for Statement",P
1180 PORT= P
1190 PRINT TAB(35);"NET WORTH"
1200 PRINT TAB(33);"STATEMENT FOR"
1210 PRINT
1220 PRINT TAB(INT((80-LEN(A$(1)))/2));A$(1)
1230 PRINT TAB(INT((80-LEN(A$(2)))/2));A$(2)
1240 PRINT TAB(INT((78-LEN(A$(3)+A$(4)))/2));A$(3);", ";A$(4)
1250 PRINT :PRINTTAB(INT((74-LEN(A$(5)))/2));"As of ";A$(5)
1260 PRINT :PRINT
1270 PRINT TAB(37);"ASSETS"
1280 PRINT TAB(5);"CURRENT ASSETS"
1290 PRINT "Cash on hand/in bank(s)";TAB(73-LEN(STR$(A(1))));"$ ";A(1)
1300 IF A(2)=0 THEN 1320
1310 PRINT "Cash value of life insurance";TAB(75-LEN(STR$(A(2))));A(2)
1320 IF A(3)=0 THEN 1340
1330 PRINT "Value of savings bonds";TAB(75-LEN(STR$(A(3))));A(3)
1340 IF A(4)=0 THEN 1360
1350 PRINT "Cash in retirement plans";TAB(75-LEN(STR$(A(4))));A(4)
1360 IF A(5)=0 THEN 1380
1370 PRINT "Market value of stocks/bonds";TAB(75-LEN(STR$(A(5))));A(5)
1380 IF C(5)=0 THEN 1430
1390 FOR J=1 TO Z
1400 PRINT C$(J);
1410 PRINT TAB(75-LEN(STR$(C(J))));C(J)
1420 NEXT J
1430 PRINT TAB(65);"-----------"
1440 PRINT "TOTAL CURRENT ASSETS";
1450 PRINT TAB(73-LEN(STR$(A)));"$ ";A
1460 PRINT :PRINTTAB(5);"OTHER ASSETS"
1470 IF A(6)=0 THEN 1490
1480 PRINT "Market value of real estate";TAB(75-LEN(STR$(A(6))));A(6)
1490 IF A(7)=0 THEN 1510
1500 PRINT "Value of car(s)";TAB(75-LEN(STR$(A(7))));A(7)
1510 IF A(8)+A(9)+A(10)+A(11)+A(12)+A(13)=0 THEN 1650
1520 PRINT "Replacement cost of:"
1530 IF A(8)=0 THEN 1550
1540 PRINT TAB(5);"Furniture";TAB(75-LEN(STR$(A(8))));A(8)
1550 IF A(9)=0 THEN 1570
1560 PRINT TAB(5);"Machinery & Tools";TAB(75-LEN(STR$(A(9))));A(9)
1570 IF A(10)=0 THEN 1590
1580 PRINT TAB(5);"Personal effects";TAB(75-LEN(STR$(A(10))));A(10)
1590 IF A(11)=0 THEN 1610
1600 PRINT TAB(5);"Hobby Equipment";TAB(75-LEN(STR$(A(11))));A(11)
1610 IF A(12)=0 THEN 1630
1620 PRINT TAB(5);"Jewelry & Furs";TAB(75-LEN(STR$(A(12))));A(12)
1630 IF A(13)=0 THEN 1650
1640 PRINT TAB(5);"Coin/Stamp Collections";TAB(75-LEN(STR$(A(13))));A(13
1650 IF A(14)=0 THEN 1670
```

```
1660 PRINT "Equity in businesses";TAB(75-LEN(STR$(A(14))));A(14)
1670 IF Y=0 THEN 1720
1680 FOR J=1TOY
1690 PRINT G$(J);
1700 PRINT TAB(75-LEN(STR$(G(J))));G(J)
1710 NEXT J
1720 PRINT TAB(65);"------------"
1730 PRINT "TOTAL ASSETS";TAB(73-LEN(STR$(C)));"$ ";C
1740 PRINT TAB(65);"==========="
1750 PRINT :PRINTTAB(30);"LIABILITIES"
1760 IF W=0THEN1840
1770 PRINT TAB(5);"CURRENT LIABILITIES"
1780 PRINT L$(1);TAB(73-LEN(STR$(L(1))));"$ ";L(1)
1790 IF W=1THEN1830
1800 FOR J=2TOW
1810 PRINT L$(J);TAB(75-LEN(STR$(L(J))));L(J)
1820 NEXT J
1830 PRINT TAB(65);"------------"
1840 PRINT "TOTAL CURRENT LIABILITIES";
1850 PRINT TAB(73-LEN(STR$(L(10))));"$ ";L(10)
1860 PRINT :PRINTTAB(5);"OTHER LIABILITIES"
1870 IF L1=0THEN1890
1880 PRINT "Real estate mortgages";TAB(75-LEN(STR$(L1)));L1
1890 IF L2=0THEN1910
1900 PRINT "Automobile loans";TAB(75-LEN(STR$(L2)));L2
1910 IF L3=0THEN1930
1920 PRINT "Furniture/Appliance Loans";TAB(75-LEN(STR$(L3)));L3
1930 IF V=0THEN1980
1940 FOR J=1TOV
1950 PRINT M$(J);
1960 PRINT TAB(75-LEN(STR$(M(J))));M(J)
1970 NEXT J
1980 PRINT TAB(65);"------------"
1990 PRINT "TOTAL LIABILITIES";
2000 PRINT TAB(73-LEN(STR$(L)));"$ ";L
2010 PRINT
2020 PRINT "NET WORTH";
2030 PRINT TAB(75-LEN(STR$(C-L)));C-L
2040 PRINT TAB(65);"==========="
2050 IF W=0THEN2080
2060  R=A/L(10)
2070 PRINT :PRINT
2080 PRINT "(Solvency/Current Ratio is ";R;")"
2090 PRINT CHR$(12)
2100 PORT= 1
2110 INPUT "Another Copy",Y$
2120 IF LEFT$(Y$,1)="Y" THEN 1170
2130 END
```

12
AUTO LOAN ANALYSIS

Automobile purchase loans take on a more significant place in the family budget scheme as car prices increase. You need to shop for loan terms with as much care as you shop for the car. This is the first of three loan-analysis routines. It is a warmup for the loan-investigation series. The output of Auto Loan Analysis is not an accounting statement; it is an informational presentation to you. You'll get a comparison of the "easy monthly payments" for different loan terms and a listing of the total sums paid over the life of the loan.

Although there's no heavy number crunching used in the program, the calculations are a bit more complex than we've seen before. In the first part of the routine, we'll calculate an estimate of the sales tax and license fees for the purchase. Generally, this will amount to multiplying the car cost by a percentage.

Automobile loans are treated a bit differently than other transactions. Usually, the interest is calculated up-front and added to the amount financed. This technique allows the lender to quote a more reasonable interest rate than the truth-in-lending rules now require. (The interest is calculated as though the total loan will be repaid in one payment at the end of the loan period. Since the loan is repaid gradually over the entire period, the effective rate is in excess of the "add-on" rate.) We'll calculate the true annual interest rate with a later program. Auto Loan Analysis is a comparison tool. You can calculate a series of payments for a given interest rate with each operation. Several program executions can compare the various interest rates.

We'll emulate the finance companies in calculating the interest and monthly payments. First, multiply the amount financed (N) by the interest rate (I) and term of the loan in years (Y) to get the interest amount. Next, add the interest amount to the amount financed, and divide by the term of the loan in months to get the monthly payment. We can combine the two operations into one equation:

$$\text{Monthly Payment} = A = \frac{N + (N * I * Y)}{12 * Y}$$

To get the total of payments, we'll retrace a step or two and multiply the monthly payment by the number of months:

$$\text{Total paid} = B = A * 12 * Y$$

PROGRAMMING NOTES

This is a short routine that you can have programmed and running in an evening. (We deserve an easy one after the length of <u>Net</u> <u>Worth</u> <u>Statement</u>.) The biggest problem you'll have with this one is making sure you get the right number of parentheses entered around some of the variables.

The first few statements contain our usual heading information. The variables used for the input routines are nonmatrix single-valued numerics. I've tried to pick some that are obvious for later manipulation (P for Price, I for Interest Rate, <u>etc</u>.).

Estimated sales tax and license fees are calculated in lines 150 and 170. The estimates are based on California's tax rates. The tax is 6 percent (0.06) of the purchase price; modify this line to use the rate in your state and locality. The California license fee is $11.00 plus 2 percent of the market value--we'll estimate that the price is the market value for this evaluation. You'll have to incorporate the rates in your home area when you adapt this program. Since this is an estimated fee, we round the number to the nearest integer in line 170. If your state's structure is more exact, you can calculate the exact amount.

The OTHER FEES question in line 200 is intended to collect "loan fees," "insurance fees," or any other extra tacked onto an auto-loan transaction in your area. If you don't have to contend with these, you can drop this step.

The "shortest" and "longest" inputs will be used later to bracket a FOR...NEXT LOOP. You may wish to add an error trap to ensure that the entries are integers--a fraction will produce an error message from BASIC when the loop hits.

Since we used P as the car-price variable, we have to use Z for the output-port selection in this routine. If you'd like to maintain the purity of P on your PRINT statements, change the car-price variable. The printing routine also takes care of the rest of the calculations in the program. There's nothing fancy about the printing, but we'll take a look at the computations.

The total of the automobile, fees, taxes, and licenses is gained in line 410. The down payment is subtracted to arrive at the amount financed in line 460. Monthly payments for each loan compared are calculated in line 510. Since we asked for entry of the interest rate in percent, we must divide by 100 to get the correct fraction. The monthly payment is printed in line 610, and the total of payments is calculated in line 620 and printed in line 630.

Line 660 allows recycling of the output routine--you can check the results on your video terminal then get a hard copy. Line 680 provides recycling of the entire program if you want to repeat the process with a different add-on interest rate.

OPERATING NOTES

You'll enjoy running Auto Loan Analysis. The basic entries of automobile data can come from newspaper advertisements. Your personal preference will govern the loan terms you'll accept. The TOTAL OF PAYMENTS column may be a little shocking to you. I hope so. The whole point of the program is to illustrate the tradeoff between lower monthly payments and higher total payments. Later loan-analysis routines will allow you an even finer look at the factors involved in borrowing.

SAMPLE CAR LOAN ANALYSIS

INPUT

READY
RUN

        CAR LOAN

CAR PRICE? 13850
INTEREST RATE (ADD-ON PERCENT)? 12
DOWN PAYMENT/TRADE-IN ALLOWANCE? 5850
OTHER FEES? 123
WHAT IS THE SHORTEST LOAN YOU WANT TO CONSIDER (YEARS)? 3
WHAT IS THE LONGEST LOAN YOU WANT TO CONSIDER (YEARS)? 7
WHAT PORT FOR OUTPUT? 2
ANOTHER COPY? N
ANOTHER ANALYSIS? NO

READY
#

OUTPUT

CAR LOAN ANALYSIS

CAR PRICE	$ 13850.00
SALES TAX	831.00
LICENSE FEES	288.00
OTHER FEES	123.00

SUBTOTAL	$ 15092.00
LESS DOWN PAYMENT/TRADE-IN ALLOWANCE	5850.00

AMOUNT FINANCED	$ 9242.00
	===========

YEARS	MONTHLY PAYMENT	TOTAL OF PAYMENTS
3	$349.14	$12569.11
4	$284.96	$13678.15
5	$246.45	$14787.19
6	$220.78	$15896.23
7	$202.44	$17005.27

```
0010 REM ***********************************
0020 REM *        AUTO LOAN ANALYSIS        *
0030 REM ***********************************
0040 REM ********* VERSION 20 *********
0050 DIGITS= 2
0060 LINE= 0
0100 PRINT :PRINT:PRINT
0110 PRINT TAB(10);"CAR LOAN"
0120 PRINT
0130 INPUT "CAR PRICE",P
0140 REM *** SALES TAX & LICENSE FEES ***
0150   T=0.06*P
0170   L=INT((0.02*P+11)+.5)
0180 INPUT "INTEREST RATE (ADD-ON PERCENT)",I
0190 INPUT "DOWN PAYMENT/TRADE-IN ALLOWANCE",D
0200 INPUT "OTHER FEES",F
0210 INPUT "What is the shortest loan you want to consider (years)",S
0220 INPUT "What is the longest loan you want to consider (years)",Y
0300 REM ****** OUTPUT SELECTION ******
0310 INPUT "What port for output",Z
0320 PRINT #Z:PRINT#Z:PRINT#Z
0330 PRINT #Z,TAB(31);"CAR LOAN ANALYSIS"
0340 PRINT #Z:PRINT#Z
0350 PRINT #Z,TAB(5);"Car Price";TAB(70-LEN(STR$(P)));"$ ";P
0360 PRINT #Z,TAB(5);"Sales Tax";TAB(72-LEN(STR$(T)));T
0370 PRINT #Z,TAB(5);"License Fees";TAB(72-LEN(STR$(L)));L
0380 IF F=0 THEN 400
0390 PRINT #Z,TAB(5);"Other Fees";TAB(72-LEN(STR$(F)));F
0400 PRINT #Z,TAB(60);"-------------"
0410   Q=P+T+L+F
0420 PRINT #Z,TAB(5);"Subtotal";TAB(70-LEN(STR$(Q)));"$ ";Q
0430 PRINT #Z,TAB(5);"Less Down Payment/Trade-in Allowance";
0440 PRINT #Z,TAB(72-LEN(STR$(D)));D
0450 PRINT #Z,TAB(60);"-------------"
0460   N=Q-D
0470 PRINT #Z,TAB(5);"Amount Financed";TAB(70-LEN(STR$(N)));"$ ";N
0480 PRINT #Z,TAB(60);"============"
0490 PRINT #Z:PRINT#Z
0500 FOR J=S TO Y
0510   A(J)=(N+(I*N*J/100))/(12*J)
0520 NEXT J
0530 PRINT #Z,"Years";
0540 PRINT #Z,TAB(35);"Monthly Payment";
0550 PRINT #Z,TAB(60);"TOTAL OF PAYMENTS"
0560 PRINT #Z
0570 FOR J=S TO Y
0580 DIGITS= 0
0590 PRINT #Z,TAB(3);J;
```

```
0600 DIGITS= 2
0610 PRINT #Z,TAB(45-LEN(STR$(A(J))));"$";A(J);
0620  B(J)=A(J)*J*12
0630 PRINT #Z,TAB(70-LEN(STR$(B(J))));"$";B(J)
0640 NEXT J
0650 PRINT #Z,CHR$(12)
0660 INPUT "Another Copy",Z$
0670 IF LEFT$(Z$,1)="Y" THEN 300
0680 INPUT "Another Analysis",Z$
0690 IF LEFT$(Z$,1)="Y" THEN 100
0700 END
```

13
CONSUMER LOAN ANALYSIS

Here is the second program in our loan-analysis trilogy. Auto Loan Analysis provided a consumer's view of the cost of an add-on loan in dollars. Consumer Loan Analysis will calculate the true annual percentage rate (APR) of interest and allow a single-number comparison of various loans. This routine will be useful to you whether you borrow or lend money. You can use the program to expand your analyses of automobile, appliance, or personal loan transactions.

BACKGROUND

When you borrow money, you pay interest (actually, rent) on the loan. The amount you repay in excess of the sum you borrowed is the interest, or finance charge. When you repay $110 a year after you borrowed $100, your finance charge is $10. Since you kept the funds for a year, the annual percentage rate is $10/$100 = 10 percent.

When you repay periodically (monthly payments), the interest calculation isn't so simple. Interest should be paid only for the time you have the cash. After the first payment of a fully amortized loan (one in which you repay principal and interest periodically), the balance has declined, and so the interest should be calculated on a smaller amount.

True annual interest is a comparison technique. The true rate, used in a declining-balance calculation, results in the repayment schedule of the original loan. All true annual interest rates are comparable (that is, you can compare the APR between various loans and know that you're making a fair comparison).

We can calculate true equivalent interest rates by determining the actual repayment schedule. We know what amount is to be borrowed. If there are loan fees, we take them into account. The loan fees are normally deducted from the proceeds before you get the money. (They may be

110

paid from separate funds at the time of the deal, but that's the same thing.) Effectively, you are paying back more principal than you received.

You know the amount being borrowed, the fees (if any), and the number of monthly payments. If the monthly payment is known, we can proceed to the APR calculation. If not, we'll calculate the monthly payment using the mathematics from <u>Auto Loan Analysis</u>.

The APR calculation will start with a standard accounting formula that relates principal (P), interest (I), number of payments (N), and payment amount (M).

$$P = M * \frac{1 - (1 + I)^{-N}}{I}$$

This relationship, which applies to fully amortized loans, will be used in other programs when we calculate compound-interest amounts. Most accounting texts can provide the derivation if you're interested in the theory behind the math.

Solving for I in the equation is a little tough because of the exponential term. Although it's a brute-force device, we'll use an iteration method. That is, we'll let the computer guess a number for the solution and then test the answer to see how close it is. The program can update the guess based on the error and try the new answer. We'll keep on estimating and trying until we have an acceptable error. I chose an error limit of one part in one million (or 0.0001 percent) for the program. The error limit is dependent on the precision of the arithmetic routines in your computer. A larger error budget will allow the routine to end earlier. A smaller one may keep the program from converging to a solution. (When you debug your version, start with a loose error limit. You can progressively tighten the error allowance while you experiment with program run time.)

There are a couple of techniques available for making the interest rate "guesses." One extreme method would have us enter every possible interest rate in DATA statements and try each until an error that we can work with is reached. (That could take 1,000 DATA statements for two-digit accuracy after the decimal point!)

By playing some algebra games with the compound-interest formula given earlier, we can derive an equation for computing the first guess (the formula derivation is in Appendix C if you want the specifics of how we arrived at this):

$$I \text{ first} = \frac{2 * (N - P/M)}{N * (N + I)}$$

We can plug the value of I first into the original equation and solve for the principal value. By comparing the actual principal with the calculation, we'll know what the error is. We can also use the two versions of the principal value to adjust our estimate of interest rate. If the

111

new principal is higher than the actual, we'll need to increase the value of I next; if the value is lower than the actual, we'll want a lower value for I next. Fortunately, one equation will do the job:

$$I \text{ next} = \frac{P \text{ calculated}}{P \text{ actual}} * I \text{ last}$$

After the initial guess, we'll use the last formula to keep refining the interest-rate number until the error is within our set limits. This refinement technique is conservative of computer memory and program run time.

PROGRAMMING NOTES

Enough arithmetic! Let's get to the keypunching. The normal program-heading information is in lines 10 through 60. Data input is handled by lines 100 through 250. The monthly payment amount computation takes up lines 300 through 380, while the rest of the routine is devoted to the APR calculation.

Two variables are given to the storage of loan principal. In line 130, the user inputs the amount borrowed to V1. When loan fees have been entered, the program calculates the true principal value and stores it in V. We'll use V1 only to determine the amount of the monthly payment. (Later, we'll reassign this variable to hold the interim value of principal for the error comparison.)

When the operator does not know the monthly-payment amount, program flow is steered to the computation at line 300. If the payment is known, it is entered in line 230. When the monthly payment is determined, program flow enters the APR calculation steps at line 400.

The add-on interest rate is converted from a percent to a decimal fraction in line 330. The actual calculation of the payment is handled by line 350 with a version of the formula used by Auto Loan Analysis. Before the amount of the payment is displayed, it is rounded up to the nearest penny by line 370. (The rounded value is for display only; the exact number is used in the APR determination.)

Since many interest rates are quoted with three digits after the decimal point, we reconfigure our printing format in line 410. Line 420 implements our "first-guess" formula for the initial estimate of the interest rate. The error comparison is made in lines 440 and 450 after the checking value of principal has been computed in line 430. When the error is outside of our limits, the second equation is brought into play. Line 560 updates the value of the trial interest rate, and line 570 bounces the program back to the calculation of principal value in line 430.

When we reach the desired accuracy, the program steps to line 460, which converts the interest from a decimal fraction representing monthly interest rate to an annual percent number. Depending on the actual interest rate, the program can take a few seconds or a few moments to produce an answer. (Annual interest rates less than 3 or 4 percent take longest.) Although I promised no "bells and whistles," line 470 sends a "bell" command to the terminal. Earlier versions of the program took so much time to calculate APR that I needed an alarm clock to tell me the job was complete; Line 470 is that alarm clock, and it is the only "bell" in the book. The refined routine really isn't long enough to lull the user to sleep, so you can delete this feature with no adverse effect on the program.

Line 500 resets the DIGITS=2 before line 510 asks if you want the routine recycled. Nothing in our ending routine should be new to you.

OPERATING NOTES

All of the inputs and outputs of Consumer Loan Analysis go through the control terminal. The sample run uses some numbers borrowed from Auto Loan Analysis samples. You can see that the "easy" 12 percent is really more than 20 percent in APR terms. You can have fun with this one by computing the APR values for advertised loans--if your numbers vary greatly from the advertised truth-in-lending statement or APR, look to the fine print for some loan fees that are hidden.

The only operational problem you may have is with the DO YOU KNOW THE MONTHLY PAYMENT? prompt. This question requires a yes-or-no response. The program expects that you know the payment, so any answer except one beginning with an "N" will be treated as a "yes" answer.

SAMPLE RUN

READY
<u>RUN</u>

                CONSUMER LOAN ANALYSIS
WHAT IS THE AMOUNT BORROWED? <u>9242</u>
WHAT ARE THE LOAN FEES? <u>0</u>
HOW MANY MONTHLY PAYMENTS? <u>36</u>
DO YOU KNOW THE MONTHLY PAYMENT? <u>YES</u>
WHAT IS THE MONTHLY PAYMENT? <u>349.14</u>

THE ANNUAL PERCENTAGE RATE OF TRUE INTEREST IS 21.199 %
ANOTHER PROBLEM? <u>Y</u>
WHAT IS THE AMOUNT BORROWED? <u>9242</u>
WHAT ARE THE LOAN FEES? <u>0</u>
HOW MANY MONTHLY PAYMENTS? <u>48</u>
DO YOU KNOW THE MONTHLY PAYMENT? <u>NO</u>
WHAT IS THE ADD-ON INTEREST RATE (PERCENT)? <u>12</u>
THE MONTHLY PAYMENT IS $284.96

THE ANNUAL PERCENTAGE RATE OF TRUE INTEREST IS 20.753 %
ANOTHER PROBLEM? <u>Y</u>
WHAT IS THE AMOUNT BORROWED? <u>9242</u>
WHAT ARE THE LOAN FEES? <u>0</u>
HOW MANY MONTHLY PAYMENTS? <u>60</u>
DO YOU KNOW THE MONTHLY PAYMENT? <u>NO</u>
WHAT IS THE ADD-ON INTEREST RATE (PERCENT)? <u>12</u>
THE MONTHLY PAYMENT IS $246.45

THE ANNUAL PERCENTAGE RATE OF TRUE INTEREST IS 20.309 %
ANOTHER PROBLEM? <u>NO</u>
THANK YOU.
READY
#

```
0010 REM ********************************
0020 REM *    CONSUMER LOAN ANALYSIS    *
0030 REM ********************************
0040 REM ********* VERSION 20 *********
0050 DIGITS= 2
0060 LINE= 0
0100 PRINT :PRINT:PRINT
0110 PRINT TAB(12);"CONSUMER LOAN ANALYSIS"
0120 PRINT
0130 INPUT "What is the amount borrowed",V1
0140 PRINT
0150 INPUT "What are the loan fees",F
0160   V=V1-F
0170 PRINT
0180 INPUT "How many monthly payments",N
0190 PRINT
0200 INPUT "Do you know the monthly payment",Z$
0210 IF LEFT$(Z$,1)="N" THEN 300
0220 PRINT
0230 INPUT "What is the monthly payment",M
0240 PRINT
0250 GOTO 400
0300 REM **** COMPUTE MONTHLY PAYMENT ***
0310 PRINT
0320 INPUT "What is the add-on interest rate (percent)",R1
0330   R=R1/100
0340 PRINT
0350   M=V1*((1/N)+(R/12))
0360 PRINT "The monthly payment is $";
0370 PRINT (INT(100*(M+0.005)))/100
0380 PRINT
0400 REM ******** CALCULATE APR *********
0410 DIGITS= 3
0420   I1=2*(N-V/M)/(N*(N+1))
0430   V1=M*(1-(1+I1)↑(-N))/I1
0440 IF V1>1.000001*V THEN 560
0450 IF V1<0.999999*V THEN 560
0460   I=I1*1200
0470 PRINT :PRINTCHR$(7)
0480 PRINT "The annual percentage rate of true interest is ";I;"%"
0490 PRINT
0500 DIGITS= 2
0510 INPUT "Another problem",Z$
0520 PRINT
0530 IF LEFT$(Z$,1)="Y" THEN 130
0540 PRINT "Thank you."
0550 END
0560   I1=I1*V1/V
0570 GOTO 430
```

14

REAL ESTATE LOAN ANALYSIS

The capstone of our loan-analysis trio is probably the most powerful routine of the three. <u>Real Estate Loan Analysis</u> will tell you everything you want to know about the payments, interest rate, and repayment period for a mortgage loan. It isn't limited to giving information about mortgages, either. Any fully amortized loan for which interest is calculated on the remaining balance can be investigated. Just about all bank, savings and loan, and credit union transactions fit the category. Some of the mathematical tricks we develop here will be used in later programs. There's also a new operator-input feature introduced so you can increase your bag of programming tricks.

BACKGROUND

The four factors in a fully amortized loan are: the principal value, or amount borrowed; the annual interest rate; the monthly payment; and the number of payments. With this program, we can calculate any one of the factors if we know the other three. For example, when you know the prevailing interest rate, you can determine how much you can afford to pay for a house based on the monthly payment you are comfortable with for a 30-year loan.

We've seen all of the arithmetic before. The heart of the computation is the compound interest formula (technically, it's a "present-value-of-an-annuity" equation). We'll solve for the loan principal by using the formula "straight" and plugging in user data for the monthly-payment amount, the number of payments, and the interest rate. The monthly-payment calculation is also straightforward. A minor algebra shuffle of the formula parts puts it into a form that allows us to plug in values to solve for the periodic payment. (The equation derivations are shown in Appendix C.) Determination of the number of payments is another easy calculation, once we've massaged the formula. (It took a little college-level algebra to accomplish that

116

trick, but you need only keypunch the program to do it.)
We lift the interest-rate-calculation routine directly from
Consumer Loan Analysis--it took too long to come up with a
memory-efficient tool that doesn't take forever to run to
change it now.

OPERATING NOTES

You'll be pleased at the ease of operation. The program
will always ask for the loan factors in the same order:

     PRINCIPAL?

     MONTHLY PAYMENT?

     NUMBER OF PAYMENTS?

     INTEREST RATE?

Enter the numbers you know, and hit "RETURN" when you come
to the unknown you're trying to find. This feature (press
"RETURN" for the unknown) saves having to go through a menu
of choices with every program exercise. It should also
amaze your computer-expert friends who know that you can't
refuse to make an entry of a numeric variable. (You can't
with most home computers, but we have a technique that
makes it look like we've suspended the input rules for
awhile.) After your answer is presented, the routine will
ask if you want another problem.

PROGRAMMING NOTES

Real Estate Loan Analysis is deceptively short for the
power it provides. You can probably have it keypunched and
debugged in an easy evening--particularly if the interest-
rate computation was done as part of Consumer Loan Anal-
sis. Refer to the program listing, and we'll go over the
high points.
    The user-input steps are in lines 100 through 400.
The unique feature of the program is also implemented in
these lines. Note that each numeric entry is put into a
character string variable (for example, "Principal amount",
V$) instead of a numeric. Character string variables will
accept a null entry (PRESS "RETURN"). We check each variable for the null entry to determine the unknown quantity.
When a null is sensed, program flow is directed to the
appropriate calculation routine. Within each calculation
routine, the input questions are continued. This structure
requires that you keypunch the same question in a few
places, but provides the operator with a standard sequence.
Once we're in a compute action, the operator shouldn't be
entering a null, so we can use standard numeric variables
for the input actions.
    If a value has been entered, we need to put it into a
numeric variable. Lines 240, 280, 320, and 360 take care

of the shift. Lines 370, 380, and 390 provide an error trap in case the user enters four knowns. Since interest rate is entered as an annual percentage, we must divide it by 100 to get a decimal that the program can handle; then, we must divide it by 12 for a monthly rate to correspond with the monthly-payment nature of our calculation. Lines 360, 1060, 2040, and 3020 handle this change in the form of the interest rate. When we're calculating interest rate, we must change the number from a monthly decimal amount to an annual percentage rate, and line 4110 handles that chore.

The actual work is handled in the computation routines located at lines 1000, 2000, 3000, and 4000. The REMark statements at the head of each routine specify the purpose of each. With the exception of the interest-rate calculation, each routine does its duty in one line of formula. The iterative-interest computation is the same one we used in the previous program--if your BASIC has a renumbering editor, you won't even need to keypunch it.

You'll note that the END statement in line 400 is only reached by a GOTO from the various routines. This follows our rule of having only one END statement per program--it also puts the final statement up near the front. When we get to the file management routine later, we will want to change all of these END statements.

You can save some keypunching and program memory by deleting lines 330 to 390 and adding a GOTO 4000 in line 330. You'll lose the error trap, but if you've made a terrible error in some other entry step, the computer will let you know. You may also wish to delete lines 100 to 160 if you're the only operator. I recommend leaving them in-memory and keypunch time spent to give user convenience are well spent.

SAMPLE RUN

READY
RUN

                    REAL ESTATE LOAN ANALYSIS

THIS ROUTINE WILL CALCULATE VARIOUS FACTORS OF A
FULLY AMORTIZED (NO BALLOON PAYMENT) REAL ESTATE
LOAN. YOU MUST KNOW THREE OF THE FOUR FACTORS
(PRINCIPAL, PAYMENT AMOUNT, NUMBER OF PAYMENTS,
AND INTEREST RATE) TO FIND THE FOURTH.

ENTER THE AMOUNTS YOU KNOW. WHEN YOU COME TO THE
UNKNOWN, PRESS 'RETURN'.

PRINCIPAL AMOUNT? 130000

MONTHLY PAYMENT?

NUMBER OF PAYMENTS? 360

ANNUAL PERCENTAGE INTEREST RATE? 14

THE MONTHLY PAYMENT IS $1540.33

ANOTHER PROBLEM? YES

ENTER THE AMOUNTS YOU KNOW. WHEN YOU COME TO THE UNKNOWN,
PRESS 'RETURN'.

PRINCIPAL AMOUNT? 95350

MONTHLY PAYMENT? 1300

NUMBER OF PAYMENTS? 360

ANNUAL PERCENTAGE INTEREST RATE?

PLEASE BE PATIENT WHILE I THINK.

THIS IS A TOUGH ONE.

THANKS FOR WAITING.

THE ANNUAL INTEREST RATE IS 16.230 %

ANOTHER PROBLEM? YES

ENTER THE AMOUNTS YOU KNOW. WHEN YOU COME TO THE
UNKNOWN, PRESS 'RETURN'.

119

PRINCIPAL AMOUNT?

MONTHLY PAYMENT? 1000

NUMBER OF PAYMENTS? 360

ANNUAL PERCENTAGE INTEREST RATE? 15

THE PRINCIPAL AMOUNT OF THE LOAN IS $79086.14

ANOTHER PROBLEM? YUP

ENTER THE AMOUNTS YOU KNOW. WHEN YOU COME TO THE
UNKNOWN, PRESS 'RETURN'.

PRINCIPAL AMOUNT? 85000

MONTHLY PAYMENT? 1000

NUMBER OF PAYMENTS?

ANNUAL PERCENTAGE INTEREST RATE? 13.5

THERE ARE 280 MONTHLY PAYMENTS.

ANOTHER PROBLEM? NO

READY
#

```
0010 REM ***********************************
0020 REM *   REAL ESTATE LOAN ANALYSIS    *
0030 REM ***********************************
0040 REM ********** VERSION 30 **********
0050 DIGITS= 2
0060 LINE= 0
0100 PRINT :PRINT:PRINT
0110 PRINT TAB(12);"REAL ESTATE LOAN ANALYSIS":PRINT
0120 PRINT "This routine will calculate various factors of a"
0130 PRINT "fully amortized (no balloon payment) real estate"
0140 PRINT "loan.  You must know three of the four factors"
0150 PRINT "(Principal, Payment Amount, Number of Payments, "
0160 PRINT "and Interest Rate) to find the fourth."
0170 PRINT
0180 PRINT "Enter the amounts you know.  When you come to the"
0190 PRINT "unknown, press 'RETURN'."
0200 PRINT
0210 INPUT "Principal amount",V$
0220 PRINT
0230 IF V$="" THEN 1000
0240   V=VAL(V$)
0250 INPUT "Monthly payment",M$
0260 PRINT
0270 IF M$="" THEN 2000
0280   M=VAL(M$)
0290 INPUT "Number of payments",N$
0300 PRINT
0310 IF N$="" THEN 3000
0320   N=VAL(N$)
0330 INPUT "Annual percentage interest rate",I$
0340 PRINT
0350 IF I$="" THEN 4000
0360   I=(VAL(I$))/1200
0370 PRINT "Sorry, I seem to have read one of your answers"
0380 PRINT "incorrectly.  Please start again."
0390 GOTO 170
0400 END
1000 REM ***** CALCULATE PRINCIPAL ******
1010 INPUT "Monthly payment",M
1020 PRINT
1030 INPUT "Number of payments",N
1040 PRINT
1050 INPUT "Annual percentage interest rate",I1
1060   I=I1/1200
1070 PRINT
1080   V=M*(1-(1/(1+I)↑N))/I
1090 PRINT "The principal amount of the loan is $";V
1100 PRINT
1110 INPUT "Another problem",Z$
1120 IF LEFT$(Z$,1)="Y" THEN 170
1130 GOTO 400
2000 REM ****** CALCULATE PAYMENT *******
2010 INPUT "Number of payments",N
2020 PRINT
```

```
2030 INPUT "Annual percentage interest rate",I1
2040  I=I1/1200
2050 PRINT
2060  M=V*(I/(1-(1+I)↑(-N)))
2070 PRINT "The monthly payment is $";M
2080 PRINT
2090 INPUT "Another problem",Z$
2100 IF LEFT$(Z$,1)="Y" THEN 170
2110 GOTO 400
3000 REM ****** NUMBER OF PAYMENTS ******
3010 INPUT "Annual percentage interest rate",I1
3020  I=I1/1200
3030 PRINT
3040  N=LOG(1/(1-I*V/M))/LOG(1+I)
3050 DIGITS= 0
3060 PRINT "There are ";INT(N+.5);"monthly payments."
3070 PRINT
3080 INPUT "Another problem",Z$
3090 IF LEFT$(Z$,1)="Y" THEN 170
3100 GOTO 400
4000 REM *** CALCULATE INTEREST RATE ****
4010 PRINT
4020 PRINT "Please be patient while I think."
4030 PRINT
4040 PRINT "This is a tough one."
4050 PRINT
4060 DIGITS= 3
4070  I1=2*(N-V/M)/(N*(N+1))
4080  V1=M*(1-(1+I1)↑(-N))/I1
4090 IF V1>1.0000001*V THEN 4200
4100 IF V1<0.9999999*V THEN 4200
4110  I=I1*1200
4120 PRINT "Thanks for waiting."
4130 PRINT
4140 PRINT "The annual interest rate is ";I;"%"
4150 PRINT
4160 INPUT "Another problem",Z$
4170 DIGITS= 2
4180 IF LEFT$(Z$,1)="Y" THEN 170
4190 GOTO 400
4200  Y=(1+I1)↑(-N)
4210  W=1-Y
4220  I1=I1*(1-(((I1*V/M)-W)/(W-(N*I1*Y/(1+I1)))))
4230 GOTO 4080
```

15
REAL ESTATE LOAN STATUS

Here's another one-evening project that will help you with your income taxes. Real Estate Loan Status will calculate the interest paid over any period and the remaining principal balance at the end of the period. It will work for any fully amortized loan on which interest is calculated on the remaining balance, so the usefulness is not limited to mortgages. You can calculate your interest expense at year-end and have your itemized deductions totalled before the bank statements come in.

BACKGROUND

It takes two separate calculations to provide the interest total and the remaining balance. Both are based on the compound-interest formula we discussed earlier. The interest calculation is made by calculating the total paid during the interval of our observation (usually the current year) and subtracting the principal reduction during the same period. The equation derived (in Appendix C) to do the job is:

$$I = M * (N2 - N1 - \frac{(1 + I)^{(N2-N)} + (1 + I)^{(N1-N)}}{I})$$

where I represents the interest paid during the interval, M is the amount of each monthly payment, N2 is the payment number for the last payment in the period, N1 is the payment number of the payment just before the first one in the period, and I is the interest rate. The total number of payments in the loan is represented by N. While this looks like a hairy formula, your computer has seen all of the elements before. The worst problem you'll have is keypunching the right number of parentheses in line 280.

The remaining-balance computation is handled with the same compound-interest formula we used in the previous programs. In this case, we know how many payments remain (the total minus the number of the last in the present period), the monthly-payment amount, and the interest rate. By calculating principal as though we were dealing with a new loan, we'll find the remaining balance. Here's how we've modified the equation:

$$\text{Balance} = M * \frac{1 - (1 + I)^{(N2-N)}}{I}$$

Both equations fit on one statement line, so the program doesn't lose any time iterating. Since exponentials are normally the slowest calculations performed by our home computers, you may expect some delays in this routine. Happily, the computer is still faster than the terminal-- there's no perceptible delay between the last user input and the answer.

OPERATING NOTES

The sample run illustrates two uses of <u>Real</u> <u>Estate</u> <u>Loan</u> <u>Status</u>. The first example employs the program to calculate the interest paid during the second year of a mythical loan (and provide the remaining balance). In the second, we have input the first and last numbers of all payments to total the interest to be paid over the life of the same loan.

About the only thing the prompting messages don't spell out is the definition of loan-payment "numbers." What is wanted by the payment-number prompt is the sequence number of the payment. The first payment is number 1, the second is 2, and so on. In the example, the first payment of the second year (number 13) and last payment of the second year (number 24) are entered in the first exercise. The second example enters the first payment (number 1), and the last payment (number 360) of a 30-year mortgage. You shouldn't have any other trouble with the operation of this routine. There's no provision for hard-copy output, but that won't be a problem if you have a printing terminal.

PROGRAMMING NOTES

As the program listing reveals, this is a very short routine. You may wish to make it even shorter--or combine it with one of the loan-analysis programs--by deleting lines 100 through 150, which are operator instructions. You could also omit some of the PRINT statements between the input questions; they are included to keep the terminal display unbusy.

We really need to calculate with the number of the payment just before the first payment in the period of concern. Rather than ask for that, we ask the operator to input the number of the first payment and include line 190 to adjust for the payment we want. Line 260 makes the conversion from annual percentage interest rate to a monthly

124

decimal that the routine can handle. Our main total-interest-calculation formula is berthed in line 280, and the remaining-balance equation is given in line 300.

Line 320 ensures that we print the integer payment number without a decimal and trailing zeroes, then line 340 converts back to a dollars-and-cents format. Our semi-standard program recycle and wrapup takes up lines 370 through 420. No program fancies in this one--you can have it keypunched between cocktails and dinner.

```
        SAMPLE RUN

READY
# RUN

            REAL ESTATE LOAN STATUS

THIS ROUTINE WILL ESTIMATE THE INTEREST PAID ON
A REAL-ESTATE LOAN FOR ANY PERIOD, AND PROVIDE
THE APPROXIMATE REMAINING PRINCIPAL BALANCE.

HOW MANY TOTAL PAYMENTS OVER THE LIFE OF THE LOAN? 360

WHAT NUMBER IS THE FIRST PAYMENT OF THE PERIOD? 13

WHAT IS THE NUMBER OF THE LAST PAYMENT IN THE PERIOD? 24

WHAT IS THE NORMAL MONTHLY PAYMENT? 550.18

WHAT IS THE ANNUAL INTEREST RATE (PERCENT)? 11.5


THE INTEREST PAID ON THE NOTE DURING THE PERIOD IS $6350.25

THE REMAINING BALANCE AFTER PAYMENT 24 IS $55080.82


ANOTHER? YES

HOW MANY TOTAL PAYMENTS OVER THE LIFE OF THE LOAN?

WHAT NUMBER IS THE FIRST PAYMENT OF THE PERIOD? 1

WHAT IS THE NUMBER OF THE LAST PAYMENT IN THE PERIOD? 360

WHAT IS THE NORMAL MONTHLY PAYMENT? 550.18

WHAT IS THE ANNUAL INTEREST RATE (PERCENT)? 11.5


THE INTEREST PAID ON THE NOTE DURING THE PERIOD IS $142507.41

THE REMAINING BALANCE AFTER PAYMENT 360 IS $0.00


ANOTHER? NO THANKS

THANK YOU!

READY
#
```

126

```
0010  REM  *********************************
0020  REM *     REAL ESTATE LOAN STATUS     *
0030  REM  *********************************
0040  REM ********** VERSION 10 **********
0050  LINE= 0
0060  DIGITS= 2
0100  PRINT TAB(12);"REAL ESTATE LOAN STATUS"
0110  PRINT
0120  PRINT "This routine will estimate the interest paid on"
0130  PRINT "a real-estate loan for any period, and provide"
0140  PRINT "the approximate remaining principal balance."
0150  PRINT
0160  INPUT "How many total payments over the life of the loan",N
0170  PRINT
0180  INPUT "What number is the first payment of the period",N1
0190    N1=N1-1
0200  PRINT
0210  INPUT "What is the number of the last payment in the period",N2
0220  PRINT
0230  INPUT "What is the normal monthly payment",M
0240  PRINT
0250  INPUT "What is the annual interest rate (percent)",R1
0260    R=R1/1200
0270  PRINT :PRINT:PRINT
0280    I=M*(N2-N1-(((1+R)↑(N2-N))/R)+(((1+R)↑(N1-N))/R))
0290  PRINT "The interest paid on the note during the period is $";I
0300    V=(M/R)*(1-(1+R)↑(N2-N))
0310  PRINT
0320  DIGITS= 0
0330  PRINT "The remaining balance after payment ";N2;
0340  DIGITS= 2
0350  PRINT "is $";V
0360  PRINT
0370  PRINT
0380  INPUT "Another",Z$
0390  IF LEFT$(Z$,1)="Y" THEN 150
0400  PRINT
0410  PRINT "Thank you!"
0420  END
```

16
LOAN RECORDS

We could as easily consider Loan Records a money-management program as a credit-control tool. Its primary purpose is one of keeping track of the various time-payment obligations important to our lives. (The program header, in fact, calls this routine Time Payment Records. Call your version whatever suits you.) We included it in this section because the mathematical manipulations fit in with the loan calculations we've just completed. The arithmetic used allows our computer to keep us abreast of the remaining balances on each loan in the record. There are no new programming tricks or mathematical techniques used here. The program will illustrate another way to recombine our resources for another task.

Loan Records is written for a system with disk-memory capability. The program routines use the disk in a "fast-cassette" mode (that is, no true random-access disk data processing is attempted). If you don't have disk capabilities yet, you can easily adapt the routine for tape-cassette data storage. If your disk-operating system (DOS) is a sophisticated one, you'll probably want to adjust the program to provide random-access data treatment and cut down the keypunching task. Whatever way you choose to modify this one, you'll find it a handy financial management tool.

OPERATING NOTES

The sample run of this routine is a bit long because I tried to illustrate each command. You'll notice that the first command given the routine isn't on the menu of tasks. Initialization of the disk won't happen often, so it has been given the "hidden-command" treatment to keep an unknowing operator from accidentally wiping out the data record. You can record as many or as few loans as you wish—just tell the program the number you plan to enter during the initialization session. On later program exercises, you may enter or delete loans.

There's no particular magic to the order of loan entries. Enter the payee, the present balance, the annual interest rate, and the normal monthly payment as the program asks for each piece of information. To classify the loan as a "conventional" or "add-on" type, enter a "C" or an "A" for each; the routine looks only at the initial letter.

After each program exercise, the data base is displayed. The DISPLAY command allows you to review the data base without making any changes or entries. You may display the record on any output device available to your computer. (In the sample, port #3 designates my printing terminal on which the entries are made.) Following the printout, the routine will ask for the disk-drive location where you wish data stored. You may wish to store the information in two separate disk slots to keep a backup record. (You can read from one and write to the other alternately.)

Posting of loan payments is illustrated as the sample continues. When a loan payment is entered into the record, the program will calculate the remaining balance. It assumes, however, that you're making regular monthly payments, so the routine doesn't adjust the balance if you miss one. (The next program addresses that problem, so you might wish to combine the two when you adapt the book programs for your own use.)

The continuation of the sample demonstrates the procedure needed to add a loan to the record. The entries are the same ones requested by the initialization routine, so no operator surprises lurk here. The display of the record shows that the loan was entered in the data base. Note that anytime an entry is changed, the LAST PAYMENT date is upgraded to reflect TODAY'S DATE.

Our final sample is a loan-remove action. You might wish to remove a loan from the record rather than enter a final payment. The deletion is almost a one-keystroke task. The program will list the loans in the data base and assign a number to each. Indicate the one to be dropped by typing the number. The final display will prove that the correct loan was deleted. The input prompts are a little wordy throughout the program, but the operator convenience should make up for that extra keypunch time.

PROGRAMMING NOTES

Refer to the listing as we discuss the high points of <u>Loan Records</u>. You'll note one minor change in the preface statements: On line 60, we set DIGITS=0 to take care of integer printing. We'll reset our normal dollars-and-cents DIGITS=2 as part of the printing routine.

Lines 190 through 270 steer program flow after the menu choice. Lines 250, 260, and 270 form an error trap to catch an operator miskey. Although it seems odd, all of

129

the statements except INITIALIZE send program flow to line 400. The apparent goof will be cleared up after the disk is read and the same inputs are used to further vector the program to appropriate routines.

The INITIALIZE routine in lines 300 through 390 is similar to others we've used. The variables are DIMensioned to the number of entries selected by the operator. A FOR...NEXT loop exercises the subroutine for data entry which is included in lines 1500 through 1700.

The data-entry subroutine doesn't present any new quirks. The D$(X)=Y$ in line 1600 stuffs TODAY'S DATE into the LAST PAYMENT variable. Lines 1640 through 1700 provide an error trap for the loan-type entry T$(X). We've got to insist on an "A" or a "C" entry.

With all initial loan data entered, line 390 sends the program to the display data base routine at line 1800. The printing segment is pretty standard, so we won't spend a lot of words on it. The routine is followed (always) by the disk-storage task. The only lines that may raise a question in the storage routine are lines 2020 and 2030. These form an error trap. There are two disk drives on my system, so the first digit in the DRIVE/SECTOR selection must be either a one or a two. There are 350 sectors on each disk, so a sector selection in excess of 350 is a no-no. (To be complete, the error trap should also check for numbers between 1350 and 1999, but my usual keypunch error occurs in the first digit--specifying the wrong drive--so I didn't go any further with the trap.)

Lines 400 through 610 provide the READ DISK procedure for all menu selections except INITIALIZE. Lines 440, 450, and 460 may raise a question. They allow the variables to be DIMensioned one number greater than the number of loans on the disk. The extra position will allow us to add a loan later without generating a BASIC error for overflowing the variable memory allocation. You could safely omit lines 550, 560, and 570. Only a major hardware problem or disastrous programming glitch would invoke these lines. (Since my programs are famous for containing some disaster in their early versions, I keep lines like this in for debugging purposes. By the time I've refined things to a final version, I've also usually scrubbed most of the disaster messages.) The error trap in lines 580 to 610 is a valid one, however. You could pick this one by entering the wrong disk drive/sector address, or by picking up the wrong disk.

Loan payments are entered by the routine in lines 1000 through 1190. This is the code segment that makes use of the loan-type entry--T$(X) that we've asked the operator to enter. If we're dealing with a conventional loan, we'll calculate the interest and add it to the balance before subtracting the payment. This operation is handled in line 1180 after the "C" in T$(X) steers the program at line 1150. For add-on loans, the interest has been included in the balance already, so the calculation is far simpler. Line 1160 calculates the new balance for add-on loans. Both lines 1160 and 1180 have two BASIC statements. The

130

first is the balance calculator; the second (after the colon) updates the last-payment variable to the current date.

The actual loan-balance updating is maneuvered by a subroutine in lines 1100 to 1190. The subroutine is called by the FOR...NEXT loop of lines 1020 through 1070. When all loans have been dealt a payment option, program flow is sent to the display routine.

Lines 1200 to 1240 provide the routine to add a loan. Here's where we take advantage of the extra number used to DIMension the loan variables. Line 1210 resets N to N+1; line 1220 sets X equal to the new N; and line 1230 calls the subroutine that will request loan entries from the user. Obviously, this loan will be tacked onto the end of the data base. After entry of the data, the program flow moves to the display, record, and end sequences.

Lines 1300 through 1460 provide the vehicle for removing a loan from the data record. The technique of numbering the loans and asking the operator to input the number of the loan to be dropped helps us in two ways. It makes the operator's task a one-keystroke job, and it saves programming by setting up a limit for the FOR...NEXT loop of lines 1370 to 1440. The purpose of the loop is to move all data for the loans with numbers higher than the one deleted to data pockets one number lower. In the sample, we deleted loan number 3. This program segment would cause loan number 4 to be recorded in the memory variables assigned to loan 3--effectively erasing all memory of loan 3. The total number of loans in the data base is reset by line 1450 before the program ambles on to the display sequence.

While this program is a little longer than average, the segment nature of the BASIC code will allow debugging to go rapidly. You can try each small piece of code immediately after keypunching to catch those glitches (and sons-of-glitches!) before any real damage is started.

We've discussed previously (in the Electronic Checkbook program) that the disk system in your hardware will need to be consulted. If yours is more sophisticated than mine, you'll need to change the disk-operation commands to fit. Your task can only be eased by the increased automation of your DOS, however, since the system I have requires the most program definitions.

SAMPLE RUN - LOAN RECORDS

READY
RUN

             TIME PAYMENT RECORDS
TODAY'S DATE (DAY-MONTH-YEAR)? 1 JAN 1984

WOULD YOU LIKE TO -

         'E'NTER PAYMENT DATA,
         'D'ISPLAY THE RECORDS,
         'A'DD A NEW LOAN, OR
         'R'EMOVE AN OLD ONE? INITIALIZE PROGRAM

HOW MANY LOANS DO YOU WISH TO RECORD? 3

WHO IS THE MORTGAGOR/PAYEE? FIRST CITY BANK

WHAT IS THE BALANCE OWING? 50000

WHAT IS THE ANNUAL INTEREST RATE? 9.5

WHAT IS THE MONTHLY PAYMENT AMOUNT? 420.43

IS IT A 'CONVENTIONAL' LOAN (LIKE A HOUSE MORTGAGE), OR
AN 'ADD-ON' LOAN (LIKE AN AUTO LOAN)? CONVENTIONAL

WHO IS THE MORTGAGOR/PAYEE? SECOND COUNTY S & L

WHAT IS THE BALANCE OWING? 5300

WHAT IS THE ANNUAL INTEREST RATE? 11.0

WHAT IS THE MONTHLY PAYMENT AMOUNT? 73.01

IS IT A 'CONVENTIONAL' LOAN (LIKE A HOUSE MORTGAGE), OR
AN 'ADD-ON' LOAN (LIKE AN AUTO LOAN)? C

WHO IS THE MORTGAGOR/PAYEE? TOWNSHIP LOAN COMPANY

WHAT IS THE BALANCE OWING? 200

WHAT IS THE ANNUAL INTEREST RATE? 15.0

WHAT IS THE MONTHLY PAYMENT AMOUNT? 100

IS IT A 'CONVENTIONAL' LOAN (LIKE A HOUSE MORTGAGE), OR
AN 'ADD-ON' LOAN (LIKE AN AUTO LOAN)? ADD-ON

WHAT OUTPUT PORT DO YOU WISH TO USE? <u>3</u>

                    LOAN PAYMENT RECORD

PAYEE	BALANCE	PAYMENT	RATE	LAST PAYMENT
FIRST CITY BANK	50000.00	420.43	9.50 %	1 JAN 1984
SECOND COUNTY S & L	5300.00	73.01	11.00 %	1 JAN 1984
TOWNSHIP LOAN COMPANY	200.00	100.00	15.00 %	1 JAN 1984

WHAT DISK DRIVE AND SECTOR (DSSS)? <u>2001</u>

READY
<u>RUN</u>

            TIME PAYMENT RECORDS
TODAY'S DATE (DAY-MONTH-YEAR)? <u>1 FEB 1984</u>

WOULD YOU LIKE TO -

            'E'NTER PAYMENT DATA,
            'D'ISPLAY THE RECORDS,
            'A'DD A NEW LOAN, OR
            'R'EMOVE AN OLD ONE? <u>ENTER</u>

WHAT DISK DRIVE AND SECTOR (DSSS)? <u>2001</u>

DID YOU MAKE A PAYMENT ON THE FIRST CITY BANK LOAN? <u>YES</u>
THE PRESENT BALANCE ON THE LOAN IS 50000
THE LAST PAYMENT WAS MADE ON 1 JAN 1984

THE RECOMMENDED MONTHLY PAYMENT IS 420.43
AMOUNT OF TODAY'S PAYMENT? <u>420.43</u>

DID YOU MAKE A PAYMENT ON THE SECOND COUNTY S & L LOAN? <u>NO</u>

DID YOU MAKE A PAYMENT ON THE TOWNSHIP LOAN COMPANY LOAN? <u>YES</u>
THE PRESENT BALANCE ON THE LOAN IS 200
THE LAST PAYMENT WAS MADE ON 1 JAN 1984

THE RECOMMENDED MONTHLY PAYMENT IS 100
AMOUNT OF TODAY'S PAYMENT? <u>100</u>

WHAT OUTPUT PORT DO YOU WISH TO USE? <u>3</u>

133

```
                LOAN PAYMENT RECORD
PAYEE                BALANCE    PAYMENT      RATE       LAST PAYMENT
FIRST CITY BANK      49975.40    420.43     9.50%      1 FEB 1984

SECOND COUNTY S & L   5300.00     73.01    11.00%      1 JAN 1984

TOWNSHIP LOAN COMPANY  100.00    100.00    15.00%      1 FEB 1984

WHAT DISK DRIVE AND SECTOR (DSSS)? 2001
READY
# RUN
                TIME PAYMENT RECORDS
TODAY'S DATE (DAY-MONTH-YEAR)? 9 FEB 1984

WOULD YOU LIKE TO -

        'E'NTER PAYMENT DATA,
        'D'ISPLAY THE RECORDS,
        'A'DD A NEW LOAN, OR
        'R'EMOVE AN OLD ONE? ADD LOAN

WHAT DISK DRIVE AND SECTOR (DSSS)? 2001

WHO IS THE MORTGAGOR/PAYEE? CREDIT UNION

WHAT IS THE BALANCE OWING? 500

WHAT IS THE ANNUAL INTEREST RATE? 12.5

WHAT IS THE MONTHLY PAYMENT AMOUNT? 25.00

IS IT A 'CONVENTIONAL' LOAN (LIKE A HOUSE MORTGAGE), OR
AN 'ADD-ON' LOAN (LIKE AN AUTO LOAN)? CONVENTIONAL
WHAT OUTPUT PORT DO YOU WISH TO USE? 3

                LOAN PAYMENT RECORD
PAYEE                BALANCE    PAYMENT      RATE       LAST PAYMENT
FIRST CITY BANK      49975.40    420.43     9.50 %     1 FEB 1984

SECOND COUNTY S & L   5300.00     73.01    11.00 %     1 JAN 1984

TOWNSHIP LOAN COMPANY  100.00    100.00    15.00 %     1 FEB 1984

CREDIT UNION           500.00     25.00    12.50 %     9 FEB 1984
```

WHAT DISK DRIVE AND SECTOR (DSSS)? <u>2001</u>

READY
<u>RUN</u>

                TIME PAYMENT RECORDS
TODAY'S DATE (DAY-MONTH-YEAR)? <u>1 MAR 1984</u>

WOULD YOU LIKE TO -

        'E'NTER PAYMENT DATA,
        'D'ISPLAY THE RECORDS,
        'A'DD A NEW LOAN, OR
        'R'EMOVE AN OLD ONE? <u>REMOVE</u>

WHAT DISK DRIVE AND SECTOR (DSSS)? <u>2001</u>

THE LOANS IN THE RECORD NOW ARE -
NR 1 - FIRST CITY BANK
NR 2 - SECOND COUNTY S & L
NR 3 - TOWNSHIP LOAN COMPANY
NR 4 - CREDIT UNION

WHICH NUMBER DO YOU WISH TO DROP? <u>3</u>
WHAT OUTPUT PORT DO YOU WISH TO USE? <u>3</u>

                    LOAN PAYMENT RECORD

PAYEE	BALANCE	PAYMENT	RATE	LAST PAYMENT
FIRST CITY BANK	49975.40	420.43	9.50 %	1 FEB 1984
SECOND COUNTY S & L	5300.00	73.01	11.00 %	1 JAN 1984
CREDIT UNION	500.00	25.00	12.50 %	9 FEB 1984

WHAT DISK DRIVE AND SECTOR (DSSS)? <u>2001</u>

READY
#

```
0010 REM *******************************
0020 REM *      TIME PAYMENT RECORDS      *
0030 REM *******************************
0040 REM ********* VERSION 10 *********
0050 LINE= 0
0060 DIGITS= 0
0080 PRINT TAB(12);"TIME PAYMENT RECORDS"
0090 INPUT "Today's date (Day-Month-Year)",Y$
0100 PRINT
0110 PRINT "Would you like to -"
0120 PRINT
0130 PRINT "          'E'nter payment data,"
0140 PRINT "          'D'isplay the records,"
0150 PRINT "          'A'dd a new loan, or"
0160 PRINT "          'R'emove an old one";
0170 INPUT Z$
0180 PRINT
0190 IF LEFT$(Z$,1)="I" THEN 300
0200 IF LEFT$(Z$,1)="E" THEN 400
0210 IF LEFT$(Z$,1)="D" THEN 400
0220 IF LEFT$(Z$,1)="A" THEN 400
0230 IF LEFT$(Z$,1)="R" THEN 400
0240 PRINT
0250 PRINT "Sorry, I don't understand your response of '";Z$;"'!"
0260 PRINT "Please try again."
0270 GOTO 120
0300 REM ********* INITIALIZE **********
0310 PRINT
0320 INPUT "How many loans do you wish to record",N
0330 PRINT
0340 DIM B(N),D$(N),M$(N),P(N),R(N),T$(N)
0350 FOR X=1 TO N
0360 GOSUB 1500
0370 NEXT X
0380 PRINT
0390 GOTO 1800
0400 REM ********* READ  DISK **********
0410 INPUT "What disk drive and sector (DSSS)",S
0420 OPEN #10,S
0430 READ #10,N\580
0440  N=N+1
0450 DIM B(N),D$(N),M$(N),P(N),R(N),T$(N)
0460  N=N-1
0470 FOR X=1 TO N
0480 READ #10,B(X),D$(X),M$(X),P(X),R(X),T$(X)\580
0490 NEXT X
0500 CLOSE #10
0510 IF LEFT$(Z$,1)="E" THEN 1000
0520 IF LEFT$(Z$,1)="D" THEN 1800
0530 IF LEFT$(Z$,1)="A" THEN 1200
0540 IF LEFT$(Z$,1)="R" THEN 1300
0550 PRINT "YOU SHOULDN'T HAVE GOTTEN HERE!"
0560 PRINT "There's a programming problem or a hardware glitch!"
0570 GOTO 2100
```

```
0580 PRINT "***** OOPS! *****"
0590 PRINT "You must have the wrong disk assignment, there's no"
0600 PRINT "data there.  Let's start again."
0610 GOTO 2100
1000 REM ****** ENTER PAYMENT DATA ******
1010 PRINT
1020 FOR X=1 TO N
1030 PRINT "Did you make a payment on the ";M$(X);" loan";
1040 INPUT Z$
1050 IF LEFT$(Z$,1)="Y" THEN GOSUB 1100
1060 PRINT
1070 NEXT X
1080 GOTO 1800
1100 PRINT "The present balance on the loan is ";B(X)
1110 PRINT "The last payment was made on ";D$(X)
1120 PRINT
1130 PRINT "The recommended monthly payment is ";P(X)
1140 INPUT "Amount of today's payment",Z
1150 IF LEFT$(T$(X),1)="C" THEN 1180
1160   B(X)=B(X)-Z: D$(X)=Y$
1170 RETURN
1180   B(X)=(B(X)*(1+R(X)/1200))-Z:D$(X)=Y$
1190 RETURN
1200 REM ***** ADD A LOAN TO RECORD *****
1210   N=N+1
1220   X=N
1230 GOSUB 1500
1240 GOTO 1800
1300 REM ** REMOVE A LOAN FROM RECORD ***
1310 PRINT "The loans in the record now are -"
1320 FOR X=1 TO N
1330 PRINT "Nr ";X;" - ";M$(X)
1340 NEXT X
1350 PRINT
1360 INPUT "Which number do you wish to drop",W
1370 FOR X=W TO N-1
1380   B(X)=B(X+1)
1390   D$(X)=D$(X+1)
1400   M$(X)=M$(X+1)
1410   P(X)=P(X+1)
1420   R(X)=R(X+1)
1430   T$(X)=T$(X+1)
1440 NEXT X
1450   N=N-1
1460 GOTO 1800
1500 REM ****** ENTER LOANS DATA ******
1510 PRINT
1520 INPUT "Who is the mortgagor/payee",M$(X)
1530 PRINT
1540 INPUT "What is the balance owing",B(X)
1550 PRINT
1560 INPUT "What is the annual interest rate",R(X)
1570 PRINT
1580 INPUT "What is the monthly payment amount",P(X)
1590 PRINT
```

```
1600    D$(X)=Y$
1610 PRINT "Is it a 'CONVENTIONAL' loan (like a house mortgage), or"
1620 PRINT "an 'ADD-ON' loan (like an auto loan)";
1630 INPUT T$(X)
1640 IF LEFT$(T$(X),1)="A" RETURN
1650 IF LEFT$(T$(X),1)="C" RETURN
1660 PRINT
1670 PRINT "Please tell me if it is a 'CONVENTIONAL' loan or"
1680 PRINT "an 'ADD-ON' loan."
1690 INPUT T$(X)
1700 GOTO 1640
1800 REM ******* PRINT THE RECORD *******
1810 DIGITS= 2
1820 INPUT "What output port do you wish to use",P
1830 PRINT #P
1840 PRINT #P,TAB(30);"LOAN PAYMENT RECORD"
1850 PRINT #P
1860 PRINT #P,"Payee";
1870 PRINT #P,TAB(30);"Balance";
1880 PRINT #P,TAB(40);"Payment";
1890 PRINT #P,TAB(50);"Rate";
1900 PRINT #P,TAB(60);"Last Payment"
1910 PRINT #P
1920 FOR X=1 TO N
1930 PRINT #P,M$(X);
1940 PRINT #P,TAB(36-LEN(STR$(B(X))));B(X);
1950 PRINT #P,TAB(46-LEN(STR$(P(X))));P(X);
1960 PRINT #P,TAB(53-LEN(STR$(R(X))));R(X);"%";
1970 PRINT #P,TAB(60);D$(X)
1980 NEXT X
1990 PRINT #P,CHR$(12)
2000 REM ******** STORE THE DATA ********
2010 INPUT "What disk drive and sector (DSSS)",S
2020 IF S<1000 THEN 2010
2030 IF S>2350 THEN 2010
2040 OPEN #10,S
2050 PRINT #10,N
2060 FOR X=1 TO N
2070 PRINT #10,B(X);D$(X);M$(X);P(X);R(X);T$(X)
2080 NEXT X
2090 CLOSE #10
2100 END
```

17
LOAN PAYMENT

We'll round out this section with one more program that deals with real estate or conventional-type loans. Loan Payment collects data on a month-by-month basis to present a record of interest paid to date and the current balance. You can use it for any loan, but it is most helpful when payments are not uniform. It will tell you how much interest and principal you've paid as a borrower, and will be a collection tool if you play the role of lender.

OPERATING NOTES

The sample run illustrates a full-year record of a loan for which receipts vary in amount. The routine will also work for partial years and for loans with regular amounts remitted. As the program stands, all operator entries are numeric except the response to ANOTHER COPY?, which requires a yes-or-no answer.

In the first user response, you may enter a year (as in the sample) or a month and year. The annual interest rate should be expressed in percent. The principal value is the loan balance at the start of the year. For subsequent years, enter the balance calculated by the program on the last record. HOW MANY PERIODS? requests the number of months covered by the report you are making. You can start in the middle of a year by telling the program the name of the first month of interest.

Enter the monetary payment amount for each month as the routine asks for it, select an output port, and watch your computer give you a complete picture of the loan transactions. If you're collecting a note, add a signature block to turn the record into a receipt. You can run the first copy on your video terminal to double-check the data; then, select your hard copy output device for the second copy. My program doesn't have provisions for recording the data inputs on disk or cassette, but you can add that feature when you adapt it to your own system.

139

This is another easy one-evening keypunch task. There are only 72 lines of code, and none should be strange to you. Glance over the listing, and we'll hit the high points.

The DIMension statement in line 70 allocates 12 memory spaces to the monthly-payment variable. There's no reason that this variable can't be added to the DIMensioning task in line 150, where the remaining variables are allocated. The first real work of the routine starts in lines 170 and 180. The READ A$(1) tries to match the first three letters of the name of the month in M$ with one of the data items. (This would be a good place for an error trap. I didn't include one because you don't have that much time invested in running the program at this point, and a "no match" will generate a BASIC error.) When a match is found, the proper initial month name is in A$(1), and the DATA pointer is aiming at the next month of the year. Lines 190 through 210 fill the remaining variables A$(X) with the names of subsequent months.

The loan balance is set to the beginning principal value in line 220. The FOR...NEXT loop of lines 230 to 350 performs the remaining calculations. Line 240 establishes the current-period balance. Line 250 calculates the current-period interest, rounding off to the nearest penny. Line 260 totals the balance and interest. Current-payment information is received by lines 270 and 280, and the new remaining balance is computed in line 290. The next five lines deal with the amount of annual interest paid. If no payment is made, no interest was paid, so line 300 steers the program flow to the NEXT X statement (line 350). If a payment is made that is less than the current-interest amount, the total payment is applied to interest and line 310 directs the program flow to the summation statement of line 340. When a normal payment is made (equal to or greater than the current-period interest), normal program flow will go to line 320, where the interest is added to the yearly total. Line 330 guides the "normal" program flow to the NEXT X statement.

Line 380 begins the output routine with a selection of the display-device control port. Line 390 calls the subroutine at line 2000 to print the heading on the output statement. If you want to personalize the routine, you can insert a letterhead segment in the heading subroutine without disturbing the main program-print segment. The remainder of the display routine is pretty standard, so we won't dwell on it.

My DATA generator didn't get into an echo mode in lines 990 and 1000. By repeating the months of the year, we've made provision for a fiscal-year form. You can have a 12-month year beginning in any month (including December) without inviting a BASIC error message.

Well, go to it! You can marry this program to any of the previous routines and have a really high-power financial tool.

SAMPLE INPUT - LOAN PAYMENT RECORD

READY
RUN

WHAT PERIOD (YEAR)? 1984
ENTER ANNUAL INTEREST RATE? 12
PRINCIPAL VALUE? 23550.23
HOW MANY PERIODS? 12
WHAT IS FIRST MONTH? JAN

FOR JAN WHAT IS PAYMENT? 240
FOR FEB WHAT IS PAYMENT? 200
FOR MAR WHAT IS PAYMENT? 265
FOR APR WHAT IS PAYMENT? 240
FOR MAY WHAT IS PAYMENT? 275
FOR JUN WHAT IS PAYMENT? 0
FOR JUL WHAT IS PAYMENT? 350
FOR AUG WHAT IS PAYMENT? 240
FOR SEP WHAT IS PAYMENT? 200
FOR OCT WHAT IS PAYMENT? 310
FOR NOV WHAT IS PAYMENT? 265
FOR DEC WHAT IS PAYMENT? 247

WHAT OUTPUT PORT? 2
ANOTHER COPY? NO

READY
#

SAMPLE OUTPUT

LOAN PAYMENT RECORD
1984

MONTH	BALANCE	INTEREST	TOTAL	(PAYMENT)
JAN	23550.23	235.50	23785.73	240.00
FEB	23545.73	235.46	23781.19	200.00
MAR	23581.19	235.81	23817.01	265.00
APR	23552.01	235.52	23787.54	240.00
MAY	23547.54	235.48	23783.02	275.00
JUN	23508.02	235.08	23743.10	0.00
JUL	23743.10	237.43	23980.54	350.00
AUG	23630.54	236.31	23866.85	240.00
SEP	23626.85	236.27	23863.12	200.00
OCT	23663.12	236.63	23899.76	310.00
NOV	23589.76	235.90	23825.66	265.00
DEC	23560.66	235.61	23796.27	247.00

TOTAL INTEREST FOR 1984 IS $2524.22

BALANCE AT 1984 IS $23549.27

```
0010 REM *********************************
0020 REM *       LOAN PAYMENT RECORD      *
0030 REM *********************************
0040 REM ********* VERSION 10 **********
0050 LINE= 0
0060 DIGITS= 2
0070 DIM P(12)
0100 INPUT "WHAT PERIOD (YEAR)",Y$
0110 INPUT "ENTER ANNUAL INTEREST RATE",I
0120  I=I/1200
0130 INPUT "PRINCIPAL VALUE",V
0140 INPUT "HOW MANY PERIODS",R
0150 DIM B(R),I(R),T(R),A$(R)
0160 INPUT "WHAT IS FIRST MONTH",M$
0170 READ A$(1)
0180 IF LEFT$(A$(1),3)<>M$ THEN 170
0190 FOR X=2 TO R
0200 READ A$(X)
0210 NEXT X
0220  B=V
0230 FOR X=1 TO R
0240  B(X)=B
0250  I(X)=B(X)*I+.005
0260  T(X)=B(X)+I(X)
0270 PRINT "FOR ";A$(X);" WHAT IS PAYMENT";
0280 INPUT P(X)
0290  B=T(X)-P(X)
0300 IF P(X)=0 THEN 350
0310 IF P(X)<I(X) THEN 340
0320  T=T+I(X)
0330 GOTO 350
0340  T=T+P(X)
0350 NEXT X
0380 INPUT "WHAT OUTPUT PORT",P
0390 GOSUB 2000
0400 FOR X=1 TO R
0410 PRINT #P,A$(X);
0420 PRINT #P,TAB(22-LEN(STR$(B(X))));B(X);
0430 PRINT #P,TAB(37-LEN(STR$(I(X))));I(X);
0440 PRINT #P,TAB(52-LEN(STR$(T(X))));T(X);
0450 PRINT #P,TAB(65-LEN(STR$(P(X))));P(X)
0460 PRINT #P
0470 NEXT X
0480 PRINT #P
0490 PRINT #P,"TOTAL INTEREST FOR ";Y$;" IS $";T
0500 PRINT #P
0510 PRINT #P,"BALANCE AT ";Y$;" IS $";B
0520 PRINT #P,CHR$(12)
0530 INPUT "Another Copy",Z$
0540 IF LEFT$(Z$,1)="Y" THEN 380
0550 END
0990 DATA JAN,FEB,MAR,APR,MAY,JUN,JUL,AUG,SEP,OCT,NOV,DEC
1000 DATA JAN,FEB,MAR,APR,MAY,JUN,JUL,AUG,SEP,OCT,NOV,DEC
2000 REM *** PAGE HEADER SUBROUTINE *****
```

```
2010 PRINT #P
2020 PRINT #P
2030 PRINT #P,TAB(26);"LOAN PAYMENT RECORD"
2040 PRINT #P,TAB((72-LEN(Y$))/2);Y$
2050 PRINT #P
2060 PRINT #P
2070 PRINT #P,"MONTH";
2080 PRINT #P,TAB(15);
2090 PRINT #P,"BALANCE";
2100 PRINT #P,TAB(30);
2110 PRINT #P,"INTEREST";
2120 PRINT #P,TAB(45);
2130 PRINT #P,"TOTAL";
2140 PRINT #P,TAB(57);
2150 PRINT #P,"(PAYMENT)"
2160 PRINT #P
2170 RETURN
```

III

MAJOR ASSET MANAGEMENT

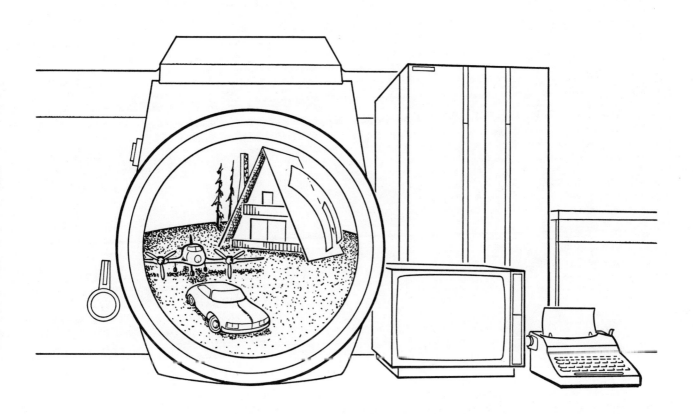

18
AUTO EXPENSE RECORDS

An important facet of financial management is the purchase and care of the major items we need (or think we need) to enjoy life. How we spend our money is as important as how we invest and earn it. It's all right to spend large sums on entertainment, fine clothes, or a frivolous ego trip as long as you realize what you're doing. Financial management helps us get the most benefit from the money we have.

The programs in this section address the analyses you may use to purchase a noninvestment asset, and methods of letting your computer help take care of the goods you acquire. You may wish to drive a large prestigious automobile, or you may be satisfied with a "transportation" vehicle. Wouldn't it be nice to know how much your car is costing? Auto Expense Records provide the cost-collection methods to let you know what your personal car is draining from your budget. The program also serves a reminder function for some needed periodic expense categories. Don't let the name deceive you, either. This routine can keep track of airplane, boat, or camper costs. With a little effort, you can alter the program to collect costs for anything important to your individual lifestyle.

Since this is a recording program, no fancy arithmetic is used. The basic four functions (addition, subtraction, multiplication, and division) will get us through the program in style. The program uses disk memory for much of its storage and data manipulation. You can implement the features with a cassette tape, but I fear the program will run too slowly to serve satisfactorily.

The structure of Auto Expense Records is a little reminiscent of our Electronic Checkbook bookkeeping entries. We'll establish eight categories of cost data (initial cost, gas, repairs, tags and licenses, lubrication, insurance, accessories, and miscellaneous). We'll also record the date and mileage figures for each entry. Program outputs include a gas-mileage calculation (most recent tankful and cumulative values), a cost-per-mile computation, a status-reminder review, and a final accounting.

This is another menu-driven program. As operator, you may elect one of seven choices. The sample run illustrates each of the options. Note that you can initialize the program by typing a zero in response to the menu display. We omitted the zero choice in the menu to prevent the casual operator from accidently destroying your date base records.

When you elect the data-entry sequence, you'll be asked to furnish the classification of the expense from another menu. You need type only the initial letter of the category name--that's all the computer stores. Although the sample doesn't show it, you may use miles and tenths, and gallons and tenths in your entries. Even though you are entering some other cost category, the program will ask for gallons of fuel. (For example, if you are entering insurance cost, the routine will ask for gallons of fuel.) Just enter a zero to satisfy the routine--or add a feature to remove the question when you keypunch the program for your system. When you elect another data-entry sequence without ending the program, the date information will be taken from your first entry of the operating session. (If you wish to enter several gasoline fillups at one session, you'll have to alternate data-entry runs with end-of-program selections to change the date for each of the several entries.) You'll also note that we use a different technique for date entry in this program. Enter one or two digits for the day, type a comma, then enter one or two digits for the month, type another comma, and key a two-digit year designator. This method of date entry will allow some flexibility in calculations of time--which we don't use in this program.

The gas-mileage computation will usually provide two output figures: the mileage on the last tankful and the cumulative miles per gallon since the vehicle was acquired. If your most recent entry has not included a gasoline fill up (such as a "repairs" cost), the program will provide only the cumulative efficiency tally.

The program is written to count real costs only. It will not calculate depreciation of the automobile until the final accounting. There are some depreciation calculations later in the book, and you may wish to add that feature to this program. Cost-per-mile numbers, therefore, are computed without regard to depreciation. They'll give you a good picture of out-of-pocket expenses as you drive.

The status-review option will tell you the mileage reading and calendar date at your last lubrication service. The same information will be given for your insurance payment and license renewal. You can add to this list easily.

The final accounting routine asks what amount you realized from the sale of the car. With this information, your computer can calculate real depreciation--the actual amount of money used up by your ownership. With this calculation, the total cost per mile of vehicle ownership is available. The numbers in our example are fictitious, so don't rely on these as standards.

Note that with my (primitive) disk-operating system (DOS), the operator must enter drive and sector information periodically. This assignment can be included in the program or left out, if your DOS is more automatic. Set up your version to suit your habits and needs.

PROGRAMMING NOTES

<u>Auto</u> <u>Expense</u> <u>Records</u> is a medium-length program, so you may wish to budget two evenings to getting it up and running. There's nothing in this routine that you haven't previously seen (and probably entered in your computer's memory), so we'll keep the program discussion rather brief.

Line 120 requests the current date information and stuffs it into three variables. In line 130, we format the date for storage. Since the year will always have two digits, we'll put it first. My version of BASIC drops leading zeroes in numerics and could confuse a later use of the date if we entered the day first (and the day were identified by a single digit). The D1 extra variable is used as a storage shelf for the date. We'll need to resurrect this information later on disk-read actions. (Since the date is stored on disk as D$, a disk read will overwrite the current date identifier. We'll overwrite the overwrite in line 1850.)

After the date entry, we get a first look at the menu of choices. The menu treatment is pretty standard. There's no error trap because the IF...THEN statements of lines 240 through 290 take care of all possible numbers equal to or greater than one. Anything else is read as an initialization command, and program operation flows right into the routine at line 300. Each record on the disk contains the following:

Variable	Contents
C	Cost in dollars and cents
C$	One-letter code
D$	Six-digit date
G	Number of gallons
M	Mileage reading

The initialization routine collects the new-car (or newly purchased used-car) mileage, date of purchase, and vehicle cost. After recording the initial cost data, the routine establishes a baseline for each of the other categories with a zero cost (except the new-car mileage and purchase date). At the end of the routine, program flow is steered back to the menu at line 140. If you want to re-enter the date for each menu exercise, change the GOTO 140 statements to GOTO 110.

149

Lines 600 through 750 hold the data-entry routine. This is the area to modify if you want to change the cost categories. Line 690 throws away all but the initial let-let of the cost category to conserve disk real estate. When you add extra categories, make sure the new categories have unique initials--no duplicates. To suppress the request for gallons of fuel information on a category other than gas, add something like:

```
0705 IF LEFT$ (C$,1)<>"G" THEN G=0: GOTO 720
```

Of course, if you occasionally purchase fuel when your car is repaired, you'll want to leave the sequence alone.

The gas-mileage calculations of lines 800 through 990 work on the assumption that you always fill the tank when you purchase fuel. If so, you are replacing the gallons that were burned to travel the mileage since the last fill up. If you usually add fuel in some different ratio, you'll need to alter the efficiency calculations to fit your method.

The first task of our calculation routine is to set flag F and variable G1 to a value of zero. Lines 840 and 850 sort through the entire disk data base to sift out only the expense categories with a G key. Variable M1 is used to hold the starting mileage. When the first mileage reading is loaded into M1, flag F is set to steer later data readings around the M1 loading statement. That initial mileage figure is the starting point, so we won't total the gallons that might be associated with it (hence, the GOTO 840 in line 890). Further G-class entries are directed to line 900, where the tankful purchases (variable G) are added to the total fuel purchased (variable G1). Line 920 shuffles the latest mileage into variable M3, after the previous reading in M3 was put into the "next-to-last" mileage variable M2 by line 910. When the disk-reading effort is finished, line 950 checks to see if the last reading was a fuel replenishment. If so, line 960 presents the calculation of miles per gallon for the most recent tankful. Cumulative fuel efficiency is calculated and displayed by line 980.

The routine that computes cost per mile (lines 1000 to 1170) looks a lot like the gas-mileage calculator. The major change is in the sorting of disk data. To arrive at the cost per mile, we sum all of the operating costs (excluding the purchase price) in C1. The initial mileage is stuffed into M1 by line 1050 through 1080. When we've read all of the data on disk, the display and compute functions are handled by lines 1130, 1140, and 1150.

For the status-reminder review of lines 1200 through 1440, we set up three matrix variables for mileage and three more for the date information. The remainder of the work is done by the disk system. We read the category code and overwrite the appropriate variable. When the disk reading is finished, the latest information is waiting to be displayed. The printing sequence of lines 1310 through 1430 puts the news on the control terminal display.

150

The final accounting steps mimic the cost-per-mile calculation. The additional information requested in line
1520 is used in line 1580 to calculate actual depreciation.
The cost calculation of line 1670 now includes total costs,
not just operating expenses.

The two-line subroutine at line 1700 is our standard
disk-write command. It is called by the initialization and
data-entry routines to store the expense information. The
subroutine at line 1800 is used by the data-entry routine
to move the disk pointer to the end-of-data mark.

You'll have another powerful tool in your computer kit
when you put Auto Expense Records on-line!

SAMPLE RUN

READY
RUN
                    AUTO EXPENSE RECORDS

TODAY'S DATE (DD,MM,YY)? 1.1.82

ENTER A: TO GET:

    '1'   DATA ENTRY
    '2'   GAS MILEAGE
    '3'   COST PER MILE
    '4'   STATUS REVIEW
    '5'   FINAL ACCOUNTING
    '6'   END OF PROGRAM
? 0

PLEASE MAKE AN ENTRY IN EACH FIELD.

COST OF VEHICLE? 8576.19
MILEAGE? 12
WHAT IS THE STARTING DRIVE AND SECTOR (DSSS)? 2001

ENTER A: TO GET:

    '1'   DATA ENTRY
    '2'   GAS MILEAGE
    '3'   COST PER MILE
    '4'   STATUS REVIEW
    '5'   FINAL ACCOUNTING
    '6'   END OF PROGRAM
? 1

STARTING DISK DRIVE AND SECTOR? 2001
ENTER THE CLASSIFICATION OF THE EXPENSE FROM THIS LIST:
    'G'AS   'L'UBRICATION/OIL
    'R'EPAIRS   'I'NSURANCE
    'T'AGS & LICENSES   'A'CCESSORIES
    'M'ISCELLANEOUS

CLASSIFICATION? GAS
MILEAGE? 15
GALLONS OF FUEL? 6
COST $? 12.25

ENTER A: TO GET:

    '1'   DATA ENTRY
    '2'   GAS MILEAGE
    '3'   COST PER MILE
    '4'   STATUS REVIEW
    '5'   FINAL ACCOUNTING
    '6'   END OF PROGRAM

? <u>1</u>
STARTING DISK DRIVE AND SECTOR? <u>2001</u>
ENTER THE CLASSIFICATION OF THE EXPENSE FROM THIS LIST:
   'G'AS   'L'UBRICATION
   'R'EPAIRS   'I'NSURANCE
   'T'AGS & LICENSES   'A'CCESSORIES
   'M'ISCELLANEOUS

CLASSIFICATION? <u>INSURANCE</u>
MILEAGE? <u>18</u>
GALLONS OF FUEL? <u>0</u>
COST $? <u>325.97</u>

ENTER A: TO GET:

   '1'   DATA ENTRY
   '2'   GAS MILEAGE
   '3'   COST PER MILE
   '4'   STATUS REVIEW
   '5'   FINAL ACCOUNTING
   '6'   END OF PROGRAM
? <u>1</u>
STARTING DISK DRIVE AND SECTOR? <u>2001</u>
ENTER THE CLASSIFICATION OF THE EXPENSE FROM THIS LIST:
   'G'AS   'L'UBRICATION
   'R'EPAIRS   'I'NSURANCE
   'T'AGS & LICENSES   'A'CCESSORIES
   'M'ISCELLANEOUS

CLASSIFICATION? <u>ACCESSORIES</u>
MILEAGE? <u>23</u>
GALLONS OF FUEL? <u>0</u>
COST $? <u>49.92</u>

ENTER A: TO GET:

   '1'   DATA ENTRY
   '2'   GAS MILEAGE
   '3'   COST PER MILE
   '4'   STATUS REVIEW
   '5'   FINAL ACCOUNTING
   '6'   END OF PROGRAM
? <u>1</u>
STARTING DISK DRIVE AND SECTOR? <u>2001</u>
ENTER THE CLASSIFICATION OF THE EXPENSE FROM THIS LIST:
   'G'AS   'L'UBRICATION
   'R'EPAIRS   'I'NSURANCE
   'T'AGS & LICENSES   'A'CCESSORIES
   'M'ISCELLANEOUS

CLASSIFICATION? <u>TAGS</u>
MILEAGE? <u>32</u>
GALLONS OF FUEL? <u>0</u>
COST $? <u>256.25</u>

```
ENTER A:              TO GET:

  '1'                 DATA ENTRY
  '2'                 GAS MILEAGE
  '3'                 COST PER MILE
  '4'                 STATUS REVIEW
  '5'                 FINAL ACCOUNTING
  '6'                 END OF PROGRAM
? 6


READY
#

READY
# RUN
                  AUTO EXPENSE RECORDS

TODAY'S DATE (DD,MM,YY)? 12.10.82

ENTER A:              TO GET:

  '1'                 DATA ENTRY
  '2'                 GAS MILEAGE
  '3'                 COST PER MILE
  '4'                 STATUS REVIEW
  '5'                 FINAL ACCOUNTING
  '6'                 END OF PROGRAM
? 2
STARTING DRIVE AND SECTOR? 2001


TOTAL FUEL MILEAGE TO DATE IS 40.21 M.P.G.

ENTER A:              TO GET:

  '1'                 DATA ENTRY
  '2'                 GAS MILEAGE
  '3'                 COST PER MILE
  '4'                 STATUS REVIEW
  '5'                 FINAL ACCOUNTING
  '6'                 END OF PROGRAM
? 3
STARTING DRIVE AND SECTOR? 2001


COST PER MILE FOR OPERATION TO DATE IS $0.14
WITHOUT REGARD TO DEPRECIATION.

ENTER A:              TO GET:

  '1'                 DATA ENTRY
  '2'                 GAS MILEAGE
  '3'                 COST PER MILE
  '4'                 STATUS REVIEW
  '5'                 FINAL ACCOUNTING
  '6'                 END OF PROGRAM
```

154

```
? 4
STARTING DRIVE AND SECTOR? 2001

                         STATUS

MOST RECENT                       MILEAGE              DATE

LUBRICATION                       14200.0          10/10/82
INSURANCE                            18.0          01/01/82
TAGS/LICENSES                        32.0          01/01/82

ENTER A:          TO GET:

   '1'            DATA ENTRY
   '2'            GAS MILEAGE
   '3'            COST PER MILE
   '4'            STATUS REVIEW
   '5'            FINAL ACCOUNTING
   '6'            END OF PROGRAM
? 5
WHAT WAS REALIZED FROM SALE OF AUTO? 4238.19
STARTING DRIVE AND SECTOR? 2001

TOTAL COST PER MILE TO OWN THE VEHICLE HAS BEEN $0.45

ENTER A:          TO GET:

   '1'            DATA ENTRY
   '2'            GAS MILEAGE
   '3'            COST PER MILE
   '4'            STATUS REVIEW
   '5'            FINAL ACCOUNTING
   '6'            END OF PROGRAM
? 6

READY
#
```

```
0010 REM ******************************
0020 REM *      AUTO EXPENSE RECORDS       *
0030 REM ******************************
0040 REM ********* VERSION 10 **********
0080 LINE= 0
0090 DIGITS= 2
0100 PRINT TAB(12);"AUTO EXPENSE RECORDS"
0110 PRINT
0120 INPUT "Today's date (DD,MM,YY)",D,M,Y
0130   D1=10000*Y+100*M+D:D$=STR$(D1)
0140 PRINT
0150 PRINT "Enter a:          To Get:"
0160 PRINT
0170 PRINT "   '1'          Data Entry"
0180 PRINT "   '2'          Gas Mileage"
0190 PRINT "   '3'          Cost Per Mile"
0200 PRINT "   '4'          Status Review"
0210 PRINT "   '5'          Final Accounting"
0220 PRINT "   '6'          End of Program"
0230 INPUT Z
0240 IF Z>5 THEN END
0250 IF INT(Z)=1 THEN 600
0260 IF INT(Z)=2 THEN 800
0270 IF INT(Z)=3 THEN 1000
0280 IF INT(Z)=4 THEN 1200
0290 IF Z>4 THEN 1500
0300 REM ********* INITIALIZATION *********
0310 PRINT
0320 PRINT "Please make an entry in each field."
0330 PRINT
0340   C$="C"
0350 INPUT "Cost of vehicle",C
0360 INPUT "Mileage",M
0370   G=0
0380 INPUT "What is the starting drive and sector (DSSS)",S
0390 OPEN #10,S
0400 GOSUB 1700
0410   C$="G"
0420   C=0
0430 GOSUB 1700
0440   C$="L"
0450 GOSUB 1700
0460   C$="R"
0470 GOSUB 1700
0480   C$="I"
0490 GOSUB 1700
0500   C$="T"
0510 GOSUB 1700
0520   C$="M"
0530 GOSUB 1700
0540 CLOSE #10
0550 GOTO 140
0600 REM ********** ENTER DATA **********
0610 GOSUB 1800
```

```
0620 PRINT "Enter the classification of the expense from this list:"
0630 PRINT "    'G'AS                    'L'UBRICATION/OIL"
0640 PRINT "    'R'EPAIRS                'I'NSURANCE"
0650 PRINT "    'T'AGS & LICENSES        'A'CCESSORIES"
0660 PRINT "    'M'ISCELLANEOUS"
0670 PRINT
0680 INPUT "Classification", C$
0690  C$=LEFT$(C$,1)
0700 INPUT "Mileage",M
0710 INPUT "Gallons of Fuel",G
0720 INPUT "Cost  $",C
0730 GOSUB 1700
0740 CLOSE #10
0750 GOTO 140
0800 REM ********* GAS   MILEAGE **********
0810  F=0:G1=0
0820 INPUT "Starting Drive and Sector",S
0830 OPEN #10,S
0840 READ #10,C,C$,D$,G,M\940
0850 IF C$<>"G" THEN 840
0860 IF F=1 THEN 900
0870  M1=M
0880  F=1
0890 GOTO 840
0900  G1=G1+G
0910  M2=M3
0920  M3=M
0930 GOTO 840
0940 CLOSE #10
0950 IF G=0 THEN 970
0960 PRINT "Fuel mileage on last tankful was ";(M-M2)/G;"m.p.g."
0970 PRINT
0980 PRINT "Total fuel mileage to date is ";(M-M1)/G1;"m.p.g."
0990 GOTO 140
1000 REM *********** COST/MILE ************
1010  F=0:C1=0
1020 INPUT "Starting Drive and Sector",S
1030 OPEN #10,S
1040 READ #10,C,C$,D$,G,M\1110
1050 IF F=1 THEN 1090
1060  M1=M
1070  F=1
1080 GOTO 1040
1090  C1=C1+C
1100 GOTO 1040
1110 CLOSE #10
1120 PRINT
1130 PRINT "Cost per mile for operation to date is $";
1140 PRINT C1/(M-M1)
1150 PRINT "Without regard to depreciation."
1160 PRINT
1170 GOTO 140
1200 REM ********* STATUS   REVIEW *********
1210  M(1)=0:M(2)=0:M(3)=0
```

```
1220 INPUT "Starting Drive and Sector",S
1230 OPEN #10,S
1240 READ #10,C,C$,D$,G,M\1290
1250 IF C$="L" M(1)=M:D$(1)=D$
1260 IF C$="I" M(2)=M:D$(2)=D$
1270 IF C$="T" M(3)=M:D$(3)=D$
1280 GOTO 1240
1290 CLOSE #10
1300 PRINT
1310 DIGITS= 1
1320 PRINT TAB(30);"STATUS"
1330 PRINT
1340 PRINT
1350 PRINT "Most Recent";TAB(35);"Mileage";TAB(55);"Date"
1360 PRINT
1370 FOR X=1 TO 3
1380   D$(X)=MID$(D$(X),5,2)+"/"+MID$(D$(X),3,2)+"/"+LEFT$(D$(X),2)
1390 NEXT X
1400 PRINT "Lubrication";TAB(42-LEN(STR$(M(1))));M(1);TAB(54);D$(1)
1410 PRINT "Insurance";TAB(42-LEN(STR$(M(2))));M(2);TAB(54);D$(2)
1420 PRINT "Tags/Licenses";TAB(42-LEN(STR$(M(3))));M(3);TAB(54);D$(3)
1430 PRINT
1440 GOTO 140
1500 REM ******** FINAL ACCOUNTING ********
1510   F=0:C1=0
1520 INPUT "What was realized from sale of auto",Z
1530 INPUT "Starting Drive and Sector",S
1540 OPEN #10,S
1550 READ #10,C,C$,D$,G,M\1630
1560 IF F=1 THEN 1610
1570   M1=M
1580   C1=C-Z
1590   F=1
1600 GOTO 1550
1610   C1=C1+C
1620 GOTO 1550
1630 CLOSE #10
1640 PRINT
1650 PRINT "Total cost per mile to own the vehicle ";
1660 PRINT "has been $";
1670 PRINT C1/(M-M1)
1680 PRINT
1690 GOTO 140
1700 REM ******* PRINT DATA TO DISK *******
1710 PRINT #10,C;C$;D$;G;M
1720 RETURN
1800 REM ****** READ THE END OF DATA ******
1810 INPUT "Starting Disk Drive and Sector",S
1820 OPEN #10,S
1830 READ #10,C,C$,D$,G,M\1850
1840 GOTO 1830
1850   D$=STR$(D1)
1860 RETURN
```

19
LEASE/BUY

Is it better to purchase or lease an automobile, airplane, or typewriter? That depends on a lot of factors that you control. How much you will use the item will make a difference, as will the type of purchase or lease contract you will sign. Your personal preferences, too, are critical to the decision. If you like the feel of owning a car, leasing may not be your cup of tea regardless of the economics. Your computer can analyze the economics of the deal. You'll need to do a little homework to compile the input information, but your computer will give you a statement of the dollars and cents that makes sense and saves dollars!

Lease/Buy is a comparison program. It will balance various types of expenses for the lease option with similar data for ownership and compute the more advantageous path for you. No complex mathematics are involved, and no program manipulations boggle the imagination. You can have this one up and running in one or two evenings and be able to carry computer-generated analysis forms to the sales or lease showroom. (Who knows? The computer report may help you drive a better bargain at the contract negotiations!)

Economics is not the only decision factor. Whenever you let your personal preference govern a decision, however, it's nice to know what your ego factors are costing. A decision is stupid only when you ignore all the options. This program will allow you to be informed.

BACKGROUND

The routine collects information on the lease expenses, then on the purchase option. Those costs that normally occur monthly are input as monthly amounts; irregular expenses are gathered on an annual basis. At output time, all expenses are put on a monthly schedule. The monthly projections are totalled, and the less expensive option is indicated. The program makes one important assumption--that the lease is a "closed-end" contract. (In a closed

159

lease, there is no residual payment at lease end. An "open-ended" contract, on the other hand, may require an additional payment or provide a rebate, depending on the market value of the leased asset.) If you are comparing an open-ended lease with the purchase option, you'll have to estimate the lease-end value of your car and include that figure in the comparison.

OPERATING NOTES

The sample run illustrates the operator inputs and computer output for a mythical analysis. In the example, identical numbers have been used for fuel expense, insurance premiums, license costs, and miscellaneous expenses. It is not necessary that these be identical in your analysis. You may wish to purchase a larger automobile than you'd lease, or vice versa. You might lease a more-fuel-efficient vehicle than you'd own. Estimate the costs based on your projected use. Separate entries are provided for taxes and license expenses. In some areas, the lease payment is subject to a sales tax, while license taxes are included in the tag fees. The lease may have an interest expense--and it may or may not be a part of the monthly payment. Insurance companies may charge a higher premium for leased vehicles--or you may elect a greater coverage for your leased car. Use the input-prompt list as a check list when you are gathering data.

Note that you would not have lease payments with the purchase choice, nor would you have depreciation with the leased vehicle. Depreciation takes the place of monthly payments on the car you buy. What the car costs you is part of the comparison, not the terms of your purchase contract. Depreciation is the annual loss in value (what you paid less what you could sell for) of the owned automobile. When you purchase with "easy monthly payments," you'll have an interest-expense entry for the purchase option.

PROGRAMMING NOTES

Just about half of the program listing is devoted to the output statement. Lease/Buy won't require much debugging, just keypunching. The function DEFinitions in lines 70 and 80 provide our usual output format. We'll save quite a bit of keypunching by using these in the output TAB functions.

Data input for the lease option takes up lines 200 through 470. The information items are stored in matrix variable L(X), but the annual amounts are collected in variable L1. The conversion to a monthly figure is made as each expense is input. For example, the insurance premiums are input to L1 in line 300. The conversion to a monthly amount is performed in line 310, where the monthly figure is stored in L(3).

The total of monthly lease expenses is computed by the FOR...NEXT loop of lines 450, 460, and 470. Purchase option costs are treated in much the same way in lines 500 through 750. P1 and P(X) are the variables used for purchase expenses.

The output routine takes up the remainder of the program, from lines 1000 to 1570. Since we used variable P for purchase expense totals, we'll use Q for the output-port designator. Throughout the printing segment, the FNA function is used for lease option TABs and the FNB for purchase options. Remember that these tabulator functions line up the decimal points in the output numerical columns to provide a professional accounting-style report.

Fancy footwork in the program is limited to the routine in lines 1500 through 1550. In line 1500, the difference between leasing and purchasing is calculated. If the difference is a minus number, indicating that leasing is more expensive, line 1510 sends the program flow to line 1540. In line 1540, the number is converted to a positive one. Line 1550 then tells the operator of the economic advantage in purchasing. Should leasing be the lesser cost, line 1520 prints the news.

When you keypunch this one, you may wish to add a letterhead and signature block so you can sell Lease/Buy analyses. You may also wish to change the number and type of categories investigated. Remember that if you add categories, you'll have to add a variable DIMensioning in the header. (My version of BASIC defaults to--or automatically assumes--a matrix size of 10 items. If more variables are needed, a DIMension statement is required.)

SAMPLE INPUT - LEASE OR PURCHASE

READY
RUN

LEASE OPTION

ENTER THE ESTIMATED MONTHLY AMOUNTS FOR:

LEASE PAYMENTS? 358.12
FUEL AND OIL EXPENSE? 100

ENTER THE ESTIMATED ANNUAL AMOUNTS FOR:

INSURANCE PREMIUMS? 620
TAXES EXPENSES? 180
LICENSE EXPENSE? 245
REPAIRS AND MAINTENANCE EXPENSE? 230
TIRES AND SUPPLIES? 200
INTEREST EXPENSE? 0
OTHER MISCELLANEOUS EXPENSES? 300

PURCHASE OPTION

ENTER THE ESTIMATED MONTHLY FUEL AND OIL EXPENSE? 100

ENTER THE ESTIMATED ANNUAL AMOUNTS FOR:

DEPRECIATION? 2000
INSURANCE PREMIUMS? 620
TAXES EXPENSE? 0
LICENSE EXPENSE? 245
REPAIRS AND MAINTENANCE EXPENSE? 250
TIRES AND SUPPLIES? 125
INTEREST EXPENSE? 850
OTHER MISCELLANEOUS EXPENSES? 300
WHAT OUTPUT PORT DO YOU WANT TO USE? 3

READY
#

SAMPLE OUTPUT

LEASE OR PURCHASE

MONTHLY ANALYSIS

ITEM	LEASE	PURCHASE
LEASE PAYMENTS	358.12	
DEPRECIATION		166.66
FUEL AND OIL	100.00	100.00
INSURANCE	51.66	51.66
TAXES EXPENSE	15.00	0.00
LICENSE EXPENSE	20.41	20.41
REPAIRS AND MAINTENANCE	19.16	20.83
TIRES AND SUPPLIES	16.66	10.41
INTEREST EXPENSE	0.00	70.83
MISCELLANEOUS EXPENSE	25.00	25.00
	-------	-------
TOTALS	606.03	465.83
	=======	=======

THE MONTHLY ADVANTAGE TO PURCHASE IS $140.20

```
0010 REM ***********************************
0020 REM *          LEASE OR BUY?         *
0030 REM ***********************************
0040 REM ********** VERSION 10 **********
0050 DIGITS= 2
0060 LINE= 0
0070 DEF FNA(X)=(45-LEN(STR$(X)))
0080 DEF FNB(X)=(75-LEN(STR$(X)))
0200 PRINT TAB(20);"LEASE OPTION"
0210 PRINT
0220 PRINT
0230 PRINT "Enter the estimated MONTHLY amounts for:"
0240 PRINT
0250 INPUT "Lease payments",L(1)
0260 INPUT "Fuel and oil expense",L(2)
0270 PRINT
0280 PRINT "Enter the estimated ANNUAL amounts for:"
0290 PRINT
0300 INPUT "Insurance premiums",L1
0310   L(3)=L1/12
0320 INPUT "Taxes expenses",L1
0330   L(4)=L1/12
0340 INPUT "License expense",L1
0350   L(5)=L1/12
0360 INPUT "Repairs and maintenance expense",L1
0370   L(6)=L1/12
0380 INPUT "Tires and supplies",L1
0390   L(7)=L1/12
0400 INPUT "Interest expense",L1
0410   L(8)=L1/12
0420 INPUT "Other miscellaneous expenses",L1
0430   L(9)=L1/12
0440   L=0
0450 FOR X=1 TO 9
0460   L=L+L(X)
0470 NEXT X
0500 PRINT TAB(20);"PURCHASE OPTION"
0510 PRINT
0520 PRINT
0530 INPUT "Enter the estimated MONTHLY fuel and oil expense",P(2)
0540 PRINT
0550 PRINT "Enter the estimated ANNUAL amounts for:"
0560 INPUT "Depreciation",P1
0570   P(1)=P1/12
0580 INPUT "Insurance premiums",P1
0590   P(3)=P1/12
0600 INPUT "Taxes expense",P1
0610   P(4)=P1/12
0620 INPUT "License expense",P1
0630   P(5)=P1/12
0640 INPUT "Repairs and maintenance expense",P1
0650   P(6)=P1/12
0660 INPUT "Tires and supplies",P1
0670   P(7)=P1/12
0680 INPUT "Interest expense",P1
```

```
0690    P(8)=P1/12
0700 INPUT "Other miscellaneous expenses",P1
0710    P(9)=P1/12
0720    P=0
0730 FOR X=1 TO 9
0740    P=P+P(X)
0750 NEXT X
1000 INPUT "What output port do you want to use",Q
1010 PRINT #Q
1020 PRINT #Q
1030 PRINT #Q
1040 PRINT #Q,TAB(31);"LEASE OR PURCHASE"
1050 PRINT #Q
1060 PRINT #Q
1070 PRINT #Q,TAB(32);"Monthly Analysis"
1080 PRINT #Q
1090 PRINT #Q,TAB(3);"Item";
1100 PRINT #Q,TAB(40);"LEASE";
1110 PRINT #Q,TAB(67);"PURCHASE"
1120 PRINT #Q
1130 PRINT #Q,"Lease Payments";
1140 PRINT #Q,TAB(FNA(L(1)));L(1)
1150 PRINT #Q,"Depreciation";
1160 PRINT #Q,TAB(FNB(P(1)));P(1)
1170 PRINT #Q,"Fuel and Oil";
1180 PRINT #Q,TAB(FNA(L(2)));L(2);
1190 PRINT #Q,TAB(FNB(P(2)));P(2)
1200 PRINT #Q,"Insurance";
1210 PRINT #Q,TAB(FNA(L(3)));L(3);
1220 PRINT #Q,TAB(FNB(P(3)));P(3)
1230 PRINT #Q,"Taxes expense";
1240 PRINT #Q,TAB(FNA(L(4)));L(4);
1250 PRINT #Q,TAB(FNB(P(4)));P(4)
1260 PRINT #Q,"License expense";
1270 PRINT #Q,TAB(FNA(L(5)));L(5);
1280 PRINT #Q,TAB(FNB(P(5)));P(5)
1290 PRINT #Q,"Repairs and maintenance";
1300 PRINT #Q,TAB(FNA(L(6)));L(6);
1310 PRINT #Q,TAB(FNB(P(6)));P(6)
1320 PRINT #Q,"Tires and supplies";
1330 PRINT #Q,TAB(FNA(L(7)));L(7);
1340 PRINT #Q,TAB(FNB(P(7)));P(7)
1350 PRINT #Q,"Interest expense";
1360 PRINT #Q,TAB(FNA(L(8)));L(8);
1370 PRINT #Q,TAB(FNB(P(8)));P(8)
1380 PRINT #Q,"Miscellaneous expense";
1390 PRINT #Q,TAB(FNA(L(9)));L(9);
1400 PRINT #Q,TAB(FNB(P(9)));P(9)
1410 PRINT #Q,TAB(38);"--------";
1420 PRINT #Q,TAB(68);"--------"
1430 PRINT #Q,"TOTALS";
1440 PRINT #Q,TAB(FNA(L));L;
1450 PRINT #Q,TAB(FNB(P));P
1460 PRINT #Q,TAB(38);"========";
1470 PRINT #Q,TAB(68);"========"
```

```
1480 PRINT #Q:PRINT#Q:PRINT#Q
1500   D=P-L
1510 IF D<0 THEN 1540
1520 PRINT #Q,"The monthly advantage to leasing is $";D
1530 GOTO 1560
1540   D=-D
1550 PRINT #Q,"The monthly advantage to purchase is $";D
1560 PRINT #Q,CHR$(12)
1570 END
```

20

TRADE STUDY

This is the program that can compare apples and oranges. Trade Study is one of my favorites in the book, because it gives you the power to compare noneconomic factors in any decision process. You can use it to decide which job offer to accept, what automobile to purchase, or what kind of fruit to take for lunch. Government and industry have used this type of study to make and justify decisions for years. Now we can implement this powerful tool at home.

BACKGROUND

From an operator standpoint, Trade Study is a free-form exercise. The user can enter any number of candidates for comparison, and any number of factors to compare. The factors can be weighted differently to acknowledge relative importance, and both words and numbers are used for the evaluation process. A variety of program outputs is available, and all are suitable for group presentations and family discussions or individual study.

In concept, the program allows the operator to enter the candidates and the important comparison factors. Each factor is assigned a numerical weight to establish relative importance. A verbal and numerical rating is given to each candidate for each factor. The numbers are multiplied by the weights, and totals for each candidate gathered. The totals help you decide what your preference is. (If you don't like the result, you can always run Trade Study again with different weightings or factors.)

OPERATING NOTES

Two sample runs are included. In the first, three candidates for comparison are evaluated with nine factors. I have tried to select my favorite fruit for a brown-bag lunch with this tongue-in-cheek exercise. When more than

167

seven factors are used, the output report is a tabulation of all of the factors for each candidate. The report includes both the verbal and numerical rankings and the weighted total of the numbers. The sample output illustrates the format. The second example evaluates four candidates for commuting vehicles over four factors. With the fewer factors, a different report format is available. The output is a tabulation of all candidates and all factors with either the verbal responses or numerical ratings. When the numerical rankings are selected, the weighted totals are also printed. (The weightings are not revealed, so a quick glance at the totals may lead you to believe your computer has forgotten how to add.)

Operation of Trade Study is straightforward. The input-prompt messages are self-explanatory. After you've entered the factor weights, the routine prints the list for your review. When you use a printing terminal, this repetition is unnecessary and a little irritating. On a video terminal, however, it's nice to be able to review the items that have already walked off the top of the screen. After the review, you may change the weightings of any or all factors. (The first sample illustrates this weighting adjustment.)

The remaining operator inputs are judgment exercises. You'll rate each candidate on a factor before moving on to the next factor. This comparison technique is implemented to reduce the "halo effect" (a good mark in one area biases the judge to give good marks in other areas) for the candidates.

If you have a long factor list, the program will ask what output port you wish and begin the printing task. If your factor list is short, you'll be asked whether you want a chart of the verbal ratings or the numbers. In either case, you can print another chart on the same or a different terminal when the first presentation is complete.

PROGRAMMING NOTES

The keypunching task for this program looks tougher than it is. Many of the program commands are PRINT messages to help the user operate. You may wish to abbreviate these when you set up your version. In any event, a PRINT is much easier to debug than a complex mathematical routine. This might be a two-evening project, but it really shouldn't take you any longer than that.

Let's discuss the high points of the listing. After the number of candidates and factors is input in lines 120 and 130, the variables are DIMensioned. Matrix character string variable $A\$(x,y)$ is dimensioned to one more than the number of candidates and one more than the number of factors. This extra row and column is used to hold the candidate names and the factor names. The main body of the matrix will keep the verbal ratings stored.

Generally, FOR...NEXT loops are used to garner user inputs. The candidate names are captured in lines 160 to 200; factor names are collected in lines 220 to 250; and numerical weights for factors are input in lines 320 to 350. The factor-weighting review is handled by lines 370 through 440. The weighting change takes place in lines 450 through 560. The error trap in lines 480 and 490 will catch a factor-number entry that is too high. You may wish to add a routine to snare noninteger inputs also. If the post-weighting review bothers you, delete line 560.

The FOR...NEXT loops in lines 700 through 800 take care of all evaluation entries. The X loop takes care of the factors, and the Y routine moves through the candidates.

The remaining BASIC code deals with the output. After the operator output-port selection of line 1020, line 1040 determines which output format should be used. If few enough factors are used to allow the all-in-one display, program flow continues to the next operator choice in lines 1050 and 1060.

Since the number of factors can vary, a variable tabulator must be used for the output. The calculation for this function is made in line 1110, where the printer width (80 columns in the example) is divided by the number of printed columns needed for the verbal display. A similar calculation is undertaken in line 1530 for the numeric display. (Note that in the numeric format we need an additional display column for the numeric totals.) If your printer has other than an 80-column capability, alter these two calculations to fit. FOR...NEXT loops take care of the printing chore. Note the TAB functions that use the T variable we computed to provide horizontal spacing for the various columns.

If we have enough factors to require the columnar display for each candidate, the printing routine in lines 2000 through 2180 takes over. Since we'll only have three printing columns, there's no need for a calculated TAB function. The calculation of the TAB in line 2030 provides a centering of the candidate name at the head of the report. Again, FOR...NEXT loops drive the data display. (If these programs seem heavy with FOR...NEXT statements, it's because I'm partial to the technique. Anytime you're looping through data, the FOR...NEXT can save a lot of keypunching and give you a whole lot of action for only a little code.)

If you debug each FOR...NEXT sequence as you keypunch the program, you should have no trouble getting Trade Study up and running. Whether your uses of this program are serious or fun, you'll get a lot of play from the code. And, if you happen to use your home computer for business, the extra profits you can grab by making better informed decisions will sweeten the pot.

169

SAMPLE INPUT #1 - TRADE STUDY

```
READY
# RUN
            TRADE STUDY
HOW MANY CANDIDATES? 3
HOW MANY FACTORS WILL YOU EVALUATE? 9

CANDIDATE NUMBER 1 ? APPLE
CANDIDATE NUMBER 2 ? ORANGE
CANDIDATE NUMBER 3 ? PEACH

FACTOR NUMBER 1 ? TASTE
FACTOR NUMBER 2 ? COLOR
FACTOR NUMBER 3 ? TEXTURE
FACTOR NUMBER 4 ? SKIN/RIND
FACTOR NUMBER 5 ? STORABILITY
FACTOR NUMBER 6 ? ODOR
FACTOR NUMBER 7 ? RESIDUE
FACTOR NUMBER 8 ? MESSINESS
FACTOR NUMBER 9 ? SEEDS

PLEASE ASSIGN A NUMERICAL WEIGHT TO EACH FACTOR,
WITH MORE IMPORTANT FACTORS HAVING HIGHER NUMBERS.

FACTOR                      WEIGHT

TASTE                       ? 10
COLOR                       ? 2
TEXTURE                     ? 4
SKIN/RIND                   ? 5
STORABILITY                 ? 2
ODOR                        ? 1
RESIDUE                     ? 3
MESSINESS                   ? 6
SEEDS                       ? 2
LET'S REVIEW THE FACTORS.

NUMBER    FACTOR                        WEIGHT

   1      TASTE                          10
   2      COLOR                          2
   3      TEXTURE                        4
   4      SKIN/RIND                      5
   5      STORABILITY                    2
   6      ODOR                           1
   7      RESIDUE                        3
   8      MESSINESS                      6
   9      SEEDS                          2
```

170

DO YOU WANT TO CHANGE ANY WEIGHTINGS? <u>YES</u>
WHICH FACTOR NUMBER? <u>1</u>
1   TASTE   10

WHAT IS THE CORRECT WEIGHTING FACTOR? <u>8</u>

ANOTHER? <u>NO</u>
LET'S REVIEW THE FACTORS.

NUMBER	FACTOR	WEIGHT
1	TASTE	8
2	COLOR	2
3	TEXTURE	4
4	SKIN/RIND	5
5	STORABILITY	2
6	ODOR	1
7	RESIDUE	3
8	MESSINESS	6
9	SEEDS	2

DO YOU WANT TO CHANGE ANY WEIGHTINGS? <u>NO</u>

I'LL PRINT THE NAME OF A FACTOR, THEN PRINT THE
VARIOUS CANDIDATES. ENTER YOUR ESTIMATE IN ONE OR
TWO WORDS OF HOW THE CANDIDATE RATES; THEN ENTER
A NUMBER REPRESENTING WHERE THE CANDIDATE RANKS ON
A SCALE OF 1 TO 10. AFTER WE FINISH ALL THE CANDIDATES,
I'LL PRINT ANOTHER FACTOR AND REPEAT THE LIST UNTIL
WE'RE DONE.

FACTOR: TASTE

    APPLE (IN WORDS) ? <u>GOOD</u>
(ON A SCALE OF 1 TO 10) ? <u>7</u>
    ORANGE (IN WORDS) ? <u>GOOD</u>
(ON A SCALE OF 1 TO 10) ? <u>7</u>
    PEACH (IN WORDS) ? <u>GREAT</u>
(ON A SCALE OF 1 TO 10) ? <u>9</u>

FACTOR: COLOR

    APPLE (IN WORDS) ? <u>RUDDY</u>
(ON A SCALE OF 1 TO 10) ? <u>8</u>
    ORANGE (IN WORDS) ? <u>WARM</u>
(ON A SCALE OF 1 TO 10) ? <u>7</u>
    PEACH (IN WORDS) ? <u>PEACHY</u>
(ON A SCALE OF 1 TO 10) ? <u>8</u>

FACTOR: TEXTURE

    APPLE (IN WORDS) ? <u>CRISPY</u>
(ON A SCALE OF 1 TO 10) ? <u>9</u>
    ORANGE (IN WORDS) ? <u>PULPY</u>
(ON A SCALE OF 1 TO 10) ? <u>7</u>
    PEACH (IN WORDS) ? <u>SMOOTH</u>
(ON A SCALE OF 1 TO 10) ? <u>8</u>

FACTOR: SKIN/RIND

     APPLE (IN WORDS) ? <u>EDIBLE</u>
(ON A SCALE OF 1 TO 10) ? <u>9</u>
     ORANGE (IN WORDS) ? <u>TROUBLESOME</u>
(ON A SCALE OF 1 TO 10) ? <u>3</u>
     PEACH (IN WORDS) ? <u>FUZZY</u>
(ON A SCALE OF 1 TO 10) ? <u>7</u>

FACTOR: STORABILITY

     APPLE (IN WORDS) ? <u>GREAT</u>
(ON A SCALE OF 1 TO 10) ? <u>9</u>
     ORANGE (IN WORDS) ? <u>FAIR</u>
(ON A SCALE OF 1 TO 10) ? <u>6</u>
     PEACH (IN WORDS) ? <u>POOR</u>
(ON A SCALE OF 1 TO 10) ? <u>3</u>

FACTOR: ODOR

     APPLE (IN WORDS) ? <u>O.K.</u>
(ON A SCALE OF 1 TO 10) ? <u>5</u>
     ORANGE (IN WORDS) ? <u>PERFUME</u>
(ON A SCALE OF 1 TO 10) ? <u>9</u>
     PEACH (IN WORDS) ? <u>BLAND</u>
(ON A SCALE OF 1 TO 10) ? <u>5</u>

FACTOR: RESIDUE

     APPLE (IN WORDS) ? <u>CORE</u>
(ON A SCALE OF 1 TO 10) ? <u>7</u>
     ORANGE (IN WORDS) ? <u>SKIN/SEEDS</u>
(ON A SCALE OF 1 TO 10) ? <u>6</u>
     PEACH (IN WORDS) ? <u>PIT</u>
(ON A SCALE OF 1 TO 10) ? <u>8</u>

FACTOR: MESSINESS

     APPLE (IN WORDS) ? <u>NEAT</u>
(ON A SCALE OF 1 TO 10) ? <u>9</u>
     ORANGE (IN WORDS) ? <u>SLOPPY</u>
(ON A SCALE OF 1 TO 10) ? <u>6</u>
     PEACH (IN WORDS) ? <u>MESSY</u>
(ON A SCALE OF 1 TO 10) ? <u>3</u>

FACTOR: SEEDS

     APPLE (IN WORDS) ? <u>IN CORE</u>
(ON A SCALE OF 1 TO 10) ? <u>8</u>
     ORANGE (IN WORDS) ? <u>TROUBLING</u>
(ON A SCALE OF 1 TO 10) ? <u>2</u>
     PEACH (IN WORDS) ? <u>ONE PIT</u>
(ON A SCALE OF 1 TO 10) ? <u>7</u>

WHAT OUTPUT PORT DO YOU WISH TO USE? <u>2</u>

172

ANOTHER? <u>YES</u>

WHAT OUTPUT PORT DO YOU WISH TO USE? <u>1</u>

ANOTHER? <u>NO</u>

READY
#
  SAMPLE OUTPUT #1 - TRADE STUDY

                         TRADE STUDY

                           APPLE

TASTE   GOOD   7
COLOR   RUDDY   8
TEXTURE   CRISPY   9
SKIN/RIND   EDIBLE   9
STORABILITY   GREAT   9
ODOR   O.K.   5
RESIDUE   CORE   7
MESSINESS   NEAT   9
SEEDS   IN CORE   8

                                          TOTAL 267

                          ORANGE

TASTE   GOOD   7
COLOR   WARM   7
TEXTURE   PULPY   7
SKIN/RIND   TROUBLESOME   3
STORABILITY   FAIR   6
ODOR   PERFUME   9
RESIDUE   SKIN/SEEDS   6
MESSINESS   SLOPPY   6
SEEDS   TROUBLING   2

                                          TOTAL 192

                           PEACH

TASTE   GREAT   9
COLOR   PEACHY   8
TEXTURE   SMOOTH   8
SKIN/RIND   FUZZY   7
STORABILITY   POOR   3
ODOR   BLAND   5
RESIDUE   PIT   8
MESSINESS   MESSY   3
SEEDS   ONE PIT   7

                                          TOTAL 222

    173

```
READY
# RUN
            TRADE STUDY
HOW MANY CANDIDATES? 4
HOW MANY FACTORS WILL YOU EVALUATE? 4

CANDIDATE NUMBER 1 ? AUTOMOBILE
CANDIDATE NUMBER 2 ? BICYCLE
CANDIDATE NUMBER 3 ? MOTORCYCLE
CANDIDATE NUMBER 4 ? SKATEBOARD

FACTOR NUMBER 1 ? FUEL COST
FACTOR NUMBER 2 ? PAYLOAD
FACTOR NUMBER 3 ? RANGE
FACTOR NUMBER 4 ? PURCHASE COST
```

PLEASE ASSIGN A NUMERICAL WEIGHT TO EACH FACTOR,
WITH MORE IMPORTANT FACTORS HAVING HIGHER NUMBERS.

FACTOR	WEIGHT
FUEL COST	? 50
PAYLOAD	? 35
RANGE	? 70
PURCHASE COST	? 40

LET'S REVIEW THE FACTORS.

NUMBER	FACTOR	WEIGHT
1	FUEL COST	50
2	PAYLOAD	35
3	RANGE	70
4	PURCHASE COST	40

DO YOU WANT TO CHANGE ANY WEIGHTINGS? NO

I'LL PRINT THE NAME OF A FACTOR, THEN PRINT THE
VARIOUS CANDIDATES. ENTER YOUR ESTIMATE IN ONE OR
TWO WORDS OF HOW THE CANDIDATE RATES; THEN ENTER
A NUMBER REPRESENTING WHERE THE CANDIDATE RANKS ON
A SCALE OF 1 TO 10. AFTER WE FINISH ALL THE CANDIDATES,
I'LL PRINT ANOTHER FACTOR AND REPEAT THE LIST UNTIL
WE'RE DONE.

FACTOR: FUEL COST

```
    AUTOMOBILE (IN WORDS) ? HIGHEST
(ON A SCALE OF 1 TO 10) ? 3
    BICYCLE (IN WORDS) ? LOWEST
```

174

```
(ON A SCALE OF 1 TO 10) ? 9
     MOTORCYCLE (IN WORDS) ? MEDIUM
(ON A SCALE OF 1 TO 10) ? 5
     SKATEBOARD (IN WORDS) ? LOWEST
(ON A SCALE OF 1 TO 10) ? 9

FACTOR: PAYLOAD

     AUTOMOBILE (IN WORDS) ? BEST
(ON A SCALE OF 1 TO 10) ? 9
     BICYCLE (IN WORDS) ? VERY SMALL
(ON A SCALE OF 1 TO 10) ? 2
     MOTORCYCLE (IN WORDS) ? SMALL
(ON A SCALE OF 1 TO 10) ? 4
     SKATEBOARD (IN WORDS) ? NONE
(ON A SCALE OF 1 TO 10) ? 1

FACTOR: RANGE

     AUTOMOBILE (IN WORDS) ? 300 MILES
(ON A SCALE OF 1 TO 10) ? 8
     BICYCLE (IN WORDS) ? 10 MILES
(ON A SCALE OF 1 TO 10) ? 4
     MOTORCYCLE (IN WORDS) ? 500 MILES
(ON A SCALE OF 1 TO 10) ? 9
     SKATEBOARD (IN WORDS) ? 10 FEET
(ON A SCALE OF 1 TO 10) ? 1

FACTOR: PURCHASE COST

     AUTOMOBILE (IN WORDS) ? GREATEST
(ON A SCALE OF 1 TO 10) ? 3
     BICYCLE (IN WORDS) ? MODERATE
(ON A SCALE OF 1 TO 10) ? 7
     MOTORCYCLE (IN WORDS) ? HIGH
(ON A SCALE OF 1 TO 10) ? 4
     SKATEBOARD (IN WORDS) ? LEAST
(ON A SCALE OF 1 TO 10) ? 9


WHAT OUTPUT PORT DO YOU WISH TO USE? 2

WOULD YOU LIKE A CHART OF THE NUMBERS OR THE
VERBAL RATINGS? VERBAL
ANOTHER? YES

WHAT OUTPUT PORT DO YOU WISH TO USE? 2

WOULD YOU LIKE A CHART OF THE NUMBERS OR THE
VERBAL RATINGS? NUMBERS
ANOTHER? NO THANKS

READY
#
```

SAMPLE OUTPUT #2

TRADE STUDY

NAME	FUEL COST	PAYLOAD	RANGE	PURCHASE COST
AUTOMOBILE	HIGHEST	BEST	300 MILES	GREATEST
BICYCLE	LOWEST	VERY SMALL	10 MILES	MODERATE
MOTORCYCLE	MEDIUM	SMALL	500 MILES	HIGH
SKATEBOARD	LOWEST	NONE	10 FEET	LEAST

TRADE STUDY

NAME	FUEL COST	PAYLOAD	RANGE	PURCHASE COST	TOTAL
AUTOMOBILE	3	9	8	3	1145
BICYCLE	9	2	4	7	1080
MOTORCYCLE	5	4	9	4	1180
SKATEBOARD	9	1	1	9	915

176

```
0010 REM *******************************
0020 REM *          TRADE STUDY          *
0030 REM *******************************
0040 REM ********** VERSION 10 **********
0050 LINE= 0
0060 DIGITS= 0
0100 REM ****** SETUP THE MATRIX *******
0110 PRINT TAB(10);"TRADE STUDY"
0120 INPUT "How many candidates",N
0130 INPUT "How many factors will you evaluate",F
0140 DIM A$((F+1),(N+1)),R(F,N),T(N),W(F)
0150 PRINT
0160 FOR X=1 TO N
0170 PRINT "Candidate Number ";X;
0180 INPUT A$((F+1),X)
0190   T(X)=0
0200 NEXT X
0210 PRINT
0220 FOR X=1 TO F
0230 PRINT "Factor Number ";X;
0240 INPUT A$(X,(N+1))
0250 NEXT X
0260 PRINT
0270 PRINT "Please assign a numerical weight to each factor,"
0280 PRINT "with more important factors having higher numbers."
0290 PRINT
0300 PRINT "Factor";TAB(30);"Weight"
0310 PRINT
0320 FOR X=1 TO F
0330 PRINT A$(X,(N+1));TAB(30);
0340 INPUT W(X)
0350 NEXT X
0360 PRINT
0370 PRINT "Let's review the factors."
0380 PRINT
0390 PRINT "Number";TAB(10);"Factor";TAB(40);"Weight"
0400 PRINT
0410 FOR X=1 TO F
0420 PRINT TAB(3);X;TAB(11);A$(X,(N+1));TAB(42);W(X)
0430 NEXT X
0440 PRINT
0450 INPUT "Do you want to change any weightings",Z$
0460 IF LEFT$(Z$,1)="N" THEN 600
0470 INPUT "Which factor number",Z
0480 IF Z>F PRINT "*** OOPS ! *** That's too high! ***"
0490 IF Z>F THEN 470
0500 PRINT Z;"   ";A$(Z,(N+1));"   ";W(Z)
0510 PRINT
0520 INPUT "What is the correct weighting factor",W(Z)
0530 PRINT
0540 INPUT "Another",Z$
0550 IF LEFT$(Z$,1)="Y" THEN 470
0560 GOTO 370
0600 REM ***** INPUT FACTOR RATINGS *****
```

```
0610 PRINT
0620 PRINT "I'll print the name of a factor, then print the"
0630 PRINT "various candidates.  Enter your estimate in one or"
0640 PRINT "two words of how the candidate rates; then enter"
0650 PRINT "a number representing where the candidate ranks on"
0660 PRINT "a scale of 1 to 10.  After we finish all the candidates,"
0670 PRINT "I'll print another factor and repeat the list until"
0680 PRINT "we're done."
0690 PRINT
0700 FOR X=1 TO F
0710 PRINT "FACTOR: ";A$(X,(N+1))
0720 PRINT
0730 FOR Y=1 TO N
0740 PRINT TAB(5);A$((F+1),Y);" ";
0750 INPUT "(in words) ",A$(X,Y)
0760 INPUT "(on a scale of 1 to 10) ",R(X,Y)
0770   T(Y)=T(Y)+(R(X,Y))*W(X)
0780 NEXT Y
0790 PRINT
0800 NEXT X
1000 REM ****** DISPLAY SELECTION *******
1010 PRINT
1020 INPUT "What output port do you wish to use",P
1030 PRINT
1040 IF (F+1)>8 THEN 2000
1050 PRINT "Would you like a chart of the NUMBERS or the"
1060 INPUT "VERBAL ratings",Z$
1070 IF LEFT$(Z$,1)="N" THEN 1500
1080 PRINT #P
1090 PRINT #P,TAB(34);"TRADE STUDY"
1100 PRINT #P
1110   T=(80/(F+1))
1120 PRINT #P,"NAME";
1130 FOR X=1 TO F
1140 PRINT #P,TAB(X*T);A$(X,(N+1));
1150 NEXT X
1160 PRINT #P:PRINT#P:PRINT#P
1170 FOR X=1 TO N
1180 PRINT #P,A$((F+1),X);
1190 FOR Y=1 TO F
1200 PRINT #P,TAB(Y*T);A$(Y,X);
1210 NEXT Y
1220 PRINT #P:PRINT#P
1230 NEXT X
1250 PRINT #P
1260 INPUT "Another",Z$
1270 IF LEFT$(Z$,1)="N" THEN END
1280 GOTO 1000
1500 PRINT #P
1510 PRINT #P,TAB(34);"TRADE STUDY"
1520 PRINT #P
1530   T=80/(F+2)
1540 PRINT #P,"NAME";
1550 FOR X=1 TO F
```

```
1560 PRINT #P,TAB(X*T);A$(X,(N+1));
1570 NEXT X
1580 PRINT #P,TAB((F+1)*T);"TOTAL"
1590 PRINT #P:PRINT#P
1600 FOR X=1 TO N
1610 PRINT #P,A$((F+1),X);
1620 FOR Y=1 TO F
1630 PRINT #P,TAB(Y*T);R(Y,X);
1640 NEXT Y
1650 PRINT #P,TAB((F+1)*T);T(X)
1660 PRINT #P
1670 NEXT X
1680 PRINT #P
1690 INPUT "Another",Z$
1700 IF LEFT$(Z$,1)="N" THEN END
1710 GOTO 1000
2000 PRINT #P,TAB(34);"TRADE STUDY"
2010 PRINT #P
2020 FOR X=1 TO N
2030 PRINT #P,TAB((80-LEN(A$((F+1),X)))/2);A$((F+1),X)
2040 PRINT #P
2050 FOR Y=1 TO F
2060 PRINT #P,A$(Y,(N+1));
2070 PRINT #P,TAB(35);A$(Y,X);
2080 PRINT #P,TAB(60);R(Y,X)
2090 NEXT Y
2100 PRINT #P
2110 PRINT #P,TAB(60);"TOTAL   ";T(X)
2120 PRINT #P
2130 NEXT X
2140 PRINT #P,CHR$(12)
2150 PRINT
2160 INPUT "Another",Z$
2170 IF LEFT$(Z$,1)="N" THEN END
2180 GOTO 1000
```

21
LIFE-CYCLE COSTING

Here is another tool of industry and government that you can use to compare the economics of purchase decisions. Government agencies procure airplanes, automobiles, and adding machines by determining the most cost-effective alternative. The costs that are compared include all costs of ownership--including training, publications, operating expenses, and maintenance factors. The original purchase cost is a factor, but not always the most important one. The least expensive television set in the showroom may not be the most economical over the long run.

Life-Cycle Costing is a home version of the extensive studies required in megamillion dollar procurements. It will allow you to collect purchase, operational, and support costs for potential purchases and compare the costs for various candidates. The results of this program do not have to be the final word, either. You can use the Life-Cycle Costing output as one of the factors in your Trade Study. One of the benefits of our Life-Cycle Costing routine is the spur it gives you to do some homework. You'll need to research cost information for your proposed purchases in areas we all usually ignore, occasionally to our sorrow.

BACKGROUND

A classic life-cycle costing exercise collects and compares data in four major areas: acquisition costs, initial logistics costs, expected lifespan, and operating expenses. Our program is true to the model. Acquisition costs are those expenditures needed to get the item out of the showroom and into our possession. They may include (in addition to the price) sales taxes, commissions, license fees, and installation costs. If we plan to sell the item after some period, the acquisition cost should be adjusted for this return of money. (Yes, that's another way of saying we're computing the depreciation!)

180

Initial logistics costs are those expenses we must suffer to prepare to operate and maintain our purchase. Initial logistics costs include publications (books, manuals, or schematic diagrams), special tools (including software), any initial spare-parts stock, and operator or maintenance training courses. We are particularly concerned with the comparison of the various candidates. If one brand requires extensive support preparation while another doesn't, that factor is significant to our purchase choice.

We need to know the expected lifespan to be able to compare the depreciation amounts on an annual basis. If the lifespan is short, a large initial logistics cost may not make much sense. A low-cost item that must be replaced every other year may not be as cost effective as an expensive asset that will last for 10 years.

Operating costs include just about everything else. Insurance, license fees, inspection fees, fuel costs (gasoline, electricity, or wood chips), lubricants, preventive maintenance, repairs, and accessories are the annual-operating-cost categories.

The classic life-cycle costing study goes one step beyond our routine. Normally, all costs past the first year are adjusted for inflation and the "cost of money" (interest fees paid to borrow the money) to convert to a "net present value" in today's dollars. We ignore that calculation in this program. There is a "net present value" routine later in this book. If you wish to combine the two, you'll have a truly professional Life-Cycle Costing program. If you elect not to combine them, this program will still be a powerful tool. The assets you and I will be comparing usually have moderate expense needs after purchase, so the error in ignoring inflation will not hurt the analysis.

OPERATING NOTES

The sample run illustrates a comparison of four computer printers (all mythical). The prompting messages are self-explanatory, and there are no special input techniques to support operator confusion. All of the sample entries are in even-dollar amounts, but you can include the cents if your research has been more precise.

The output is a tabular listing that presents totals for the three major cost areas, a total life-cycle cost, and an annual cost. The projected annual cost is the meaningful number for comparison. The sample also illustrates a common result. None of the items is significantly less expensive than the others. When a case such as this arises, you can rest assured that your personal preference is a valuable selection tool. (In the example, annual cost of the least and most expensive options are within 15 percent of each other.)

Life-Cycle Costing should be another one-evening project. The program listing reveals that it is a straightforward routine. Each major data-entry segment is a FOR...NEXT loop driven by the number of candidates (variable N) under comparison. The only numbers that survive the entry routines are the totals of costs collected in the matrices defined in line 140. Note that the salvage value amount is subtracted from the acquisition cost in line 400; otherwise, the arithmetic is a lot of addition.

This is an ideal opportunity to change the prompts and input fields to suit your personality. You can expand or compress the data-entry categories while you keypunch Life-Cycle Costing. If you want to add a "net present value" calculation, I'd recommend putting it in a subroutine. You can call the subroutine immediately after each category summation.

The printing routine is standard. You may wish to add a sorting routine to print the candidates in order of increasing (or decreasing) annual life-cycle costs. It would also be easy to add a judgment statement at the bottom of the presentation sheet to point out the most cost effective of the candidates.

LIFE CYCLE COST ANALYSIS

HOW MANY ITEMS DO YOU WISH TO COMPARE? <u>4</u>

WHAT IS THE NAME OF ITEM 1 ? <u>PRINTER #1</u>

WHAT IS ITS COST? <u>600</u>
WHAT WILL ITS SALVAGE VALUE BE? <u>50</u>
SALES TAXES/COMMISSIONS ON PURCHASE? <u>36</u>
LICENSE FEES ON PURCHASE? <u>0</u>
INSTALLATION COSTS? <u>0</u>

WHAT IS THE NAME OF ITEM 2 ? <u>PRINTER #2</u>

WHAT IS ITS COST? <u>1000</u>
WHAT WILL ITS SALVAGE VALUE BE? <u>125</u>
SALES TAXES/COMMISSIONS ON PURCHASE? <u>60</u>
LICENSE FEES ON PURCHASE? <u>0</u>
INSTALLATION COSTS? <u>0</u>

WHAT IS THE NAME OF ITEM 3 ? <u>PRINTING TERM.</u>

WHAT IS ITS COST? <u>1500</u>
WHAT WILL ITS SALVAGE VALUE BE? <u>400</u>
SALES TAXES/COMMISSIONS ON PURCHASE? <u>90</u>
LICENSE FEES ON PURCHASE? <u>0</u>
INSTALLATION COSTS? <u>50</u>

WHAT IS THE NAME OF ITEM 4 ? <u>DELUX PRINTER</u>

WHAT IS ITS COST? <u>2500</u>
WHAT WILL ITS SALVAGE VALUE BE? <u>500</u>
SALES TAXES/COMMISSIONS ON PURCHASE? <u>150</u>
LICENSE FEES ON PURCHASE? <u>0</u>
INSTALLATION COSTS? <u>100</u>

FOR ITEM #1, PRINTER #1, ENTER THE COSTS FOR --
BOOKS, MANUALS, SCHEMATIC DIAGRAMS? <u>25</u>
SPECIAL TOOLS? <u>15</u>
INITIAL SPARE PARTS STOCK? <u>30</u>
OPERATOR/MAINTENANCE TRAINING? <u>0</u>

FOR ITEM #2, PRINTER #2, ENTER THE COSTS FOR --
BOOKS, MANUALS, SCHEMATIC DIAGRAMS? <u>30</u>
SPECIAL TOOLS? <u>0</u>
INITIAL SPARE PARTS STOCK? <u>0</u>
OPERATOR/MAINTENANCE TRAINING? <u>0</u>

FOR ITEM #3, PRINTING TERM., ENTER THE COSTS FOR --
BOOKS, MANUALS, SCHEMATIC DIAGRAMS? 48
SPECIAL TOOLS? 125
INITIAL SPARE PARTS STOCK? 90
OPERATOR/MAINTENANCE TRAINING? 0

FOR ITEM #4, DELUX PRINTER, ENTER THE COSTS FOR --
BOOKS, MANUALS, SCHEMATIC DIAGRAMS? 0
SPECIAL TOOLS? 0
INITIAL SPARE PARTS STOCK? 0
OPERATOR/MAINTENANCE TRAINING? 0

WHAT IS THE EXPECTED LIFE IN YEARS OF -
PRINTER #1? 3
PRINTER #2? 4
PRINTING TERM.? 6
DELUX PRINTER? 8

ENTER THE EXPECTED ANNUAL COSTS
FOR PRINTER #1
INSURANCE? 0
LICENSE FEES? 0
MAINTENANCE/INSPECTION FEES? 50
FUEL? 0
LUBRICANTS? 10
PREVENTIVE MAINTENANCE (FILTERS, TUNE-UPS, ETC.)? 10
UNSCHEDULED MAINTENANCE (REPAIRS)? 60
ACCESSORIES/OTHER RELATED COSTS? 50

FOR PRINTER #2
INSURANCE? 0
LICENSE FEES? 0
MAINTENANCE/INSPECTION FEES? 50
FUEL? 0
LUBRICANTS? 12
PREVENTIVE MAINTENANCE (FILTERS, TUNE-UPS, ETC.)? 25
UNSCHEDULED MAINTENANCE (REPAIRS)? 60
ACCESSORIES/OTHER RELATED COSTS? 50

FOR PRINTING TERM.
INSURANCE? 0
LICENSE FEES? 0
MAINTENANCE/INSPECTION FEES? 75
FUEL? 0
LUBRICANTS? 0
PREVENTIVE MAINTENANCE (FILTERS, TUNE-UPS, ETC.)? 0
UNSCHEDULED MAINTENANCE (REPAIRS)? 0
ACCESSORIES/OTHER RELATED COSTS? 60

FOR DELUX PRINTER
INSURANCE? 0
LICENSE FEES? 0
MAINTENANCE/INSPECTION FEES? 85
FUEL? 0
LUBRICANTS? 0

PREVENTIVE MAINTENANCE (FILTERS, TUNE-UPS, ETC.)? 0
UNSCHEDULED MAINTENANCE (REPAIRS)? 0
ACCESSORIES/OTHER RELATED COSTS? 50

WHAT OUTPUT PORT DO YOU WISH? 2
ANOTHER COPY? NO

SAMPLE OUTPUT

LIFE CYCLE COST COMPARISON

CANDIDATE	ACQUISITION COST	LOGISTICS COST	OPERATING COST	LIFE CYCLE COST	ANNUAL LCC
PRINTER #1	586.00	70.00	540.00	1196.00	398.66
PRINTER #2	935.00	30.00	788.00	1753.00	438.25
PRINTING TERM.	1240.00	263.00	810.00	2313.00	385.50
DELUX PRINTER	2250.00	0.00	1080.00	3330.00	416.25

185

```
0010 REM *********************************
0020 REM *       LIFE CYCLE COSTING       *
0030 REM *********************************
0040 REM ********* VERSION 20 *********
0050 LINE= 0
0060 DIGITS= 0
0100 PRINT :PRINT:PRINT
0110 PRINT TAB(10);"LIFE CYCLE COST ANALYSIS"
0120 PRINT
0130 INPUT "How many items do you wish to compare",N
0140 DIM A$(N),A(N),I(N),N(N),O(N),L(N)
0150 PRINT
0200 REM ****** ACQUISITION COST ******
0210 FOR Q=1 TO N
0220 PRINT "What is the name of item ";Q;
0230 INPUT A$(Q)
0240 PRINT
0250 INPUT "What is its cost",C
0260 INPUT "What will its salvage value be",S
0270 INPUT "Sales taxes/commissions on purchase",T
0280 INPUT "License fees on purchase",F
0290 INPUT "Installation costs",M
0300   A(Q)=C-S+T+F+M
0310 PRINT
0320 NEXT Q
0400 REM **** INITIAL LOGISTICS COST ****
0410 FOR Q=1 TO N
0420 PRINT "For item #";Q;", ";A$(Q);", Enter the costs for --"
0430 INPUT "Books, Manuals, Schematic Diagrams",B
0440 INPUT "Special Tools",T
0450 INPUT "Initial spare parts stock",S
0460 INPUT "Operator/Maintenance Training",M
0470   I(Q)=B+T+S+M
0480 PRINT
0490 NEXT Q
0500 REM ******* EXPECTED  LIFE ********
0510 PRINT "What is the expected life in years of -"
0520 FOR Q=1 TO N
0530 PRINT A$(Q);
0540 INPUT N(Q)
0550 NEXT Q
0560 PRINT
0600 REM ****** OPERATING  COSTS ******
0610 PRINT "Enter the expected ANNUAL costs "
0620 FOR Q=1 TO N
0630 PRINT "For ";A$(Q)
0640 INPUT "Insurance",I
0650 INPUT "License Fees",F
0660 INPUT "Maintenance/Inspection Fees",M
0670 INPUT "Fuel",G
0680 INPUT "Lubricants",B
0690 INPUT "Preventive Maintenance (filters, tune-ups, etc.)",P
0700 INPUT "Unscheduled Maintenance (Repairs)",R
0710 INPUT "Accessories/Other Related Costs",X
```

```
0720   O(Q)=N(Q)*(I+F+M+G+B+P+R+X)
0730 PRINT
0740 NEXT Q
0750 FOR Q=1 TO N
0760   L(Q)=A(Q)+I(Q)+O(Q)
0770 NEXT Q
0800 REM ********** PRINTOUT **********
0810 DIGITS= 2
0820 INPUT "What output port do you wish",P
0830 PRINT #P:PRINT#P:PRINT#P
0840 PRINT #P,TAB(27);"LIFE CYCLE COST COMPARISON"
0850 PRINT #P:PRINT#P
0860 PRINT #P,"Candidate";
0870 PRINT #P,TAB(20);"Acquisition";
0880 PRINT #P,TAB(33);"Logistics";
0890 PRINT #P,TAB(45);"Operating";
0900 PRINT #P,TAB(57);"LIFE CYCLE";
0910 PRINT #P,TAB(70);"Annual"
0920 PRINT #P,TAB(23);"Cost";
0930 PRINT #P,TAB(35);"Cost";
0940 PRINT #P,TAB(47);"Cost";
0950 PRINT #P,TAB(60);"COST";
0960 PRINT #P,TAB(71);"LCC"
0970 PRINT #P:PRINT#P
0980 FOR Q=1 TO N
0990 PRINT #P,A$(Q);
1000 PRINT #P,TAB(28-LEN(STR$(A(Q))));A(Q);
1010 PRINT #P,TAB(40-LEN(STR$(I(Q))));I(Q);
1020 PRINT #P,TAB(53-LEN(STR$(O(Q))));O(Q);
1030 PRINT #P,TAB(66-LEN(STR$(L(Q))));L(Q);
1040   X=L(Q)/N(Q)
1050 PRINT #P,TAB(76-LEN(STR$(X)));X
1060 PRINT #P
1070 NEXT Q
1080 PRINT #P,CHR$(12)
1090 INPUT "Another Copy",Z$
1100 IF LEFT$(Z$,1)="Y" THEN 800
1110 END
```

22

HOME INSURANCE INVENTORY

Management of your assets includes keeping records that will describe your holdings. Most of us maintain insurance policies that will reimburse our losses in case of disaster. We've got to know what the losses are, however, to take full advantage of this insurance. Your computer is a potential record book, and the Home Insurance Inventory program is the stylus with which to inscribe your holdings.

This program requires disk-memory capability. While you may be able to reconfigure the effort for tape-cassette data storage, the operating time may be unacceptably long. Each minidiskette will hole 1,400 entries. The listing of household possessions will fit one side of a disk for most of us. Keep a copy at home and one in your safety deposit box to ease the preparation of any insurance claim. The program provides a hard-copy listing of the inventory also, and you should file such a copy in your deposit box. Another hard copy should also be furnished to your insurance agent. (After all, a truly major disaster may involve all or part of your computer hardware.)

One of the major advantages in this program may be the spur it gives us to prepare the inventory. It's awfully easy to put off until "tomorrow" any job like an inventory. No sense in inviting disaster by preparing for it! Somehow, though, disasters still happen.

OPERATING NOTES

Home Insurance Inventory is another menu-driven program. No mathematics; it's strictly a data-management routine. The four information items collected by the program are the key data pieces most requested by insurance claim forms: What is it? How can you identify it? When did you buy it? How much did it cost?

While you should record the facts for all of your important possessions, our sample run illustrates an initialization with three assets and the deletion of one of

188

the three. The addition of assets uses the same code and entry sequence as initialization, so there is no separate addition example. Each program exercise ends with a listing of the file, so we haven't included demonstration of the list sequence.

To configure the variables for controlled storage, each field of entry is limited to a specific number of characters. If your entries run over the allotment, the program will cut them off at the limit:

Variable	Contents	Characters
N$	Name of asset	21
S$	Serial number	14
D$	Date of purchase	17
C$	Purchase price/cost	8

The large number of characters allocated to the purchase date allows you to enter full spellings for the month. The eight characters devoted to purchase price will allow entries up to $99,999.99. You can restructure these limits if necessary.

You'll note that a menu choice of zero is not advertised by the display, but will result in the initialization routine. As usual, our purpose is to prevent an operator unfamiliar with the program from destroying your records. Most of the remaining prompts are self-explanatory. Before you can delete an item, the program will print the name and identification number of the asset it thinks you wish to delete. This is another double-check to catch possible operator errors.

PROGRAMMING NOTES

No new programming wrinkles are introduced in Home Insurance Inventory. Remember that the disk system used for the examples is probably more primitive than yours; you'll have to include the disk commands your system likes.

Program flow always starts and ends in the menu segment of lines 140 through 260. Variable A$ is defined as holding 20 spaces in line 150. This command definition could be placed earlier in the listing, as the definition is needed only once in any run. We'll use A$ to help format our entries later for precise disk-memory allocation.

The initialization sequence, which starts at line 300, flows into the output-listing segment at line 410. Except for the disk OPEN command, the initialization sequence is used for inventory additions, also. Line 320 calls the subroutine at line 700 for data entry and formatting. You can juggle the character allowances for the variables by changing lines 720, 750, 780, and 820. To keep the disk storage clean, make sure that the total characters allowed for the four variables is 60.

189

The addition routine uses lines 920 and 930 to move the disk-data pointer along to the end-of-data mark. With the next open real estate available, the routine passes program flow back to the initialization routine. Initialization continues to collect and format data, record it, and ask the operator if further entries are desired. You could probably initialize by going directly to the addition sequence, but a new disk might generate an error in line 920.

The deletion segment encores a technique we've used before. We read an entry in line 1060 and check the asset name with the user's entry in line 1070. If we haven't found the desired item, line 1150 will re-record the data. When we locate the proper deletion, program flow will by-pass the re-record step and continue to restack the assets. The flag set in line 1130 is used to guide the printing of the "Sorry, I can't find" message. If F=0, we didn't find any item meeting the criteria. When all deletions are accomplished, program flow is directed to the printing routine by line 1240.

As your inventory diskette fills, the printing list may get too long. You can add a question around line 410 to ignore the printing at user option. Something like the following will do the trick:

```
0411 INPUT "Want to print the list",Z$
0412 IF LEFT$(Z$,1)="N" THEN 140
```

If you only open the disk once a month, you'll probably want the listing with each program exercise. When you're doing your initial home inventory, you may be making entries once a day. The once-a-day list could get tiresome.

If you've managed to get previous disk programs running, this one will be up and running in one evening. Having that inventory disk complete can help your peace of mind.

SAMPLE INPUT - HOME INVENTORY

                HOME INSURANCE INVENTORY

STARTING DISK DRIVE/SECTOR (DSSS) ? <u>2200</u>

     ENTER A: TO:

        '1'   ADD ITEMS
        '2'   DELETE ITEMS
        '3'   LIST THE INVENTORY
        '4'   END.
? <u>0</u>

ITEM NAME OR DESCRIPTOR? <u>CLOCK</u>

IDENTIFICATION NUMBER OR SERIAL NUMBER? <u>S12345</u>

DATE OF PURCHASE (DAY-MONTH-YEAR) ? <u>12 DEC 76</u>

PURCHASE PRICE/COST? <u>355.89</u>

ANOTHER ITEM? <u>YES</u>

ITEM NAME OR DESCRIPTOR? <u>SUPER STEREO</u>

IDENTIFICATION NUMBER OR SERIAL NUMBER? <u>SS18-345</u>

DATE OF PURCHASE (DAY-MONTH-YEAR) ? <u>16 DEC 80</u>

PURCHASE PRICE/COST? <u>789.21</u>

ANOTHER ITEM? <u>YUP</u>

ITEM NAME OR DESCRIPTOR? <u>VIOLIN</u>

IDENTIFICATION NUMBER OR SERIAL NUMBER? <u>NONE</u>

DATE OF PURCHASE (DAY-MONTH-YEAR) ? <u>21 DEC 80</u>

PURCHASE PRICE/COST? <u>650</u>

ANOTHER ITEM? <u>NO</u>

THANK YOU

191

```
WHAT OUTPUT PORT? 2

      ENTER A:            TO:

      '1'           ADD ITEMS
      '2'           DELETE ITEMS
      '3'           LIST THE INVENTORY
      '4'           END
? 2

WHAT ITEM DO YOU WISH TO DELETE? CLOCK

IS THIS THE ONE YOU WANT TO DELETE-

CLOCK                 I.D. NR.: S12345        ? YES


ANOTHER DELETION? NO

WHAT OUTPUT PORT? 2

      ENTER A:            TO:

      '1'           ADD ITEMS
      '2'           DELETE ITEMS
      '3'           LIST THE INVENTORY
      '4'           END
? 4

READY
#
SAMPLE OUTPUT - FIRST RUN
```

HOME INSURANCE INVENTORY

ITEM	I.D. NR.	DATE ACQUIRED	COST
CLOCK	S12345	12 DEC 76	355.89
SUPER STEREO	SS18-345	16 DEC 80	789.21
VIOLIN	NONE	21 DEC 80	650.00

```
SAMPLE OUTPUT - SECOND RUN
```

HOME INSURANCE INVENTORY

ITEM	I.D. NR.	DATE ACQUIRED	COST
SUPER STEREO	SS18-345	16 DEC 80	789.21
VIOLIN	NONE	21 DEC 80	650.00

```
0010 REM ***********************************
0020 REM *    HOME INSURANCE INVENTORY    *
0030 REM ***********************************
0040 REM ********** VERSION 10 **********
0050 LINE= 0
0060 DIGITS= 0
0070 PRINT
0080 PRINT
0090 PRINT
0100 PRINT TAB(12);"HOME INSURANCE INVENTORY"
0110 PRINT
0120 INPUT "Starting Disk Drive/Sector (DSSS)",S
0130 IF S<1000 THEN 120
0140 PRINT
0150   A$="                    ":REM *** 20 SPACES ***
0160 PRINT "    Enter a:         To:"
0170 PRINT
0180 PRINT "       '1'           ADD items"
0190 PRINT "       '2'           DELETE items"
0200 PRINT "       '3'           LIST the inventory"
0210 PRINT "       '4'           END."
0220 INPUT Z
0230 IF INT(Z)=1 THEN 900
0240 IF INT(Z)=2 THEN 1000
0250 IF INT(Z)=3 THEN 410
0260 IF Z>3 THEN END
0300 REM ********** INITIALIZE **********
0310 OPEN #10,S
0320 GOSUB 700
0330 PRINT
0340 PRINT #10,C$;D$;N$;S$
0350 PRINT
0360 INPUT "Another item",Z$
0370 IF LEFT$(Z$,1)="Y" THEN 320
0380 PRINT
0390 PRINT "Thank you"
0400 CLOSE #10
0410 PRINT
0420 INPUT "What output port",P
0430 PRINT #P:PRINT#P
0440 PRINT #P,TAB(28);"HOME INSURANCE INVENTORY"
0450 PRINT #P:PRINT#P
0460 DIGITS= 2
0470 PRINT #P,TAB(8);"Item";
0480 PRINT #P,TAB(30);"I.D. Nr.";
0490 PRINT #P,TAB(50);"Date Acquired";
0500 PRINT #P,TAB(68);"Cost"
0510 PRINT #P
0520 OPEN #10,S
0530 READ #10,C$,D$,N$,S$\600
0540 PRINT #P,N$;
0550 PRINT #P,TAB(30);S$;
0560 PRINT #P,TAB(50);D$;
0570   C=VAL(C$)
```

```
0580 PRINT #P,TAB(72-LEN(STR$(C)));C
0590 GOTO 530
0600 PRINT #P,CHR$(12)
0610 CLOSE #10
0620 GOTO 140
0700 REM ******** INPUT SEQUENCE ********
0710 INPUT "Item name or descriptor",N$
0720   N$=LEFT$(N$+A$,21)
0730 PRINT
0740 INPUT "Identification number or serial number",S$
0750   S$=LEFT$(S$+A$,14)
0760 PRINT
0770 INPUT "Date of Purchase (Day-Month-Year)",D$
0780   D$=LEFT$(D$+A$,17)
0790 PRINT
0800 INPUT "Purchase price/cost",C
0810   C$=STR$(C)
0820   C$=LEFT$(C$+A$,8)
0830 PRINT
0840 RETURN
0900 REM ********* ADD  ITEMS *********
0910 OPEN #10,S
0920 READ #10,C$,D$,N$,S$\940
0930 GOTO 920
0940 GOTO 320
1000 REM ******** DELETE ITEMS ********
1010 PRINT
1020 PRINT "What item do you wish to delete";
1030 INPUT I$
1040   F=0
1050 OPEN #10,S:OPEN#11,S
1060 READ #10,C$,D$,N$,S$\1170
1070 IF LEFT$(N$,LEN(I$))<>I$ THEN 1150
1080 PRINT "Is this the one you want to delete-"
1090 PRINT N$;" I.D. Nr.: ";S$;
1100 INPUT Z$
1110 IF LEFT$(Z$,1)<>"Y" THEN 1150
1120 PRINT
1130   F=1
1140 GOTO 1060
1150 PRINT #11,C$;D$;N$;S$
1160 GOTO 1060
1170 PRINT
1180 IF F=1 GOTO 1200
1190 PRINT "Sorry, I can't find ";I$
1200 PRINT
1210 CLOSE #10:CLOSE#11
1220 INPUT "Another deletion",Z$
1230 IF LEFT$(Z$,1)="Y" THEN 1000
1240 GOTO 410
```

IV
INVESTMENT FACTORS

23

SAVINGS ACCOUNT ANALYSIS

Picking an investment always seems like more fun than any other facet of financial management. Perhaps it's the feeling of power available when we have spare cash. Maybe the thrill comes from the leisure available for investigation. We know that our money can work for us. To make it work most effectively, we've got to pick the right investment.

As a general rule, the larger the return on an investment, the greater the risk involved. One of the prime rules of investing should be, "Pick an investment you are comfortable with." The extra return may not be worth ulcers. The programs in this section address many types of opportunities. We'll explore the "safe-and-sane" savings accounts as well as the excitement of the options markets. Whatever you decide about where to put your money, you'll have the help of your computer.

Initially, we'll look at savings accounts. You can invest your savings with a credit union, bank, savings and loan, or thrift association for a guaranteed interest return. If you'll promise to leave your money for a specific period, you'll receive a higher interest rate. At a glance, all savings plans seem to be the same. They're not! Fractional interest rate differences can mean dollars to you. Different compounding periods will change the yield of seemingly identical interest rates. Savings Account Analysis provides a tool to compare the variety of rates and yields available. You may compare any reasonable number of account types simultaneously (my BASIC will allow 255 at once). The program will calculate the effective yield from the quoted annual interest rate and compounding period, and will calculate the actual yield of a sample investment.

BACKGROUND

Our magical mathematical formula is another of those compound-interest manipulations. The future value (V) of an amount (A) deposited at any interest rate (I) is determined by:

$$V = A * (1 + I)^N$$

where N is the number of compounding periods. We can use a minor modification of the formula to compute periodic true-interest yield. Let the amount deposited be 1 dollar and subtract the dollar from a calculation of 1 year's future value. The result is the effective annual interest rate:

$$R = (1 + I)^N - 1$$

Both I and N need to be adjusted for the various compounding times. (For quarterly compounding, for example, the interest rate used in the formula is one-fourth of the quoted annual rate and the number of periods is four.)

OPERATING NOTES

There are three inputs needed for each account analyzed. Enter the name of the depository or savings plan, the quoted annual interest rate, and a letter indicating the compounding period. After all of the information is entered, you can pick a sample investment amount and term. The rest is up to your digital doer. You'll get a table reporting effective yields and totals for your sample deposit. The sample output illustrates the different results available for a set annual interest rate with different compounding periods. The totals help put the different effective yields in proper perspective.

PROGRAMMING NOTES

No new programming wrinkles are introduced with this routine. The input-prompting messages are more conversational than usual to help the user. Savings Account Analysis is another straightforward program, so no complicated flow is encountered.

Lines 10 through 60 take care of the heading information and initial configuration. The operator input starts in line 100, which leads to the variable DIMensioning of line 130. FOR...NEXT loops are used for the input routine. The loop of lines 170 through 190 collects the plan names. The names are used in the prompt messages in the second loop. Lines 280 through 340 are an error trap. We must have a D, Q, or A in the "period" variable to drive the computation routine later.

The remaining BASIC code handles the computation and report output. After the port is selected in line 410, lines 430 to 570 print the report heading. The body of the comparison table is managed by another FOR...NEXT loop. Lines 600, 650, and 660 use a TAB calculation to line up the decimal points in the numeric output. The daily, quarterly, and annual compounding calculations are fetched by the IF... statements of lines 620, 630, and 640. If you prefer, use a GOSUB for these. (The GOTOs work because the routines are called from a single point in the program.)

Compounding-calculation segments in lines 700, 800, and 900 mechanize the formulas we discussed earlier. You'll note an extra "divide-by-one-hundred" notation, which is included to convert the percentage rates to decimal fractions. The effective yields are reconverted to percents in lines 720 and 820.

SAMPLE INPUT - SAVINGS ANALYSIS

LET'S SEE WHICH SAVINGS ACCOUNTS REALLY PROVIDE
THE BEST INVESTMENT. TELL ME HOW MANY ACCOUNTS
YOU WISH TO CONSIDER? 6

START BY TELLING ME THE SAVINGS PLAN NAMES.

BANK OR PLAN NAME? S&L #1
BANK OR PLAN NAME? S&L #2
BANK OR PLAN NAME? S&L #3
BANK OR PLAN NAME? SAVINGS BANK
BANK OR PLAN NAME? BANK SAVINGS
BANK OR PLAN NAME? CREDIT UNION

NOW, FOR EACH PLAN LET'S COLLECT THE FACTS.

FOR THE S&L #1 PLAN -

QUOTED ANNUAL INTEREST RATE (PERCENTAGE)? 5.25
IS COMPOUNDING PERIOD 'D'AILY, 'Q'UARTERLY, OR 'A'NNUAL? D

FOR THE S&L #2 PLAN -

QUOTED ANNUAL INTEREST RATE (PERCENTAGE)? 5.25
IS COMPOUNDING PERIOD 'D'AILY, 'Q'UARTERLY, OR 'A'NNUAL? Q

FOR THE S&L #3 PLAN -

QUOTED ANNUAL INTEREST RATE (PERCENTAGE)? 5.25
IS COMPOUNDING PERIOD 'D'AILY, 'Q'UARTERLY, OR 'A'NNUAL? A

FOR THE SAVINGS BANK PLAN -

QUOTED ANNUAL INTEREST RATE (PERCENTAGE)? 5.0
IS COMPOUNDING PERIOD 'D'AILY, 'Q'UARTERLY, OR 'A'NNUAL? Q

FOR THE BANK SAVINGS PLAN -

QUOTED ANNUAL INTEREST RATE (PERCENTAGE)? 4.75
IS COMPOUNDING PERIOD 'D'AILY, 'Q'UARTERLY, OR 'A'NNUAL? D

FOR THE CREDIT UNION PLAN -

QUOTED ANNUAL INTEREST RATE (PERCENTAGE)? 7.5
IS COMPOUNDING PERIOD 'D'AILY, 'Q'UARTERLY, OR 'A'NNUAL? Q

WHAT AMOUNT HAD YOU INTENDED TO INVEST? 10000
HOW MANY YEARS DID YOU PLAN TO LEAVE IT? 3

WHAT OUTPUT PORT? 3

SAMPLE OUTPUT - SAVINGS ANALYSIS

SAVINGS ACCOUNT ANALYSIS

(FOR AN EXAMPLE INVESTMENT OF $10000.00 FOR 3.00 YEARS.)

BANK/PLAN	INTEREST RATE	COMPOUNDING PERIOD	EFFECTIVE YIELD	EXAMPLE TOTAL
S&L #1	5.25	D	5.38	11705.60
S&L #2	5.25	Q	5.35	11693.82
S&L #3	5.25	A	5.25	11659.13
SAVINGS BANK	5.00	Q	5.09	11607.54
BANK SAVINGS	4.75	D	4.86	11531.33
CREDIT UNION	7.50	Q	7.71	12497.16

```
0010 REM **********************************
0020 REM *    SAVINGS ACCOUNT ANALYSIS    *
0030 REM **********************************
0040 REM ********** VERSION 10 **********
0050 LINE= 0
0060 DIGITS= 2
0100 PRINT "Let's see which savings accounts really provide"
0110 PRINT "the best investment.  Tell me how many accounts"
0120 INPUT "you wish to consider",N
0130 DIM B$(N),P$(N),I(N)
0140 PRINT
0150 PRINT "Start by telling me the savings plan names."
0160 PRINT
0170 FOR X=1 TO N
0180 INPUT "Bank or plan name",B$(X)
0190 NEXT X
0200 PRINT
0210 PRINT "Now, for each plan let's collect the facts."
0220 FOR X=1 TO N
0230 PRINT
0240 PRINT "For the ";B$(X);" plan - "
0250 PRINT
0260 INPUT "Quoted annual interest rate (percentage)",I(X)
0270 INPUT "Is compounding period 'D'aily, 'Q'uarterly, or 'A'nnual",P$(X)
0280 IF LEFT$(P$(X),1)="D" THEN 350
0290 IF LEFT$(P$(X),1)="Q" THEN 350
0300 IF LEFT$(P$(X),1)="A" THEN 350
0310 PRINT "OOPS, I don't understand '";P$(X);"'."
0320 PRINT
0330 PRINT "Please try again."
0340 GOTO 270
0350 NEXT X
0360 PRINT
0370 INPUT "What amount had you intended to invest",A
0380 INPUT "How many years did you plan to leave it",Y
0390 PRINT
0400 REM ******* OUTPUT ROUTINE *******
0410 INPUT "What output port",P
0420 PRINT
0430 PRINT #P:PRINT#P:PRINT#P
0440 PRINT #P,TAB(30);"SAVINGS ACCOUNT ANALYSIS"
0450 PRINT #P
0460 PRINT #P,"(For an example investment of $";A;" for ";Y;"years.)"
0470 PRINT #P
0480 PRINT #P,"Bank/Plan";
0490 PRINT #P,TAB(28);"Interest";
0500 PRINT #P,TAB(40);"Compounding";
0510 PRINT #P,TAB(53);"Effective";
0520 PRINT #P,TAB(67);"Example"
0530 PRINT #P,TAB(30);"Rate";
0540 PRINT #P,TAB(42);"Period";
0550 PRINT #P,TAB(55);"Yield";
0560 PRINT #P,TAB(68);"Total"
0570 PRINT #P
```

```
0580 FOR X=1 TO N
0590 PRINT #P,B$(X);
0600 PRINT #P,TAB(34-LEN(STR$(I(X))));I(X);
0610 PRINT #P,TAB(44);P$(X);
0620 IF LEFT$(P$(X),1)="D" THEN 700
0630 IF LEFT$(P$(X),1)="Q" THEN 800
0640 IF LEFT$(P$(X),1)="A" THEN 900
0650 PRINT #P,TAB(60-LEN(STR$(R)));R;
0660 PRINT #P,TAB(75-LEN(STR$(V)));V
0670 NEXT X
0680 PRINT #P,CHR$(12)
0690 END
0700 REM ****** DAILY COMPOUNDING *******
0710   R=((1+I(X)/36500)↑(365))-1
0720   R=R*100
0730   V=A*(1+I(X)/36500)↑(365*Y)
0740 GOTO 650
0800 REM **** QUARTERLY COMPOUNDING *****
0810   R=((1+I(X)/400)↑4)-1
0820   R=R*100
0830   V=A*(1+I(X)/400)↑(4*Y)
0840 GOTO 650
0900 REM ****** ANNUAL COMPOUNDING ******
0910   R=I(X)
0920   V=A*(1+I(X)/100)↑Y
0930 GOTO 650
```

24
SAVINGS ACCOUNT RECORDS

Most investment portfolios include some savings deposits. Many of us maintain more than one savings account. Spreading our demand deposits around promises a few benefits. For one thing, you build a "track record" with various financial instituations which may help when that next loan application is needed. The convenience of having some money in the bank just down the street can compensate for an unfavorable compounding period or a slightly inferior rate of interest. You may wish to balance earnings and liquidity by keeping some cash in long-term (high-interest) accounts, and some in lower-interest (no-minimum-deposit term) accounts. I like to keep an account in a nearby banking institution that compounds on a daily basis for my "ready-cash float." Your preferences will govern how you spread (or don't spread) your savings deposits.

With a few diversified savings, we need to know how much cash is where. As income tax time approaches, we'd also like to know how much interest will be earned by each account. <u>Savings</u> <u>Account</u> <u>Records</u> will help. The program will keep a record of each deposit account throughout the year, and, when you want it, will estimate the amount of interest that will be earned to year-end.

BACKGROUND

Not much mathematics in this program; in fact, we don't even use all of the interest-calculation knowledge we have. Since the estimate will always be for a total period of less than a year--and usually much less than a year, we'll cheat a bit. In the routine, we calculate only simple interest and ignore the effects of compounding. With the annual interest rate (I) known, we'll find the estimated interest for the rest of the year (E) with the following formula:

$$E = \frac{B * I * P}{N}$$

204

Where B is the present account balance, P is the number of compounding periods left in the current year, and N is the number of periods in a full year. Our approximation error will be the interest calculated on the interest to be earned--the compounding amount. If your computer has a real-time clock/calendar feature, you could set the program to calculate interest exactly. In fact, you could let it calculate your account balance and interest earned for the entire year in real time. With periodic deposits and withdrawals, this task needs to be done almost every day to be accurate. (You may also need to take into account additional rules: "Deposits by the tenth of a month earn interest from the first" is one policy of some depositories which can drive a general-purpose computer program batty!)

OPERATING NOTES

The sample run shows the full gamut of program operation. We start with a disk initiation, update the records, request a printing of the data base, and end the program. (Actually, we end the program twice--once after the initialization step.) The program always begins and ends on the menu of choices. Generally, all of the input prompts are self-explanatory. You'll need to answer the initial question carefully--you must read the disk unless you're initializing a new disk. The only other critical entry is the date. Follow the prompt, and you'll have no trouble. Enter two digits for the day, the month, and the year separated by slashes (/). The interest-estimation routine needs the date in an exact format, so this one entry can make or break your operation.

PROGRAMMING NOTES

While the listing looks a bit long, this should be another one-evening project. There's very little fancy footwork, and the program is broken into small bite-sized chunks of code. You've adapted other disk programs, and this one isn't any different.

The starting routine, including the menu, is contained in lines 100 through 390. The disk-read routine is almost a part of the start, so you may wish to move it from lines 4000 through 4130 up to the program heading. The date is requested in line 170, and put to use almost immediately by the subroutine at lines 4200 through 4320.

The date-conversion subroutine uses the DATA statements of lines 4400 and 4410. The DATA format is "month number," "days in month," "quarters remaining." The subroutine reads the first set (1, 31, 4) and compares the month with the month entered by the user. If no match is found, the days are added to variable D and the next DATA set is gathered. When a match is found, D is set to the number of days remaining in the year at the beginning of the month (by line 4270). Next, the number of days is adjusted once more in line 4280 to subtract the current day of the month. Variable M is set to the number of months left in the year in line 4290, and Q is set to the number of remaining quarters by line 4300.

With the date converted into a useful form by the program, the menu is ready for any contingency. No error trap is included in the menu area, because all numbers are acceptable--to the computer, if not the operator. A number equal to or greater than four is counted as a four to direct the end of the program. Any entry of less than two is counted as a one, which drives the routine to program initialization in lines 1000 to 1150.

One feature included in the program-end sequence is the disk-drive and sector input. Since you may enter the disk address both at program beginning and ending, you have the capability to maintain a history file. You might alternate between two disk addresses so that the latest "old" file is still on the disk to help you recover from a disaster while adjusting the "new" file.

The data base initiation is handled in lines 1000 through 1150. Note the error trap of lines 1100 and 1110, which ensure a proper interest-accrual entry. (Yes, it's another of my FOR...NEXT loops.)

Accounts are updated and the interest estimate is made in lines 2000 through 2320. (If you want an interest estimate without an update, select the update and add/withdraw zeroes.) The update segment is straightforward. The estimates are made during the printing action. Lines 2200, 2210, and 2220 call the appropriate interest-estimating subroutine. These subroutines mechanize our approximation equation.

Printing of the data base is addressed in lines 3000 through 3280. Our standard decimal-justifying TABs are used to provide accounting columns in line 3130 and 3190. The total interest is calculated by line 3200 and presented in line 3240.

SAMPLE INPUT - SAVINGS RECORDS

DO YOU WANT TO READ FROM DISK? <u>NO</u>

HOW MANY ACCOUNTS? <u>5</u>

TODAY'S DATE (DD/MM/YY)? <u>02/02/84</u>

SAVINGS ACCOUNT RECORDS

TYPE: '1' TO INITIATE THE RECORDS
         '2' TO UPDATE THE RECORDS
         '3' TO PRINT THE RECORDS
         '4' TO END.
? <u>1</u>

FOR ACCOUNT #1
WHAT BANK? <u>FIRST LOCAL BANQUE</u>
ACCOUNT NUMBER? <u>00-00000-01234</u>
DOES INTEREST ACCRUE DAILY, MONTHLY, OR QUARTERLY? <u>QUARTERLY</u>
ANNUAL INTEREST RATE? <u>5.90</u>
WHAT IS PRESENT BALANCE? <u>102.50</u>
FOR ACCOUNT #2
WHAT BANK? <u>THIRD COUNTY BANK</u>
ACCOUNT NUMBER? <u>00-000-0246810-0</u>
DOES INTEREST ACCRUE DAILY, MONTHLY, OR QUARTERLY? <u>MONTHLY</u>
ANNUAL INTEREST RATE? <u>5.85</u>
WHAT IS PRESENT BALANCE? <u>483.21</u>
FOR ACCOUNT #3
WHAT BANK? LOCAL <u>S & L</u>
ACCOUNT NUMBER? <u>0-012-00045</u>
DOES INTEREST ACCRUE DAILY, MONTHLY, OR QUARTERLY? <u>DAILY</u>
ANNUAL INTEREST RATE? <u>7.50</u>
WHAT IS PRESENT BALANCE? <u>1253.88</u>
FOR ACCOUNT # 4
WHAT BANK? <u>TOWN THRIFT ASSOCIATION</u>
ACCOUNT NUMBER? <u>00-000-1234/1</u>
DOES INTEREST ACCRUE DAILY, MONTHLY, OR QUARTERLY? <u>MONTHLY</u>
ANNUAL INTEREST RATE? <u>7.55</u>
WHAT IS PRESENT BALANCE? <u>1530.05</u>
FOR ACCOUNT #5
WHAT BANK? <u>CREDIT UNION</u>
ACCOUNT NUMBER? <u>20352/0</u>
DOES INTEREST ACCRUE DAILY, MONTHLY, OR QUARTERLY? <u>QUARTERLY</u>
ANNUAL INTEREST RATE? <u>8.25</u>
WHAT IS PRESENT BALANCE? <u>2556.80</u>

TYPE: '1' TO INITIATE THE RECORDS
         '2' TO UPDATE THE RECORDS
         '3' TO PRINT THE RECORDS
         '4' TO END.

? <u>4</u>

WHAT DRIVE AND SECTOR (DSSS)? <u>1100</u>
RECORDS STORED.
READY
#

DO YOU WANT TO READ FROM DISK? <u>YES</u>
WHAT DRIVE AND SECTOR (DSSS)? <u>1100</u>
TODAY'S DATE (DD/MM/YY)? <u>23/10/84</u>

       SAVINGS ACCOUNT RECORDS

TYPE: '1' TO INITIATE THE RECORDS
         '2' TO UPDATE THE RECORDS
         '3' TO PRINT THE RECORDS
         '4' TO END.
? <u>2</u>
BANK AND ACCOUNT NR: FIRST LOCAL BANQUE - 00-00000-01234
PRESENT BALANCE: $102.50
DEPOSITS AND ACCRUALS? <u>24.50</u>

WITHDRAWALS? <u>0</u>

BANK AND ACCOUNT NR: THIRD COUNTY BANK - 00-000-0246810-0
PRESENT BALANCE: $483.21
DEPOSITS AND ACCRUALS? <u>66.79</u>

WITHDRAWALS? <u>50</u>

BANK AND ACCOUNT NR: LOCAL S & L - 0-012-00045
PRESENT BALANCE: $1253.88
DEPOSITS AND ACCRUALS? <u>93.50</u>

WITHDRAWALS? <u>200</u>

BANK AND ACCOUNT NR: TOWN THRIFT ASSOCIATION - 00-000-1234/1
PRESENT BALANCE: $1530.05
DEPOSITS AND ACCRUALS? <u>170.20</u>

WITHDRAWALS? <u>50</u>

BANK AND ACCOUNT NR: CREDIT UNION - 20352/0
PRESENT BALANCE: $2556.80
DEPOSITS AND ACCRUALS? <u>250.10</u>

WITHDRAWALS? <u>0</u>

WHAT PORT FOR OUTPUT OF INTEREST ESTIMATE? <u>3</u>

TYPE: '1' TO INITIATE THE RECORDS
         '2' TO UPDATE THE RECORDS
         '3' TO PRINT THE RECORDS
         '4' TO END.

```
? 3
WHAT OUTPUT PORT DO YOU WISH TO USE? 3

TYPE:       '1' TO INITIATE THE RECORDS
            '2' TO UPDATE THE RECORDS
            '3' TO PRINT THE RECORDS
            '4' TO END.
? 4
WHAT DRIVE AND SECTOR (DSSS) ? 1100
RECORDS STORED.

READY
#
```

SAMPLE OUTPUT - INTEREST ESTIMATE

INTEREST ESTIMATE
FOLLOWING IS AN ESTIMATE OF THE INTEREST TO BE ACCRUED
FOR THE REMAINDER OF THE YEAR.

BANK	ACCOUNT	INTEREST
FIRST LOCAL BANQUE	00-00000-01234	1.87
THIRD COUNTY BANK	00-000-0246810-0	4.87
LOCAL S & L	0-012-00045	16.26
TOWN THRIFT ASSOCIATION	00-000-1234/1	20.76
CREDIT UNION	20352/0	57.89

TOTAL		$ 101.67
		==========

SAMPLE OUTPUT - PRINT THE RECORD

SAVINGS ACCOUNTS

BANK	ACCOUNT NUMBER	BALANCE
FIRST LOCAL BANQUE	00-00000-01234	$ 127.00
THIRD COUNTY BANK	00-000-0246810-0	500.00
LOCAL S & L	0-012-00045	1147.38
TOWN THRIFT ASSOCIATION	00-000-1234/1	1650.25
CREDIT UNION	20352/0	2806.90

TOTAL		$ 6231.53
		==========

AS OF 23/10/84

```
0010 REM ************************************
0020 REM *          SAVINGS ACCOUNTS        *
0030 REM ************************************
0040 REM ********* VERSION 10 *********
0050 LINE= 0
0060 DIGITS= 0
0100 REM ************ START ************
0110 INPUT "Do you want to read from disk",Z$
0120 IF LEFT$(Z$,1)="Y" THEN 4000
0130 PRINT
0140 INPUT "How many accounts",N
0150 DIM A$(3,N),R(N),B(N)
0160 PRINT
0170 INPUT "Today's date (DD/MM/YY)",D$
0180 GOSUB 4200
0190 PRINT
0200 PRINT TAB(10);"SAVINGS ACCOUNT RECORDS"
0210 PRINT
0220 PRINT "Type:      '1' to INITIATE the records"
0230 PRINT "           '2' to UPDATE the records"
0240 PRINT "           '3' to PRINT the records"
0250 PRINT "           '4' to END."
0260 INPUT Z
0270 IF Z<2 THEN 1000
0280 IF Z<3 THEN 2000
0290 IF Z<4 THEN 3000
0300 PRINT
0310 INPUT "What Drive and Sector (DSSS)",S
0320 OPEN #10,S
0330 PRINT #10,N;D$
0340 FOR X=1 TO N
0350 PRINT #10,A$(1,X);A$(2,X);A$(3,X);R(X);B(X)
0360 NEXT X
0370 CLOSE #10
0380 PRINT "Records Stored."
0390 END
1000 REM ****** INITIATE DATA BASE ******
1010 PRINT
1020 FOR X=1 TO N
1030 PRINT "For account #";X
1040 INPUT "What bank",A$(1,X)
1050 INPUT "Account number",A$(2,X)
1060 INPUT "Does interest accrue Daily, Monthly, or Quarterly",A$(3,X)
1070 IF LEFT$(A$(3,X),1)="Q" THEN 1120
1080 IF LEFT$(A$(3,X),1)="M" THEN 1120
1090 IF LEFT$(A$(3,X),1)="D" THEN 1120
1100 PRINT "Sorry, I don't understand '";A$(3,X);"'. Try again."
1110 GOTO 1060
1120 INPUT "Annual interest rate",R(X)
1130 INPUT "What is present balance",B(X)
1140 NEXT X
1150 GOTO 210
2000 REM ****** UPDATE   ACCOUNTS ******
2010  E=0: DIGITS=2
```

```
2020 FOR X=1 TO N
2030 PRINT "Bank and Account Nr: ";A$(1,X);" - ";A$(2,X)
2040 PRINT "Present balance: $";B(X)
2050 INPUT "Deposits and accruals",D4
2060 PRINT
2070  B(X)=B(X)+D4
2080 INPUT "Withdrawals",D5
2090 PRINT
2100  B(X)=B(X)-D5
2110 NEXT X
2120 INPUT "What port for output of interest estimate",P
2130 PRINT #P,TAB(10);"INTEREST ESTIMATE"
2140 PRINT #P,"Following is an estimate of the interest to be accrued"
2150 PRINT #P,"for the remainder of the year."
2160 PRINT #P
2170 PRINT #P,"BANK";TAB(30);"ACCOUNT";TAB(60);"INTEREST"
2180 PRINT #P
2190 FOR X=1 TO N
2200 IF LEFT$(A$(3,X),1)="D" THEN GOSUB 5000
2210 IF LEFT$(A$(3,X),1)="M" THEN GOSUB 5100
2220 IF LEFT$(A$(3,X),1)="Q" THEN GOSUB 5200
2230 PRINT #P,A$(1,X);TAB(29);A$(2,X);
2240 PRINT #P,TAB(70-LEN(STR$(E1)));E1
2250  E=E+E1
2260 NEXT X
2270 PRINT #P,TAB(60);"-----------"
2280 PRINT #P,"TOTAL";TAB(68-LEN(STR$(E)));"$ ";E
2290 PRINT #P,TAB(60);"==========="
2300 PRINT #P
2310 DIGITS= 0
2320 GOTO 210
3000 REM ****** PRINT THE RECORD ******
3010 INPUT "What output port do you wish to use",P
3020 PRINT #P
3030 PRINT #P
3040 PRINT #P,TAB(30);"SAVINGS ACCOUNTS"
3050 PRINT #P
3060 PRINT #P,TAB(5);"BANK";
3070 PRINT #P,TAB(33);"ACCOUNT NUMBER";
3080 PRINT #P,TAB(62);"BALANCE"
3090 DIGITS= 2
3100 PRINT #P
3110 PRINT #P,A$(1,1);
3120 PRINT #P,TAB(34);A$(2,1);
3130 PRINT #P,TAB(68-LEN(STR$(B(1))));"$ ";B(1)
3140  T1=B(1)
3150 FOR X=2 TO N
3160 PRINT #P
3170 PRINT #P,A$(1,X);
3180 PRINT #P,TAB(34);A$(2,X);
3190 PRINT #P,TAB(70-LEN(STR$(B(X))));B(X)
3200  T1=T1+B(X)
3210 NEXT X
3220 PRINT #P,TAB(60);"-----------"
```

211

```
3230 PRINT #P,"TOTAL";
3240 PRINT #P,TAB(68-LEN(STR$(T1)));"$ ";T1
3250 PRINT #P,TAB(60);"=========="
3260 PRINT #P,"As of ";D$
3270 PRINT #P,CHR$(12)
3280 GOTO 210
4000 REM ******* READ DISK DATA ********
4010 INPUT "What Drive and Sector (DSSS)",S
4020 OPEN #10,S
4030 READ #10,N,D$\4100
4040 DIM A$(4,N),R(N),B(N)
4050 FOR X=1 TO N
4060 READ #10,A$(1,X),A$(2,X),A$(3,X),R(X),B(X)\4100
4070 NEXT X
4080 CLOSE #10
4090 GOTO 170
4100 PRINT "OOPS!   Got the wrong disk - no data."
4110 PRINT
4120 PRINT "Let's try again."
4130 END
4200 REM ****** CONVERT THE DATE ******
4210 PRINT
4220  D=0
4230 READ D1,D2,D3
4240 IF VAL(MID$(D$,4,2))=D1 THEN 4270
4250  D=D+D2
4260 GOTO 4230
4270  D=365-D
4280  D=D-(VAL(LEFT$(D$,2)))
4290  M=12-D1
4300  Q=D3
4310 RESTORE
4320 RETURN
4400 DATA 1,31,4,2,28,4,3,31,3,4,30,3,5,31,3,6,30,2
4410 DATA 7,31,2,8,31,2,9,30,1,10,31,1,11,30,1,12,31,0
5000 REM *** CALCULATE DAILY INTEREST ***
5010  E1=B(X)*R(X)*D/36500
5020 RETURN
5100 REM ** CALCULATE MONTHLY INTEREST **
5110  E1=B(X)*R(X)*M/1200
5120 RETURN
5200 REM * CALCULATE QUARTERLY INTEREST *
5210  E1=B(X)*R(X)*Q/400
5220 RETURN
```

25
RETIREMENT FUND

What are your investment goals? Do you want to establish
a personal retirement fund? How about a college tuition
fund for the children? All investment programs need aiming
points. When you decide what your program should do for
you, you're well on the way to success. Your computer can
help provide a roadmap to your financial destination. Tell
Retirement Fund where your investment program should take
you, and the program will calculate the monthly savings
needed. Although the program is intended primarily as a
savings guide, you can use it with any investment vehicle.

BACKGROUND

The same mathematics that provided answers about loan payments will help us plot our savings plan. We'll use the
loan-repayment version to calculate what we'll need, and an
annuity-accumulation version to determine the periodic
investments.

Our savings goals are stated in terms of the monthly
payment we'd like to get. We can elect a fixed monthly
payment for a certain number of months, or for an indefinite period. If we opt for the indefinite payments, we're
telling the routine that we'd like to amass a sum such that
the monthly interest payments equal the desired receipts.
That's easy. Since the payment (A) equals the monthly
interest rate (I1) times the principal value (V), we'll
solve the equation for principal:

$$V = \frac{A}{I1}$$

If we want a certain payment for a fixed number of months,
the return will include some interest and some principal.
Our earlier formula for loan repayment is applicable:

$$V = A * \frac{1 - (1 + I1)^{-M}}{I1}$$

213

where M is the number of monthly payments desired.

The accumulation calculation is known in accounting circles as the "future value of an annuity." We're using a "working-backward" technique again. First, we tell the program what we want so it can compute the lump sum needed to satisfy that goal. Then, we tell it how long we want to pay into the fund to build that lump sum so it can calculate the amount of the payment. The basic future-value equation is:

$$V = P1 * \frac{(1 + I1)^{N-1}}{I1}$$

where P1 is the monthly payment, and N is the number of months we're willing to make payments. In the routine, we've used a little algebra to restructure the equation for P1 instead of V.

OPERATING NOTES

The sample run illustrates two annuity calculations. First, we ask for a fixed-period return to be paid us for 20 years. We are willing to pay into the fund for 30 years. The prompt messages are fairly clear, and there are no special reasons to cross your fingers when making keyboard entries.

Our second example uses the same monthly-payment return, but asks for an indefinite series of checks. The 30-year funding term and expected rate of interest hold constant. One nice feature in managing your savings plan-- and having the program in your personal computer--is the flexibility you have to change when interest rates and your needs vary. You could recompute your plan parameters each year to ensure meeting your financial goals. (And, you won't pay management fees or commissions to yourself!)

PROGRAMMING NOTES

You can just about keypunch Retirement Plan on a lunch hour. If you ignore the REMarks, there are fewer than 50 lines of code. All of the flow footwork is centered around the arithmetic segment, so debugging will normally be a trial run.

Lines 100 through 290 handle all of the operator input. The messages that prompt responses are a little wordy, so you may wish to simplify them when you keypunch. The operator answer to the fixed/indefinite question is used twice. Line 190 checks the answer to skip a question on the number of payments to be received. Later, the choice is used again in line 290 to route program progress to the appropriate calculation of savings needed. There is no error trap for Z$. Any response except one that starts with the letter "I" will be read as a fixed-period option. Program-run time is so short that an error trap probably isn't worth the time needed to keypunch it.

All of the calculations are housed in lines 300 to 410. The "need" equations depend on the type of payout wanted. Once the savings sum is certain, however, only one formula is used. Program output isn't long enough to justify a hard-copy report (unless you work with a printing terminal), so no provision is included for one. Change the output messages to suit yourself.

SAMPLE RUN – RETIREMENT FUND

ANNUITY PLAN

WHEN PAYMENTS START, HOW MUCH DO YOU WANT TO BE PAID MONTHLY? 1000

SHOULD THE PAYMENTS BE FOR A FIXED PERIOD, OR INDEFINITE? FIXED

HOW MANY MONTHLY PAYMENTS DO YOU WISH TO RECEIVE? 240

WHAT INTEREST RATE (ANNUAL PER CENT) DO YOU EXPECT
TO EARN ON YOUR SAVINGS? 8.75

HOW MANY MONTHLY PAYMENTS WILL BE MADE BEFORE RECEIPTS START? 360

TO RECEIVE A MONTHLY PAYMENT OF $1000.00 PER MONTH FOR 240 MONTHS,
YOU MUST SAVE $65.10 PER MONTH FOR THE 360 MONTHS PRECEDING THE
FIRST PAYMENT TO BE RECEIVED, ASSUMING YOUR SAVINGS EARN A STEADY
8.75 % INTEREST RATE.

ANOTHER CALCULATION? YUP

ANNUITY PLAN

WHEN PAYMENTS START, HOW MUCH DO YOU WANT TO BE PAID MONTHLY? 1000

SHOULD THE PAYMENTS BE FOR A FIXED PERIOD, OR INDEFINITE? INDEFINITE

WHAT INTEREST RATE (ANNUAL PER CENT) DO YOU EXPECT
TO EARN ON YOUR SAVINGS? 8.75

HOW MANY MONTHLY PAYMENTS WILL BE MADE BEFORE RECEIPTS START? 360

TO RECEIVE A MONTHLY PAYMENT OF $1000.00 INDEFINITELY,
YOU MUST SAVE $78.90 PER MONTH FOR THE 360 MONTHS PRECEDING THE
FIRST PAYMENT TO BE RECEIVED, ASSUMING YOUR SAVINGS EARN A STEADY
8.75 % INTEREST RATE.

ANOTHER CALCULATION? NO THANKS

216

```
0010 REM ********************************
0020 REM *         RETIREMENT PLAN        *
0030 REM ********************************
0040 REM ********* VERSION 20 *********
0050  Z=0
0060 LINE= 0
0100 REM ********* PAYOUT DATA *********
0110 PRINT TAB(34);"ANNUITY PLAN"
0120 PRINT
0130 PRINT "When payments start, how much do you want to be paid monthly";
0140 INPUT A
0150 PRINT
0160 PRINT "Should the payments be for a FIXED PERIOD, or INDEFINITE";
0170 INPUT Z$
0180 PRINT
0190 IF LEFT$(Z$,1)="I" THEN 220
0200 INPUT "How many monthly payments do you wish to receive",M
0210 PRINT
0220 PRINT "What interest rate (annual per cent) do you expect ";
0230 INPUT "to earn on your savings",I
0240 PRINT
0250 PRINT "How many monthly payments will be made before receipts start";
0260 INPUT N
0270 PRINT
0280  I1=I/1200
0290 IF LEFT$(Z$,1)="I" THEN 340
0300 REM ***** FIXED PERIOD PAYOUT ******
0310 REM *** Calculate Savings Needed ***
0320  V=A*(1-(1+I1)↑(-M))/I1
0330 GOTO 400
0340 REM ****** INDEFINITE PAYOUT *******
0350 REM *** Calculate Savings Needed ***
0360  V=A/I1
0370 GOTO 400
0400 REM ******* ANNUITY PAYMENT ********
0410  P1=V*(I1/((1+I1)↑(N)-1))
0420 PRINT
0500 REM ****** PRINT THE RESULTS *******
0510 DIGITS= 2
0520 PRINT
0530 PRINT "To receive a monthly payment of $";A;
0540 IF LEFT$(Z$,1)="I" THEN 580
0550 DIGITS= 0
0560 PRINT "per month for ";M;"months,"
0570 GOTO 590
0580 PRINT "indefinitely,"
0590 DIGITS= 2
0600 PRINT "You must save $";P1;"per month for the ";
0610 DIGITS= 0
0620 PRINT N;"months preceding the"
0630 PRINT "first payment to be received, ";
0640 PRINT "assuming your savings earn a steady "
0650 PRINT I;"% interest rate."
0660 PRINT
```

217

```
0670 PRINT
0680 INPUT "Another calculation",Z$
0690 IF LEFT$(Z$,1)="Y" THEN 110
0700 END
```

218

26
BOND INVESTMENT ANALYSIS

If savings accounts are too tame for you, bond investing may be your cup of tea. With bonds, you can choose your interest rate and corresponding risk within fairly moderate limits. The federal government, local governments (municipalities), and corporations issue bonds. Bonds are notes on which the issuer promises to pay a fixed annual rate of interest during the life of the bond, and at maturity to pay back the principal or par value to the holder. Corporate and municipal bonds are frequently sold on the financial market. Municipals usually carry a lower rate of interest than corporation paper, but the municipal interest is usually exempt from federal income taxes. Many respected financial analysts rate the security of corporate and municipal bonds. Your securities broker can explain the ratings and what they imply.

Although the interest rate is fixed, you can earn more or less than the guaranteed amount on a bond investment. Bond prices fluctuate (usually inversely) as the money market or commercial loan-interest rates vary. When interest rates go up, bond prices go down. Generally, the rates move to make a bond investment compare with a loan investment. (If you buy a 6-percent bond at a healthy discount, you will earn more than 6 percent on your investment.) In a roller-coaster market, you can make short-term gains by buying bonds when the interest rate is high and selling when interest rates bottom out. The safety factor is that a bond will bring its par value at maturity. The usual par value is $1,000.00. No matter what you pay for a bond, you'll get the par value at maturity. You will also get some interest along the way.

Bond pricing isn't quite as cut and dried as the interest-rate explanation might indicate. The security rating of a bond, recent corporate performance, and even the phases of the moon seem to affect bond prices. A bond will fluctuate more widely when it is young than when it nears maturity. All-in-all, you can have some of the fun

219

of investing and watching the financial quotations without a lot of risk when you dip into the bond market.

Our Bond Investment Analysis program is designed to help you investigate these golden pieces of paper. This routine will consider various factors and compute a rate of return for the bond. We will assume that the investment is for interest, and ignore any gain or loss on par value at maturity. (If you buy a $1,000 bond for $950, you'll still get $1,000 for it at maturity.) We are looking at the annual return only.

When you get this gem keypunched, you'll have fun trying it out. Look up the market quotations in your daily paper, and try some of the bond calculations listed. A typical quote might look like this:

ONM CORP 7s 99 at 97 19-32

This shorthand notation tells us that the bond is issued by the ONM Corporation, with a guaranteed interest rate of 7 percent (lower-case "s" is used instead of a percent sign), and will mature in the year 1999 (as represented by the last two digits of the year). Bond prices are quoted in percentages of par value, so this bond is selling for 97 and 19/32 percent of par (usually $1,000.00). In dollars and cents, the bond price would be $975.94. (I know our currency doesn't divide evenly by 32, but that is the fraction base used.)

BACKGROUND

Bond Investment Analysis doesn't use any fancy mathematics. We'll calculate the real cost of the bond by computing the price and adding the broker's commission:

Cost = (Par * Quoted Percent) + Commission

To get the actual yield (in money), we'll multiply the par value by the stated interest rate:

Yield = Par * Interest Rate

The return on investment (ROI) is the yield divided by the actual cost:

ROI = Yield/Cost

To bring the return into common terms, we multiply by one hundred to achieve a percentage.

OPERATING NOTES

Two samples are included. In the first, we enter the data on a bond for which the price is quoted in fractional notation. As a user, you need only follow the prompt messages. Enter any set of descriptors you wish for the bond--this will put a title on your output report. There is a provision to enter the par value--just in case you're investigating a nonstandard bond. Typing a "D" or "F" will tell the program whether the quote is in decimals or fractions. If you are dealing with a fractional quote, the program assumes the standard fraction base of 32, so you need enter only the numerator. The broker's commission is entered in dollars (and cents, if needed), and the stated yield is entered in percent. The routine has provision to send the output to various ports for hard-copy reports or video displays. The rest is automatic.

The second example uses decimal pricing to illustrate the slightly different input sequence. At the conclusion of the display, the program asks if you wish to analyze another bond to provide a continuous-operation feature.

PROGRAMMING NOTES

The 55 lines of BASIC code should make this another lunch-hour-special keypunch task. After lines 10 through 90 take care of the heading chore, operator input starts. The GOTO in line 150 is an error trap to insure that only a "D" or "F" gets by the input sequence. Two different price input messages are employed to straighten out the decimal/fraction entry procedure.

All of the calculations are performed in lines 270 through 320. The divide-by-100 parts of the equations convert percentages to decimal fractions.

Display is handled in lines 330 to 520. The TAB calculation in line 370 centers the bond description on an 80-column printer. Change the "80" in the line if necessary to match your system's output device. The TAB calculations in lines 390, 410, 440, 470, and 500 provide right-justification for the numerics to line up the decimal points in accounting format.

Line 520 is a form-feed command to advance the printer paper to the next perforation. Lines 530 and 540 provide our wraparound continuous-operation feature.

The worst part of debugging this routine will probably be checking the correct number of parentheses in the TAB calculations. Although it's frustrating, your BASIC will help here by giving you an error message if you've misplaced a keystroke.

```
READY
# RUN


          BOND INVESTMENT ANALYSIS

BOND DESCRIPTION? ONM CORP
FACE/PAR AMOUNT ($)? 1000
IS PRICE QUOTED IN 'D'ECIMAL OR 'F'RACTIONS? FRACTIONS
ENTER CURRENT PRICE AS INTEGER <COMMA> FRACTION, WHERE
THE FRACTION IS THE NUMBER OF 32NDS? 91,17

BROKER'S COMMISSION (PER BOND)? 12

STATED YIELD OF BOND? 8.7

WHAT OUTPUT PORT? 3
```

           BOND INVESTMENT ANALYSIS

                  ONM CORP

PAR VALUE	$ 1000.00	
QUOTED	91.53 %	
COST (WITH COMMISSION)		$ 927.31
ANNUAL INTEREST PAYMENT		$ 87.00
ACTUAL RETURN ON INVESTMENT		9.38%
		=========

ANOTHER BOND? <u>YES</u>

                    BOND INVESTMENT ANALYSIS

BOND DESCRIPTION? <u>MNOP CORP - 7S 98</u>
FACE/PAR AMOUNT ($)? <u>1000</u>
IS PRICE QUOTED IN 'D'ECIMAL OR 'F'RACTIONS? <u>D</u>
CURRENT PRICE (%)? <u>98.6</u>

BROKER'S COMMISSION (PER BOND)? <u>11</u>

STATED YIELD OF BOND? <u>7</u>

WHAT OUTPUT PORT? <u>3</u>

                    BOND INVESTMENT ANALYSIS

                       MNOP CORP - 7S 98

PAR VALUE $ 1000.00

QUOTED   98.60 %

COST (WITH COMMISSION) $ 997.00

ANNUAL INTEREST PAYMENT $ 70.00

ACTUAL RETURN ON INVESTMENT   7.02%
                                                   =========

```
0010 REM **********************************
0020 REM *    BOND INVESTMENT ANALYSIS    *
0030 REM **********************************
0040 REM ********** VERSION 10 **********
0050 LINE= 0
0060 DIGITS= 2
0070 PRINT :PRINT:PRINT
0080 PRINT TAB(12);"BOND INVESTMENT ANALYSIS"
0090 PRINT
0100 INPUT "Bond Description",B$
0110 INPUT "Face/Par amount ($)",B(1)
0120 INPUT "Is price quoted in 'D'ecimal or 'F'ractions",Z$
0130 IF LEFT$(Z$,1)="D" THEN 160
0140 IF LEFT$(Z$,1)="F" THEN 190
0150 GOTO 120
0160 INPUT "Current price (%)",B(2)
0170 PRINT
0180 GOTO 230
0190 PRINT "Enter current price as INTEGER <comma> FRACTION, where"
0200 INPUT "the fraction is the number of 32nds",I,F
0210   B(2)=I+F/32
0220 PRINT
0230 INPUT "Broker's commission (per bond)",B(3)
0240 PRINT
0250 INPUT "Stated yield of bond",B(4)
0260 PRINT
0270 REM ******** COST OF BOND ********
0280   C=(B(1)*B(2)/100)+B(3)
0290 REM ******** ACTUAL YIELD ********
0300   Y=B(1)*B(4)/100
0310 REM ***** RETURN ON INVESTMENT *****
0320   R=Y*100/C
0330 INPUT "What output port",P
0340 PRINT #P:PRINT#P:PRINT#P
0350 PRINT #P,TAB(27);"BOND INVESTMENT ANALYSIS"
0360 PRINT #P:PRINT#P
0370 PRINT #P,TAB((80-LEN(B$))/2);B$
0380 PRINT #P
0390 PRINT #P,"Par value";TAB(40-LEN(STR$(B(1))));"$ ";B(1)
0400 PRINT #P
0410 PRINT #P,"Quoted";TAB(42-LEN(STR$(B(2))));B(2);"%"
0420 PRINT #P
0430 PRINT #P,"Cost (with commission)";
0440 PRINT #P,TAB(70-LEN(STR$(C)));"$ ";C
0450 PRINT #P
0460 PRINT #P,"Annual interest payment";
0470 PRINT #P,TAB(70-LEN(STR$(Y)));"$ ";Y
0480 PRINT #P
0490 PRINT #P,"ACTUAL RETURN ON INVESTMENT";
0500 PRINT #P,TAB(72-LEN(STR$(R)));R;"%"
0510 PRINT #P,TAB(62);"=========="
0520 PRINT #P,CHR$(12)
0530 INPUT "Another bond",Z$
0540 IF LEFT$(Z$,1)="Y" THEN 70
0550 END
```

27
RETURN ON INVESTMENT

No matter what investment you consider, the potential
return on your risk is an important factor. The interest
rate quoted for savings accounts is a fair assessment of
return on investment (ROI). Many of the opportunities
available, however, aren't accompanied by a nice percentage
figure. Return on Investment will help you boil things
down to a percentage number.

This routine is really two short programs under one
heading. The two popular methods of computing investment
return are the operator's method and the investor's method.
Each is useful in a different situation. With both at your
command, you're ready for anything.

The operator's method is a tool of industry. It is
employed when the return is expected to vary from year to
year. Only the earnings from the investment are considered
in arriving at the return percentage. Business owners
would use this method to evaluate the wisdom of installing
a new machine or process. You will find it helpful when a
real estate or other limited-partnership chance comes your
way. The method is applicable when your annual return in
dollars will vary, and when your investment will be re-
funded in a separate transaction. In a real estate
partnership, for example, your annual return will vary with
rental receipts and expenses. At the end of a predetermined time, the local market for real property will
determine additional gain or loss. When you are comparing
several investments in the same geographical area, the annual ROI is your best evaluation tool. All properties will
gain or lose by a comparable amount at the end of the
venture.

The investor's method is used by accountants and
financial advisors. It's most appropriate for situations
in which your annual return is uniform from year to year,
and when your annual return includes repayment of your
original investment. A mortgage investment is an example
of this situation. (Although your interest rate would be
an easier way of evaluating the prospect.) Business people

225

might use the underline(investor's) underline(method) in examining a prospective purchase of a machine or process that is used up in a manufacturing line. You'd have to recover your original payments plus profits to make the purchase sensible. (If the payout results in a negative ROI, the calculation routine will cause a BASIC error. That's all right, since few of us wish to invest in a losing proposition.)

BACKGROUND

The mathematics should be familiar to you. For the investor's method, we resurrect the formula to calculate the rate of compound interest. It's basically the same equation used in Real Estate Loan Analysis. We'll use original investment instead of principal amount of the loan, annual cash inflow instead of monthly payment, and years of investment instead of years of loan. The calculation and approximation solution are the same, and the answer is the percent return on investment.

For the operator's method, the arithmetic is even simpler. We'll sum the various annual returns, divide by the number of years to get an average annual return, and divide the average return by the original investment to get the ROI figure. There's no magic in the calculations (although your computer will seem to perform supernaturally fast), just basic accounting.

OPERATING NOTES

The sample run illustrates one exercise of each method. The prompts are self-explanatory, and operator responses are underlined. The key difference between the two methods is the scope of the annual cash flow. In the investor's method, the annual cash inflow includes a payback of the original investment. With the operator's method, the original cost is not considered in the yearly figure. (You can include it if you want to and still have a valid comparison figure, provided that you report the same type numbers for all candidates.) No provision is made for a hard-copy report of the output, since the output is a one-liner, but you could easily alter the program to provide a formal analysis statement. Just repeat the input values in a semiformal statement. (You'll dazzle the investment sales representatives when they call. You may also be able to get some additional information on the business opportunities offered as input data for your computer.)

PROGRAMMING NOTES

If your BASIC editor is working, this will be a coffee-break keypunch task. Even if you punch each character

226

anew, you should have Return On Investment up and running in a couple of coffee breaks.

After our normal heading steps, the user-input statements take up lines 100 to 150. There's no error trap for the Z$ input. You could probably omit line 150 without any serious mishap. In that case, any response to the method question other than one starting with the letter "O" will result in an investor's analysis.

Lines 1000 through 1150 take the investor's method through its paces. The code is so similar to the Real Estate Loan Analysis program that it doesn't deserve additional discussion.

Lines 2000 through 2140 contain the operator's method. The calculation of average annual return is handled within the FOR...NEXT loop of lines 2060 to 2110. Each annual cash flow is divided by the number of payments to acquire the average. The computation of ROI is performed in line 2120. Line 2140 sends the program back to the output step (line 1140) and program end.

If you elect to provide a formalized output report, you'll probably want to write separate formats for each method. The reports won't take much code, and if you need to use your computer as an intimidation tool, the extra keypunch time will be well spent. In any case, Return On Investment will be a valuable addition to your bag of financial analysis tricks.

SAMPLE RUN - RETURN ON INVESTMENT

THIS ROUTINE CALCULATES RETURN ON INVESTMENT (ROI)
BY THE OPERATOR'S METHOD OR THE INVESTOR'S METHOD.

DO YOU WISH TO USE THE OPERATOR'S OR INVESTOR'S METHOD? INVESTOR
WHAT IS THE ORIGINAL INVESTMENT? 100000

WHAT IS THE ANNUAL CASH INFLOW? 30000

WHAT IS THE PERIOD IN YEARS OF THE INVESTMENT? 5

THE RETURN ON INVESTMENT IS 15.238 %

ANOTHER ROI PROBLEM? YES

THIS ROUTINE CALCULATES RETURN ON INVESTMENT (ROI)
BY THE OPERATOR'S METHOD OR THE INVESTOR'S METHOD.

DO YOU WISH TO USE THE OPERATOR'S OR INVESTOR'S METHOD? OPERATOR
WHAT IS THE ORIGINAL INVESTMENT? 100000

WHAT IS THE PERIOD IN YEARS OF THE INVESTMENT? 8
WHAT ARE THE EARNINGS FOR YEAR 1 ? 2100

WHAT ARE THE EARNINGS FOR YEAR 2 ? 4350

WHAT ARE THE EARNINGS FOR YEAR 3 ? 5850

WHAT ARE THE EARNINGS FOR YEAR 4 ? 7800

WHAT ARE THE EARNINGS FOR YEAR 5 ? 8930

WHAT ARE THE EARNINGS FOR YEAR 6 ? 9500

WHAT ARE THE EARNINGS FOR YEAR 7 ? 11240

WHAT ARE THE EARNINGS FOR YEAR 8 ? 8330

THE RETURN ON INVESTMENT IS 7.262 %

ANOTHER ROI PROBLEM? NO

```
0010 REM ********************************
0020 REM *      RETURN ON INVESTMENT      *
0030 REM ********************************
0040 REM ********* VERSION 10 *********
0050 DIGITS= 2
0100 PRINT "This routine calculates Return On Investment (ROI)"
0110 PRINT "by the Operator's method or the Investor's method."
0120 PRINT
0130 INPUT "Do you wish to use the Operator's or Investor's method",Z$
0140 IF LEFT$(Z$,1)="O" THEN 2000
0150 IF LEFT$(Z$,1)="I" THEN 1000
1000 REM ****** INVESTOR'S  METHOD ******
1010 INPUT "What is the original investment",V
1020 PRINT
1030 INPUT "What is the annual cash inflow",M
1040 PRINT
1050 INPUT "What is the period in years of the investment",N
1060 PRINT
1070 DIGITS= 3
1080  I1=2*(N-V/M)/(N*(N+1))
1090  V1=M*(1-(1+I1)↑(-N))/I1
1100 IF V1<0.9999999*V THEN 1200
1110 IF V1>1.0000001*V THEN 1200
1120  I=I1*100
1130 PRINT
1140 PRINT "The return on investment is ";I;"%"
1150 PRINT
1160 INPUT "Another ROI problem",Z$
1170 IF LEFT$(Z$,1)="N" THEN END
1180 DIGITS= 2
1190 GOTO 100
1200  I1=I1*V1/V
1210 GOTO 1090
2000 REM ****** OPERATOR'S  METHOD ******
2010 INPUT "What is the original investment",V
2020 PRINT
2030 INPUT "What is the period in years of the investment",N
2040 DIGITS= 0
2050  M=0
2060 FOR X=1 TO N
2070 PRINT "What are the earnings for year ";X;
2080 INPUT M1
2090  M=M+M1/N
2100 PRINT
2110 NEXT X
2120  I=(M/V)*100
2130 DIGITS= 3
2140 GOTO 1130
```

229

28
NET PRESENT VALUE

Another investment evaluation tool is the disounted cash flow, or net-present-value analysis. The technique converts all the future (estimated) cash receipts and expenditures to today's value for a comparison of return on investment against a standard. Our program will use the rate of inflation, the expected rate of return, or both to investigate the wisdom of any proposed package. The opportunity that promises "two-and-a-half times your original investment in 10 years" may be giving you a mediocre return on your investment. Net Present Value will help you with limited partnerships, machine-tool purchases, stock investments, and a host of other variable-return financial opportunities.

BACKGROUND

The program provides a combination of the operator's method and investor's method of computing return on investment. It will analyze a variable annual cash flow. It assumes that the return of your original cash is included in the annual receipts, and it has provision for further investment along the way (cash outflow, or a "negative cash flow").

A slight variation on a formula we've seen before provides the program magic. Savings Account Analysis introduced the "future-value" formula:

$$FV = PV * (1 + I)^N$$

where FV is future value, PV is present value, I is the periodic rate of compounding, and N is the number of periods. A little high-school algebra will allow us to turn the formula around and solve for present value:

$$PV = \frac{FV}{(1 + I)^N}$$

The periodic interest rate in the formula is the return on investment that you desire. You can enter the interest rate when you run the program, as well as the number of years you expect the proposition to run. As each annual cash flow figure is entered, the computer will convert the future amount to its present value. If the investment is going to be sufficiently profitable to repay your original cost with the additional return you want, you'll get a message reporting the happy news. In all cases, the program will present a tabular listing of the anticipated status of your cash each year. If the deal is not going to generate the desired income, you'll know just how far short of the mark it is.

OPERATING NOTES

The sample run demonstrates an analysis of a 10-year $1,000 investment program. Returns vary each year, and the program tells us that the overall opportunity will pay off at the end of the sixth year. An inspection of the output report reveals that the return is better than a 12-percent ROI in each year past the fifth. (Remember, though, that you'll be dealing with estimates. One of the best uses will be the refutation of sales claims. In the example, a total return of about $2,660.00 would produce a 12-percent return on investment. "More than two-and-a-half times your investment" sounds better than "12-percent ROI.")

You won't have any trouble following the input prompts to use the program. Enter the initial investment and the annual cash flow figures in dollars. For any year with a negative cash flow, type a minus sign before the dollar entry. Years are entered in units, and the rate of return in percent.

After your first output report, the program will ask if you want another. You may change output-device selections from display to printer with each report.

PROGRAMMING NOTES

Net Present Value (or Discounted Cash Flow, as the program header calls it) should be another one-evening keypunch task. The header includes two DEFine functions that we'll use to format the columns of numbers in the output report.

Lines 100 through 390 take care of the operator input and present-value calculation. The C(N) variable for annual cash flow and the V(N) variable for net present value after the annual cash flow are DIMensioned in line 190, after the entry of number of years. The total investment package is treated as a negative (cash outflow) quantity, with the burden on annual cash inflow present value to switch the profit picture to positive. Line 260 sets the initial investment to a negative cash flow to start the whole thing. Line 270 converts the percentage return desired to a decimal fraction. The FOR...NEXT loop of lines 280 through 390 guides the real work for the program.

The present-value computation is performed by line 310, and the result is stuffed in the appropriate matrix pigeonhole in line 330--after we round out the fractions of pennies in line 320. Lines 340 through 380 provide our input terminal message of profitability. F is used as a flag to suppress the printing after the routine once determines the opportunity to be viable. (Actually, if the investment proves to be profitable in 1 year and then becomes unprofitable, the flag will be reset. This will allow the message to be printed a second time when the tide turns again to profit.) Both lines 340 and 370 contain multiple statements, separated by a colon. If your BASIC won't digest multiple statements, add the following:

```
0345   IF V<0   GOTO 380
0375   F = 1
```

(You could, of course, leave out the flags and message to cut down your keypunch time. You'll know the answer to the profitability question as soon as the report is ready.) Lines 400 through 720 contain the report-printing commands. Variable T is set to zero in line 400 to allow the print routine to total the annual receipts.

Since we've specified the return we wish on our investment, a net present value of zero indicated that we've achieved the goal. All of the present values of the cash flows are balanced, and our initial investment has been returned with the desired increase. Lines 680 to 710 of the output statement give us another word report. If V is equal to or greater than zero, line 700 reports the proposition as valid. Otherwise, line 710 tells us that our investment opportunity is not what we hope.

Lines 730 and 740 provide the program steering to get a repeat copy of our analysis. With a printing terminal, you may not need extra copies and can delete these steps to streamline the keypunching.

DISCOUNTED CASH FLOW ANALYSIS

THIS PROGRAM WILL CALCULATE THE NET PRESENT VALUE
OF INVESTMENT CASH FLOW AND DETERMINE THE MERIT OF
THE INVESTMENT.

WHAT IS THE INITIAL INVESTMENT? 1000

HOW MANY YEARS DO YOU WISH TO ANALYZE? 10

WHAT RATE OF RETURN (ANNUAL PERCENT) IS DESIRED? 12

ENTER THE EXPECTED CASH FLOW FOR EACH YEAR, WITH THE
NET CASH IN POSITIVE, AND THE NET CASH OUT NEGATIVE (-).

WHAT IS CASH FLOW FOR YEAR 1 ? 100

WHAT IS CASH FLOW FOR YEAR 2 ? 200

WHAT IS CASH FLOW FOR YEAR 3 ? 250

WHAT IS CASH FLOW FOR YEAR 4 ? 300

WHAT IS CASH FLOW FOR YEAR 5 ? 376

WHAT IS CASH FLOW FOR YEAR 6 ? 450

OVERALL INVESTMENT PROFITABLE IN YEAR 6

WHAT IS CASH FLOW FOR YEAR 7 ? 400

WHAT IS CASH FLOW FOR YEAR 8 ? 500

WHAT IS CASH FLOW FOR YEAR 9 ? 450

WHAT IS CASH FLOW FOR YEAR 10 ? 350

WHAT OUTPUT PORT DO YOU WISH TO USE? 2
ANOTHER COPY? NO

SAMPLE OUTPUT

DISCOUNTED CASH FLOW ANALYSIS

YEAR	CASH FLOW	NET PRESENT VALUE
1	100.00	-910.71
2	200.00	-751.27
3	250.00	-573.33
4	300.00	-382.67
5	376.00	-169.32
6	450.00	58.66
7	400.00	239.60
8	500.00	441.54
9	450.00	603.81
10	350.00	716.50
TOTALS	3376.00	716.50

WITH A DESIRED YIELD OF 12.00 % AND AN INVESTMENT OF $1000.00
THE PROPOSED OPPORTUNITY IS PROFITABLE.

```
0010 REM ****************************
0020 REM *      DISCOUNTED CASH FLOW      *
0030 REM ****************************
0040 REM ********* VERSION 10 *********
0050 LINE= 0
0060 DIGITS= 0
0070 DEF FNA(X)=(43-LEN(STR$(X)))
0080 DEF FNB(X)=(70-LEN(STR$(X)))
0100 PRINT TAB(10);"DISCOUNTED CASH FLOW ANALYSIS"
0110 PRINT
0120 PRINT "This program will calculate the net present value"
0130 PRINT "of investment cash flow and determine the merit of"
0140 PRINT "the investment."
0150 PRINT
0160 INPUT "What is the initial investment",C
0170 PRINT
0180 INPUT "How many years do you wish to analyze",N
0190 DIM C(N),V(N)
0200 PRINT
0210 INPUT "What rate of return (annual percent) is desired",R
0220 PRINT
0230 PRINT "Enter the expected cash flow for each year, with the"
0240 PRINT "net cash IN positive, and the net cash OUT negative (-)."
0250 PRINT
0260  V=-C
0270  R1=R/100
0280 FOR X=1 TO N
0290 PRINT "What is cash flow for year ";X;
0300 INPUT C(X)
0310  V=V+C(X)/((1+R1)↑X)
0320 IF ABS(V)<0.01 THEN V=0
0330  V(X)=V
0340 IF V<0 THEN F=0: GOTO 380
0350 IF F=1 THEN 380
0360 PRINT
0370 PRINT "Overall investment profitable in year ";X : F=1
0380 PRINT
0390 NEXT X
0400  T=0
0410 INPUT "What output port do you wish to use",P
0420 PRINT #P
0430 PRINT #P
0440 PRINT #P,TAB(25);"DISCOUNTED CASH FLOW ANALYSIS"
0450 PRINT #P
0460 PRINT #P,TAB(10);"YEAR";
0470 PRINT #P,TAB(35);"CASH FLOW";
0480 PRINT #P,TAB(57);"NET PRESENT VALUE"
0490 PRINT #P
0500 FOR X=1 TO N
0510 PRINT #P,TAB(13-LEN(STR$(X)));X;
0520 DIGITS= 2
0530 PRINT #P,TAB(FNA(C(X)));C(X);
0540 PRINT #P,TAB(FNB(V(X)));V(X)
```

```
0550 DIGITS= 0
0560 PRINT #P
0570   T=T+C(X)
0580 NEXT X
0590 PRINT #P,TAB(35);"-----------";
0600 PRINT #P,TAB(62);"-----------"
0610 DIGITS= 2
0620 PRINT #P,"TOTALS";
0630 PRINT #P,TAB(FNA(T));T;
0640 PRINT #P,TAB(FNB(V));V
0650 PRINT #P,TAB(35);"==========";
0660 PRINT #P,TAB(62);"=========="
0670 PRINT #P
0680 PRINT #P,"With a desired yield of ";R;"% and an investment of $";C
0690 PRINT #P,"the proposed opportunity is ";
0700 IF V>=0 PRINT#P,"profitable."
0710 IF V<0 PRINT#P,"NOT profitable."
0720 PRINT #P,CHR$(12)
0730 INPUT "Another copy",Z$
0740 IF LEFT$(Z$,1)="Y" THEN 400
0750 END
```

29
STOCK ANALYSIS

There are two sources of potential income return with a stock market investment. You will normally receive cash dividends while you own the stock, and when you sell you may reap a profit on the transaction. Stocks are pieces of ownership in business. When you buy a share, you become part owner of a corporation. The dividends that companies pay represent shares of corporate profits. (Other dividends are paid, of course. Some companies pay far less in dividends than profits permit in order to have money for expansion and for payment of dividends in years when profits are low.) Shares of stock are traded on various markets and "over the counter." As the condition of the economy changes, the potential for growth and profit for the various corporations changes. When people guess that a corporation will make more money in the future, they are willing to pay more for a share in that firm. The stock price rises. If a company seems to be falling on hard times, the price of the stock reflects that dismal projection. The classic advice to the stock-market investor is still, "Buy low, sell high."

Many factors should be considered in selecting a stock for investment. The next few programs in our financial-management system illustrate methods for analyzing potential purchases. In Stock Analysis, we'll look at a "snapshot" technique. The data analyzed won't investigate immediate trends, but will look at the stock performance over the past year. The program will allow us to compare a number of stocks simultaneously.

The purpose of this routine is analysis of the earning potential of a stock and warning of the probability of a price swing. Until we can add a "psychic module" to our personal computers, prediction of the future is still a guessing game. We can, however, look at past performance as an indication of stability.

The specific factors we'll investigate are price, earnings, and dividends. By comparing the current dividends paid with the present price, we derive a percentage return on investment figure. When we compare earnings with current price, we can judge how well the corporation is doing with respect to others in its industry. (Most companies in an industry segment--electronics, oils, or autos, for example--tend to have similar price/earnings ratios. If a firm varies significantly from the group's overall ratio, that variance may influence our investment decision.) We look at the price spread of a stock over the past year to achieve a figure of merit that I call "volatility." A stock with a higher volatility number may provide greater opportunity for large gains (or losses) at trading time. (Note that our volatility figure is not the same one used by stock-market analysts to describe the leverage factor of mutual funds.)

OPERATING NOTES

In the sample run of Stock Analysis, four mythical stocks are run through the routine. The input-prompt messages are fairly self-explanatory. Get the entry information for your candidates from the pages of your favorite financial newspaper, the financial pages of your favorite daily newspaper, or publications from your stockbroker. The program is not intended to be a substitute for qualified financial-investment advice; it is, however, a supplement. You are responsible for your investments, not your advisor. The Stock Analysis program will help you make intelligent decisions.

Note that all of the numbers used for input are on a per-share basis. We've also ignored the broker's commission, since that would bias all computations by a similar amount. The output table lists your candidate stocks with the analysis results. The output report could be a valuable "talking paper" to kick off a discussion with your stock brokerage representative.

PROGRAMMING NOTES

There are no new techniques used here. About an evening of keypunch and debugging should have Stock Analysis up and humming. There are a lot of words in the prompt messages, but that should help operator input. The critical statements in the input routine include the variable DIMensioning of line 160, and the FOR...NEXT loops of lines 200 to 220 and 240 to 330.

The output routine is also the calculation segment. Lines 440 through 530 take care of the report heading. The FOR...NEXT sequence from lines 540 to 650 handles the stock-data output. Line 580 calculates percent return on investment for dividends, line 600 computes price to earnings ratio, and line 620 derives our volatility figure of merit. Volatility is the price swing over the last year (calculated by subtracting the lowest price from the highest) divided by the current cost. We multiply the result

238

by 100 to provide a percentage figure and stay away from fractional answers.

All of the TAB calculations in the numerics are the familiar ones we use to line up the decimal points and provide a professional-looking report. Lines 670 and 700 allow user options for more copies of the same analysis, or another analysis. You may wish to delete the copy routine if you'll be using the program for home analysis only. Another change you might like to include is a repeat of the input data on the output report. The information is still present in the input variables, so the additional printing routines should be easy for you.

BONUS PROGRAM

A number of studies over the years have "proved" that a random selection of your stock portfolio will produce greater financial success than another stock-picking scheme. Without endorsing the random theory, I'd like to give you a bonus program to implement "dart-throwing" stock selection on your computer. The listing shown here will take you only a few minutes to keypunch. It might take a couple of hours to run, though. Depending on your computer's DIMensioning limit, you may enter hundreds of stocks. (My system will let me keypunch up to 255 at one operation.)

```
0010 REM ********************************
0020 REM *      RANDOM STOCKS PICKER      *
0030 REM ********************************
0040 REM ********* VERSION 00 *********
0050 LINE= 0
0100 PRINT TAB(12);"STOCK PICKER"
0110 PRINT
0120 INPUT "HOW MANY STOCKS DO YOU WISH TO CONSIDER",N
0130 DIM S$(N)
0140 PRINT
0150 PRINT "PLEASE ENTER THE CANDIDATES ONE-BY-ONE"
0160 FOR J=1 TO N
0170 PRINT "STOCK NUMBER ";J;
0180 INPUT S$(J)
0190 NEXT J
0200 PRINT
0210 INPUT "WHEN YOU'RE READY TO SELECT A STOCK, PRESS 'RETURN'",Z$
0220   X=INT((N*RND)+1)
0230 IF S$(X)="" THEN 220
0240 FOR J=1 TO 100
0250 NEXT J
0260 PRINT
0270 PRINT "I HAVE SELECTED ";S$(X);" FOR YOU."
0280   S$(X)=""
0290 PRINT
0300 INPUT "WOULD YOU LIKE ANOTHER SELECTION",Z$
0310 IF LEFT$(Z$,1)="Y" THEN 210
0320 END
```

239

Your computer will give you a random selection of stocks. You may limit your choice to one per program run, or ask for a list at run time. Since this is a tongue-in-cheek program, we won't devote any further discussion to it. (But your stock brokerage representative might like a copy of <u>Random Stocks Picker</u> to frame and hang on the office wall!)

SAMPLE INPUT - STOCK ANALYSIS

GIVE ME THE NAMES OF THE STOCKS YOU WISH TO ANALYZE.
I'LL ASK FOR SOME DATA ON THEM AND GIVE YOU A LISTING
THAT SHOULD HELP YOU DETERMINE WHICH ARE THE BETTER
INVESTMENTS FOR YOUR SITUATION.

HOW MANY STOCKS DO YOU WISH TO EVALUATE? 4

FIRST GIVE ME THE NAMES/IDENTIFICATIONS OF YOUR CANDIDATES.

STOCK NAME? SUPER STOCK
STOCK NAME? LITTLE COMPUTERS
STOCK NAME? BIG COMPUTERS
STOCK NAME? CLASS INVESTMENTS

FOR SUPER STOCK--

CURRENT PRICE? 100
HIGHEST PRICE IN PAST YEAR? 102
LOWEST PRICE IN PAST YEAR? 41
ANNUAL PER SHARE EARNINGS? 8
ANNUAL PER SHARE DIVIDENDS? 2.50

FOR LITTLE COMPUTERS--

CURRENT PRICE? 10
HIGHEST PRICE IN PAST YEAR? 12
LOWEST PRICE IN PAST YEAR? 9
ANNUAL PER SHARE EARNINGS? 1.75
ANNUAL PER SHARE DIVIDENDS? .50

FOR BIG COMPUTERS--

CURRENT PRICE? 104
HIGHEST PRICE IN PAST YEAR? 133
LOWEST PRICE IN PAST YEAR? 82
ANNUAL PER SHARE EARNINGS? 10
ANNUAL PER SHARE DIVIDENDS? 3.75

FOR CLASS INVESTMENTS--

CURRENT PRICE? 82
HIGHEST PRICE IN PAST YEAR? 107
LOWEST PRICE IN PAST YEAR? 82
ANNUAL PER SHARE EARNINGS? 22
ANNUAL PER SHARE DIVIDENDS? 8.10

WHAT OUTPUT PORT DO YOU WISH TO USE? <u>3</u>

ANOTHER COPY? <u>NO</u>

ANOTHER ANALYSIS? <u>NOPE</u>

READY
#

SAMPLE OUTPUT - STOCK ANALYSIS

STOCK ANALYSIS

STOCK NAME	PRICE	DIVIDENDS	% RETURN	P.E.RATIO	VOLATILITY
SUPER STOCK	100.00	2.50	2.50	12.50	61.00
LITTLE COMPUTERS	10.00	0.50	5.00	5.71	30.00
BIG COMPUTERS	104.00	3.75	3.60	10.40	49.03
CLASS INVESTMENTS	82.00	8.10	9.87	3.72	30.48

```
0010 REM **********************************
0020 REM *          STOCK ANALYSIS         *
0030 REM **********************************
0040 REM ********* VERSION 20 *********
0050 LINE= 0
0060 DIGITS= 2
0090 PRINT :PRINT:PRINT
0100 PRINT "Give me the names of the stocks you wish to analyze."
0110 PRINT "I'll ask for some data on them and give you a listing"
0120 PRINT "that should help you determine which are the better"
0130 PRINT "investments for your situation."
0140 PRINT
0150 INPUT "How many stocks do you wish to evaluate",N
0160 DIM N$(N),D(N),E(N),H(N),L(N),P(N)
0170 PRINT
0180 PRINT "First give me the names/identifications of your candidates."
0190 PRINT
0200 FOR X=1 TO N
0210 INPUT "Stock name",N$(X)
0220 NEXT X
0230 PRINT
0240 FOR X=1 TO N
0250 PRINT "For ";N$(X);"--"
0260 PRINT
0270 INPUT "Current price",P(X)
0280 INPUT "Highest price in past year",H(X)
0290 INPUT "Lowest price in past year",L(X)
0300 INPUT "Annual per share earnings",E(X)
0310 INPUT "Annual per share dividends",D(X)
0320 PRINT
0330 NEXT X
0400 REM ******* OUTPUT ROUTINE *******
0410 PRINT
0420 INPUT "What output port do you wish to use",P
0430 PRINT
0440 PRINT #P:PRINT#P:PRINT#P
0450 PRINT #P,TAB(33);"STOCK ANALYSIS"
0460 PRINT #P:PRINT#P
0470 PRINT #P,"Stock Name";
0480 PRINT #P,TAB(25);"Price";
0490 PRINT #P,TAB(35);"Dividends";
0500 PRINT #P,TAB(46);"% Return";
0510 PRINT #P,TAB(57);"P.E.Ratio";
0520 PRINT #P,TAB(68);"Volatility"
0530 PRINT #P
0540 FOR X=1 TO N
0550 PRINT #P,N$(X);
0560 PRINT #P,TAB(30-LEN(STR$(P(X))));P(X);
0570 PRINT #P,TAB(41-LEN(STR$(D(X))));D(X);
0580  R=(D(X)/P(X))*100
0590 PRINT #P,TAB(52-LEN(STR$(R)));R;
0600  E=P(X)/E(X)
0610 PRINT #P,TAB(64-LEN(STR$(E)));E;
0620  V=100*(H(X)-L(X))/P(X)
```

243

```
0630  PRINT #P,TAB(76-LEN(STR$(V)));V
0640  IF N<25 PRINT#P
0650  NEXT X
0660  PRINT #P,CHR$(12)
0670  INPUT "Another Copy",Z$
0680  IF LEFT$(Z$,1)="Y" THEN 400
0690  PRINT
0700  INPUT "Another Analysis",Z$
0710  IF LEFT$(Z$,1)="Y" THEN RUN
0720  END
```

30
TEN-DAY AVERAGE

Stock options and commodity futures may appeal to you as an investment vehicle. These highly volatile speculations provide a great deal of investor excitement, quick profits, and sudden loss. Options and futures are short-lived investments. They cover a set period of time--usually months--and are traded often. Options and futures don't pay dividends. Income (or loss) is realized at the time you sell. Because of the rapid fluctuations of these gambles, people dealing in this arena spend a lot of time watching their investments. The "10-day moving average" is a favorite tool for managing stock options. Many traders set guidelines to buy or sell when the current price reaches a preset fraction of the 10-day average. It's a moving average, because we're only interested in the most recent 10 days. Each day, the new price causes the average to move along. (Talk with your stock brokerage representative about options and commodities to get the background and ground rules for the game.)

BACKGROUND

Ten-Day Average is designed to be implemented with a disk-memory feature, but you can make do with tape-cassette storage and not lose too much operational capability. Daily use makes the disk more convenient.

You must initialize the routine with 10 day's worth of price data; then, update your investment information with a few daily keystrokes. The program stores 10 separate prices and the total of the 10 for as many stocks as you wish to track. When you add a new daily price, the program drops the oldest figure and stores the new. The new moving average is also taken from the totals on a daily basis. The mathematical manipulations are pretty simple. We do the averaging by summing all 10 entries into an eleventh memory slot. At display time, multiplying the total by one-tenth gives us the average of the 10 days. Updating

245

the average means subtracting the oldest figure from the total and adding the newest.

OPERATING NOTES

We've used four separate stock options--with commodity names--and some mythical prices for the example. The first part of the input exercise is initialization. We get to the initialize routine by declining to read disk data. Since the previous day's prices will probably be available as a listing by option, we'll enter all 10 of the prices for a stock before moving to the next stock.

With the intitial entries in, the program asks us for an output-port selection and the current date. The output report is shown in the sample output; it includes stock names, the current price for each, and the 10-day average. For reference, the last date included in the list is reported. The routine ends with the statement DATA STORED.

In the second sample, we do read the disk. The program gives an immediate output report to show us what is on the disk--including the last-date information. The second sample output is identical to the first (as it should be). In this case, however, we tell the program that we wish to update the prices. The third output report reflects our updates. There are no real problem areas in the operating sequence, so Ten-Day Average is a pleasure to run.

PROGRAMMING NOTES

If you've already adapted one of the previous disk programs, this one will present no new challenges. The disk-read segment is in lines 130 through 320. Since we should not encounter the end-of-data mark on the disk unless there's an error, lines 180 and 190 send the program to line 300 if an end-of-data mark is sensed. A disk-read error is either a true reading error or a case of using the wrong disk, so the error routine of lines 300 to 320 ends the program. If this should happen, start over after checking the disk label.

The initialization routine is in lines 350 to 490. A set of nested FOR...NEXT loops garners the information needed. The X loop cycles through the stocks while the Y loop collects the pricing data for each stock. Line 450 provides the summation of all 10 prices.

Lines 500 through 680 provide the output report. Since the total of the 10 prices is kept in variable $A(11,X)$, we can print the average by multiplying the total by one-tenth. Line 610 takes care of that chore while printing the average. If you plan to monitor more than about 30 stocks, you might delete line 620 and single space the output. If you'll be tracking more than about 60 options, add a counter-step within the FOR...NEXT loop to total the number of lines printed. When the counter senses a full page, you can print a form-feed command to have your printer skip over the end-of-sheet perforation. I'd recommend keeping the double-space format and adding the skip routine to keep the output readable. You'll have to try it with your printer, but 60 single-spaced lines should be a full page. Since I like the double-space format, and since the FOR...NEXT loop provides its own counter, I'd add something like this:

```
0625 IF (X/30) = INT(X/30) THEN PRINT #P,CHR$(12)
```

The only time that one-thirtieth of X and the integer part of one-thirtieth of X are equal is when X is a multiple of 30. Experiment with this; your output may look better when you skip after 25 or 35 lines.

The daily-update routine starts in line 700. Line 740 removes the oldest price from the total; the FOR...NEXT of lines 750, 760, and 770 move all prices back by one variable (wiping out the oldest data); and line 800 adds the new price to the total.

The disk-save routine finishes our listing and program. It's not much different from other disk-write segments. We must OPEN the files before writing and CLOSE them afterward. After a FOR...NEXT loop stuffs the price information on the disk media, line 1000 adds the current date to the platter. We include line 1020 to let the operator know that the disk operation is complete.

SAMPLE INPUT - 10 DAY AVERAGE

DO YOU WANT TO READ THE DISK? NO
HOW MANY STOCKS DO YOU WANT TO TRACK? 4
STOCK NAME? PEAS
PRICE FOR PERIOD #1 ? 10
PRICE FOR PERIOD #2 ? 10
PRICE FOR PERIOD #3 ? 11
PRICE FOR PERIOD #4 ? 12
PRICE FOR PERIOD #5 ? 11
PRICE FOR PERIOD #6 ? 12
PRICE FOR PERIOD #7 ? 13
PRICE FOR PERIOD #8 ? 14
PRICE FOR PERIOD #9 ? 14
PRICE FOR PERIOD #10 ? 13

STOCK NAME? SPROUTS
PRICE FOR PERIOD #1 ? 1.50
PRICE FOR PERIOD #2 ? 1.70
PRICE FOR PERIOD #3 ? 1.70
PRICE FOR PERIOD #4 ? 1.40
PRICE FOR PERIOD #5 ? 1.30
PRICE FOR PERIOD #6 ? 1.25
PRICE FOR PERIOD #7 ? 1.10
PRICE FOR PERIOD #8 ? 1.00
PRICE FOR PERIOD #9 ? 1.25
PRICE FOR PERIOD #10 ? 1.10

STOCK NAME? GARLIC
PRICE FOR PERIOD #1 ? .25
PRICE FOR PERIOD #2 ? .50
PRICE FOR PERIOD #3 ? .75
PRICE FOR PERIOD #4 ? 1
PRICE FOR PERIOD #5 ? 1.50
PRICE FOR PERIOD #6 ? 1.25
PRICE FOR PERIOD #7 ? 1.05
PRICE FOR PERIOD #8 ? .90
PRICE FOR PERIOD #9 ? 1.10
PRICE FOR PERIOD #10 ? 1

STOCK NAME? TIRES
PRICE FOR PERIOD #1 ? 35.4
PRICE FOR PERIOD #2 ? 35.6
PRICE FOR PERIOD #3 ? 37
PRICE FOR PERIOD #4 ? 35.5
PRICE FOR PERIOD #5 ? 29
PRICE FOR PERIOD #6 ? 35
PRICE FOR PERIOD #7 ? 35
PRICE FOR PERIOD #8 ? 36
PRICE FOR PERIOD #9 ? 34
PRICE FOR PERIOD #10 ? 35

```
TODAY'S DATE? JAN 14

WHAT OUTPUT PORT DO YOU WISH TO USE? 3
DO YOU WISH TO UPDATE PRICES? NO
DO YOU WISH TO SAVE DATA ON DISK? YES
WHAT DRIVE AND SECTOR (DSSS)? 1200
DATA STORED

READY
#
DO YOU WANT TO READ THE DISK? YES
WHAT DRIVE AND SECTOR (DSSS)? 1200

WHAT OUTPUT PORT DO YOU WISH TO USE? 2
DO YOU WISH TO UPDATE PRICES? YES
STOCK:  PEAS
WHAT IS CURRENT PRICE? 12
STOCK:  SPROUTS
WHAT IS CURRENT PRICE? 1.5
STOCK:  GARLIC
WHAT IS CURRENT PRICE? .78
STOCK:  TIRES
WHAT IS CURRENT PRICE? 34

WHAT IS THE DATE OF THE INFORMATION? JAN 15

WHAT OUTPUT PORT DO YOU WISH TO USE? 2
DO YOU WISH TO UPDATE PRICES? NO
DO YOU WISH TO SAVE DATA ON DISK? YES
WHAT DRIVE AND SECTOR (DSSS)? 1200
DATA STORED

READY
#
```

SAMPLE OUTPUTS - 10 DAY AVERAGE

FIRST RUN:

STOCK NAME	CURRENT PRICE	10 DAY AVERAGE
PEAS	13.00	12.00
SPROUTS	1.10	1.33
GARLIC	1.00	0.93
TIRES	35.00	34.75

LAST DATE INCLUDED IN LIST - JAN 14

INITIAL DISPLAY - SECOND RUN:

STOCK NAME	CURRENT PRICE	10 DAY AVERAGE
PEAS	13.00	12.00
SPROUTS	1.10	1.33
GARLIC	1.00	0.93
TIRES	35.00	34.75

LAST DATE INCLUDED IN LIST - JAN 14

FINAL DISPLAY - SECOND RUN:

STOCK NAME	CURRENT PRICE	10 DAY AVERAGE
PEAS	12.00	12.20
SPROUTS	1.50	1.33
GARLIC	0.78	0.98
TIRES	34.00	34.61

LAST DATE INCLUDED IN LIST - JAN 15

```
0010 REM ********************************
0020 REM *     TEN DAY MOVING AVERAGE     *
0030 REM ********************************
0040 REM ********** VERSION 10 **********
0050 LINE= 0
0060 DIGITS= 0
0070 DEF FNA(X)=(45-LEN(STR$(X)))
0080 DEF FNB(X)=(70-LEN(STR$(X)))
0100 REM *********** START ************
0110 INPUT "Do you want to read the disk",Z$
0120 IF LEFT$(Z$,1)="N" THEN 350
0130 INPUT "What drive and sector (DSSS)",S
0140 OPEN #10,S
0150 READ #10,N\200
0160 DIM A$(N),A(11,N)
0170 FOR X=1 TO N
0180 READ #10,A$(X),A(1,X),A(2,X),A(3,X),A(4,X),A(5,X)\300
0190 READ #10,A(6,X),A(7,X),A(8,X),A(9,X),A(10,X),A(11,X)\300
0200 NEXT X
0210 PRINT
0220 READ #10,D$\20
0230 PRINT
0240 CLOSE #10
0250 GOTO 500
0300 PRINT "OOPS!!! - LOOKS LIKE THE WRONG DISK."
0310 PRINT "I CAN'T READ THE DATA.  LET'S TRY AGAIN."
0320 END
0350 INPUT "How many stocks do you want to track",N
0360 DIM A$(N),A(11,N)
0400 FOR X=1 TO N
0410 INPUT "Stock name",A$(X)
0420 FOR Y=1 TO 10
0430 PRINT "Price for period #";Y;
0440 INPUT A(Y,X)
0450   A(11,X)=A(11,X)+A(Y,X)
0460 NEXT Y
0470 PRINT
0480 NEXT X
0490 INPUT "Today's Date",D$
0500 REM ***** DISPLAY CURRENT DATA *****
0510 PRINT
0520 INPUT "What output port do you wish to use",P
0530 DIGITS= 2
0540 PRINT #P,"Stock Name";
0550 PRINT #P,TAB(35);"Current Price";
0560 PRINT #P,TAB(60);"10 Day Average"
0570 PRINT #P
0580 FOR X=1 TO N
0590 PRINT #P,A$(X);
0600 PRINT #P,TAB(FNA(A(10,X)));A(10,X);
0610 PRINT #P,TAB(FNB(.1*A(11,X)));(.1*A(11,X))
0620 PRINT #P
0630 NEXT X
0640 PRINT #P
```

```
0650 DIGITS= 0
0660 PRINT #P
0670 PRINT #P,"Last date included in list - ";D$
0680 PRINT #P,CHR$(12)
0700 REM ****** UPDATE STOCK PRICE ******
0710 INPUT "Do you wish to update prices",Z$
0720 IF LEFT$(Z$,1)="N" THEN 900
0730 FOR X=1 TO N
0740   A(11,X)=A(11,X)-A(1,X)
0750 FOR Y=1 TO 9
0760   A(Y,X)=A(Y+1,X)
0770 NEXT Y
0780 PRINT "STOCK:   ";A$(X)
0790 INPUT "What is current price",A(10,X)
0800   A(11,X)=A(11,X)+A(10,X)
0810 NEXT X
0820 PRINT
0830 INPUT "What is the date of the information",D$
0840 GOTO 500
0900 REM ****** SAVE DATA ON DISK *******
0910 INPUT "Do you wish to save data on disk",Z$
0920 IF LEFT$(Z$,1)="N" THEN 1030
0930 INPUT "What drive and sector (DSSS)",S
0940 OPEN #10,S
0950 PRINT #10,N
0960 FOR X=1 TO N
0970 PRINT #10,A$(X),A(1,X),A(2,X),A(3,X),A(4,X),A(5,X)
0980 PRINT #10,A(6,X),A(7,X),A(8,X),A(9,X),A(10,X),A(11,X)
0990 NEXT X
1000 PRINT #10,D$
1010 CLOSE #10
1020 PRINT "Data stored"
1030 END
```

31
STOCK PLOTTER

To many investors, dividends are unimportant. They purchase stocks, bonds, and commodities for the profits to be made when the price varies. Of course they cash the dividend checks, but that part of investing isn't the driving factor. Lots of these traders subscribe to the cyclic theory of market performance. The cyclic school believes that the market in general--and each stock in particular--follows a stable pattern of high and low prices in a repeating cycle. Some stocks may reach peaks and valleys of price every month, some every year, and some every 90 days.

One advantage of cyclic-theory investing is that you must do some research before you put your money down. You'll have to look over years of stock quotations for each candidate stock to find out what the time constant of the cycle is. (There are publications for various stocks, so this task is not so immense as it might seem.) Surprisingly enough, many stocks appear to follow a fairly rigid cycle despite world events and "other market factors." The cyclic theorists may have a good thing.

If you believe in the cyclic theories of stock investing, you will love Stock Plotter. This program will give you a plot of the high and low market transactions for any investment vehicle for any reasonable period of time. (My BASIC will only allow a maximum of 255 separate days at any single exercise.)

BACKGROUND

There's very little arithmetic here. Stock Plotter provides a graphic representation of stock prices on your alphanumeric terminal or printer. The two mathematical calculations performed in the program are simple. The first is a scaling computation to permit the spread of high and low prices to be printed over a wide range of the printer space. The second provides an "average" trading

253

price that should make registered stock-market representatives grind their teeth.

The scaling calculation selects the highest high price entered and divides it by 50. The graphic presentation is based on 60 divisions (columns) of printer space. The highest price we enter for our stock candidate will, therefore, be plotted at about 10 divisions from the right margin.

The averaging calculation sums all of the high and low prices to arrive at an average price. Since the highs and lows do not necessarily occur in the market with equal frequency, don't put too much faith in the average. The greatest use of the average is in comparing plots of the same stock over different periods of time. It will indicate a general trend up or down.

OPERATING NOTES

The sample program run shows a 10-trading-day exercise for a mythical stock. In practice, you may wish to plot stock prices by the week or month. The day-to-day change in prices will be a fair guide of the interval. If a stock changes radically and often, plot days; if price variances are infrequent, plot weeks or month.

WHAT DATE? suggests a complete day-month-year response. You may, however, enter whatever is most meaningful to you. In the example, only the month and day are used. You should restrict your entry to about 12 or 13 characters to keep the date from interfering with the price plot. The STOCK LOW? and STOCK HIGH? entries are self-explanatory. While it is proper to enter the dollars and cents of stock price, the cents could be rounded off at entry time. The plot is generally not fine enough to distinguish between a few cents (for example, $88.23 and $88.48).

PROGRAMMING NOTES

Stock Plotter should be another lunch-time special; you can keypunch this one with a sandwich in either hand. The 53 lines of BASIC code don't hold any surprises. There's no provision for disk storage of price data, but you could use the disk routines from Ten-Day Average if you'd like a long-term analysis package.

The really important entry in the first dozen lines is the number of trading days in line 140. The number is used to DIMension variables in line 150. The stock-price information is collected by the FOR...NEXT loop of lines 190 through 240. The loop from lines 260 to 280 sets variable R1 to the highest price. Actually, you could cut down a few steps by deleting lines 240, 250, and 260. This would combine the two FOR...NEXT loops into one and still retain the proper setting of R1.

254

The scaling computation is performed in line 290. We add 49 to R1 to ensure that we have a scale factor if the highest stock price is less than 50. The scaling constant R is used in all of the plotting and a value of zero would be sure to generate errors.

The report-output segment of lines 320 to 560 is standard. Line 350 centers the name of the stock on an 80-column printer. Remember to change these TABs if your printer has something other than an 80-column capability. The actual plotting uses columns 15 through 75. The PRINTs in lines 370 through 430 put the scale at the top of the graph. Lines 460 to 480 print the stock values.

Lines 490 and 500 total the low and high figures. The formula in line 520 computes our "average" trading price. If you are a purist, you may wish to delete this entire calculation and enjoy the graphics alone.

However you choose to employ Stock Plotter, you'll find that it's a fun program. With a little amendment, it will plot rainfall, bowling scores, or the height attained by the backyard garden corn.

STOCK PLOTTER

WHAT IS THE NAME OF THE STOCK? GARLIC TIRES
HOW MANY TRADING DAYS DO YOU WISH TO PLOT? 10

O.K., LET'S GATHER THE DATA.

WHAT DATE (DD/MM/YY)? JAN 10
STOCK LOW? 34
STOCK HIGH? 38

WHAT DATE (DD/MM/YY)? JAN 11
STOCK LOW? 36
STOCK HIGH? 39

WHAT DATE (DD/MM/YY)? JAN 12
STOCK LOW? 36
STOCK HIGH? 41

WHAT DATE (DD/MM/YY)? JAN 13
STOCK LOW? 39
STOCK HIGH? 42

WHAT DATE (DD/MM/YY)? JAN 14
STOCK LOW? 40
STOCK HIGH? 43

WHAT DATE (DD/MM/YY)? JAN 17
STOCK LOW? 41
STOCK HIGH? 46

WHAT DATE (DD/MM/YY)? JAN 18
STOCK LOW? 40
STOCK HIGH? 48

WHAT DATE (DD/MM/YY)? JAN 19
STOCK LOW? 38
STOCK HIGH? 45

WHAT DATE (DD/MM/YY)? JAN 20
STOCK LOW? 36
STOCK HIGH? 42

```
WHAT DATE (DD/MM/YY)?  JAN 21
STOCK LOW?  34
STOCK HIGH?  39

WHAT OUTPUT PORT?  2

READY
#
      SAMPLE OUTPUT - STOCK PLOT




                          STOCK PLOT

                         GARLIC TIRES


            0         10        20        30        40        50        60
JAN 10                                      L   H
JAN 11                                     L   H
JAN 12                                     L       H
JAN 13                                       L   H
JAN 14                                        L   H
JAN 17                                         L     H
JAN 18                                       L           H
JAN 19                                     L         H
JAN 20                                   L       H
JAN 21                                   L     H

AVERAGE TRADING PRICE OVER PERIOD IS $39.85
```

```
0010 REM ********************************
0020 REM *          STOCK  PLOTTER          *
0030 REM ********************************
0040 REM ********* VERSION 20 *********
0050 LINE= 0
0060 DIGITS= 0
0100 PRINT :PRINT:PRINT
0110 PRINT TAB(12);"STOCK PLOTTER"
0120 PRINT
0130 INPUT "What is the name of the stock",N$
0140 INPUT "How many trading days do you wish to plot",N
0150 DIM D$(N),L(N),H(N)
0160 PRINT
0170 PRINT "O.K., Let's gather the data."
0180 PRINT
0190 FOR X=1 TO N
0200 INPUT "What date (DD/MM/YY)",D$(X)
0210 INPUT "Stock Low",L(X)
0220 INPUT "Stock High",H(X)
0230 PRINT
0240 NEXT X
0250  R1=H(1)
0260 FOR X=1 TO N
0270 IF H(X)>R1 THEN R1=H(X)
0280 NEXT X
0290  R=INT((R1+49)/50)
0300 PRINT
0310 INPUT "What output port",P
0320 PRINT #P:PRINT#P:PRINT#P
0330 PRINT #P,TAB(35);"STOCK PLOT"
0340 PRINT #P
0350 PRINT #P,TAB((80-LEN(N$))/2);N$
0360 PRINT #P:PRINT#P
0370 PRINT #P,TAB(15);"0";
0380 PRINT #P,TAB(24);R*10;
0390 PRINT #P,TAB(34);R*20;
0400 PRINT #P,TAB(44);R*30;
0410 PRINT #P,TAB(54);R*40;
0420 PRINT #P,TAB(64);R*50;
0430 PRINT #P,TAB(74);R*60
0440 PRINT #P
0450 FOR X=1 TO N
0460 PRINT #P,D$(X);
0470 PRINT #P,TAB(15+(L(X))/R);"L";
0480 PRINT #P,TAB(15+(H(X))/R);"H"
0490  L=L+L(X)
0500  H=H+H(X)
0510 NEXT X
0520  A=(L+H)/(2*N)
0530 DIGITS= 2
0540 PRINT #P:PRINT#P
0550 PRINT #P,"Average trading price over period is $";A
0560 PRINT #P,CHR$(12)
0570 END
```

32
STOCK RECORDS

As your stock-market investing activity increases, the records you must keep increase in number and complexity. You must stay on top of the paperwork to manage your portfolio properly. Each year, the Internal Revenue Service wants a report of your dividends, gains, and losses on your income tax return. Stock Records is a comprehensive program that will allow you to store pertinent data. You'll be able to list your portfolio, retrieve sales records, or print your dividend payments with a few keystrokes. The dividend and sales reports are excellent attachments to your tax return.

BACKGROUND

Stock Records is more a data base manager than a calculation program. At first glance, it looks like a formidable keypunch task. Like many other programs, however, this one is simply a collection of short routines. By this point, you've keypunched and debugged each individual routine a couple of times. As much as I detest flow charts, I've included a couple here. The first one is an overview of Stock Records. Each program operation is begun with a menu of choices--the "master menu." Your selection drives program flow to a second, specific menu. The second level of option produces a data base change or report.

Each of the routines in the program follows a similar sequence. The second flow chart illustrates a typical program routine, specifically, the "dividend-posting routine."

To update the data base, we'll use two disk files. The first file (#10) is called by the main program, the second (#11) by the specific routine needing the capability. Each stock record is read and displayed for the user as the next step in dividend posting. If the record is an end-of-data mark, the routine closes the disk file and returns program flow to the main-routine END sequence. With a valid stock record on display, the program asks the

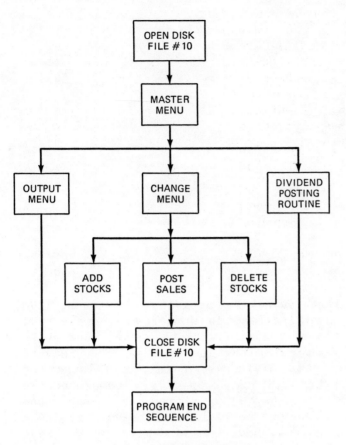

STOCK RECORDS FLOW CHART OVERVIEW

FLOW CHART OF TYPICAL ROUTINE

user if dividends are to be added. Negative responses cause the record to be reprinted on the disk with no change. A positive answer triggers the program to ask for dividends received for the stock. The payment is added to the file before it is reprinted on the disk. The most complicated mathematics used in the program is addition, so your computer won't strain any number crunchers here.

OPERATING NOTES

The sample run is a bit lengthy because it illustrates each major action possible with Stock Records. On the printing terminal, the repetition of the menu is a little boring, although you'll like the constant reminder with a video display.

The first action you'll take with Stock Records is a familiar "INITIATE" sequence. While the action is not included in the menu, it can be selected from the master-menu sequence only. "INITIATE" (and later, "ADD") asks for all stock data. When you've just purchased a stock, you won't have a DATE SOLD entry. Just hit "RETURN" for DATE SOLD? and enter a zero for AMOUNT RECEIVED?. ANY MORE? is the gate for new stock entries. MORE? will direct the program to END or recycle back to the master menu, depending on your response.

260

The second example demonstrates the addition of a stock to the file. The input sequence is identical to "INITIATE." (The same BASIC code is used for both.)

A stock-sale transaction is posted by our third sample. Since the purchase information is already in the file, the prompts indicate an abbreviated input task. You don't need to type the entire stock name: The program can accept a partial description, so long as the letters in the partial name are in the same order as the stock name on file.

Next, our sample illustrates the posting of dividends. One possible problem area occurs in the first question. DIVIDENDS RECEIVED ON... requires a yes-or-no answer. If you insert a numeric response, the program will assume a "NO" and plow ahead.

The next three examples exercise the PRINT function. First, we ask for a portfolio listing, then a sales report, and finally a report of dividends.

Our final "CHANGE" sequence is used to remove a stock from the file. (We don't automatically remove stocks when they are sold because you will want the information to prepare your income tax return. You can remove the entry after your tax return is complete.) To prove that we removed the stock, our final PRINT example again lists the portfolio, this time without "Garlic Tires."

The program will store up to 700 separate stock entries on a minidiskette, so it should be an adequate data store for even the most active trader. It would be prudent to make backup copies of the disk. (In fact, it would be downright foolish not to!)

PROGRAMMING NOTES

If you keypunch and debug Stock Records a segment at a time, it will be up and running in short order. You've seen most of the BASIC code before, so there are no surprises. The master-menu segment (lines 100 through 290), the change menu (lines 300 to 430), and the printing menu (lines 1200 through 1330) are so similar that you could keypunch one and use your BASIC editor to produce the other two.

The next code input should probably be the subroutine from lines 9000 through 9240. Since this input sequence is used for both initialization and adding stock data, debug it first to ease the validation task for the later code. Some of the same code is used in the sell routine also, so you'll have a leg up on that one when you've finished the subroutine.

The ADD, SELL, REMOVE, and RECORD DIVIDENDS routines are similar. Note that all numerics are converted to character string variables before disk recording to allow us to maintain precise control of disk real estate allocation. If we fail to specify exactly the same number of bytes for each stock record, the change of any record can wipe out the rest.

261

The PRINT routines are also similar to each other.
Alter the information content of these to suit yourself.
The "Sales Report," for example, should include a notation
of the number of shares to make it a fully useful income
tax return attachment. If you deal with a number of different stock brokerages, you may wish to include the name
of your broker on the portfolio listing. You may also add
a "Name" and "Taxpayer I.D." heading to the reports.

When you keypunch the END sequence, you may wish to
amplify the MORE? prompt to something like "MORE PROGRAM?"
to reduce potential operator confusion. Line 2320 could be
changed to "...THEN 140" instead of ...THEN RUN (I used RUN
to make certain everything was initialized properly).

Although there are a number of error traps included,
there's always room for one more. The dividend input routine is a good place to implement one. You could add a
step like:

```
1065 IF LEFT$ (Z$,1)<>"N" THEN 1030
```

to prevent an inadvertant "NO" response. The number of
traps you include should depend on the frequency with
which you'll use the program. If you don't use Stock
Records often, more error traps will help jog your operator
memory.

You'll find Stock Records worth the keypunch time if
you're at all active in the market. You can keep records
of your options, commodities, and stock shares in the computer. The satisfaction of letting your computer get ready
for income tax time while you watch is unmatched!

STOCK RECORDS

PLEASE PUT THE RECORD DISK IN DRIVE #2

DO YOU WISH TO:

    'C'HANGE THE RECORD
    'R'ECORD DIVIDEND PAYMENTS, OR
    'P'RINT THE FILE

? INITIATE
NAME OF STOCK? GARLIC TIRES
NUMBER OF SHARES? 100
NET COST OF SHARES? 4050
DIVIDENDS RECEIVED THIS YEAR? 0
DATE PURCHASED (DD MMM YY)? 13 MAR 82
DATE SOLD (DD MMM YY)? ____
AMOUNT RECEIVED FROM SALE? 0
BROKER? B. ROKER

ANY MORE? YES
NAME OF STOCK? LITTLE COMPUTERS
NUMBER OF SHARES? 500
NET COST OF SHARES? 522
DIVIDENDS RECEIVED THIS YEAR? 0
DATE PURCHASED (DD MMM YY)? 21 SEP 82
DATE SOLD (DD MMM YY)? ____
AMOUNT RECEIVED FROM SALE? 0
BROKER? O.T.C.

ANY MORE? NO
MORE? YES

STOCK RECORDS

PLEASE PUT THE RECORD DISK IN DRIVE #2

DO YOU WISH TO:

    'C'HANGE THE RECORD
    'R'ECORD DIVIDEND PAYMENTS, OR
    'P'RINT THE FILE

263

? <u>CHANGE</u>

DO YOU WANT TO:

    'ADD'   -   ADD A STOCK TO THE RECORD
    'SELL' - REPORT A STOCK SALE
    'REMOVE' - REMOVE A STOCK FROM RECORD

? <u>ADD</u>

NAME OF STOCK? <u>ORANGE SPROUTS</u>
NUMBER OF SHARES? <u>200</u>
NET COST OF SHARES? <u>2200</u>
DIVIDENDS RECEIVED THIS YEAR? <u>0</u>
DATE PURCHASED (DD MMM YY)? <u>23 MAR 84</u>
DATE SOLD (DD MMM YY)? <u>   </u>
AMOUNT RECEIVED FROM SALE? <u>0</u>
BROKER? <u>B. ROKER</u>

ANY MORE? <u>NOPE</u>
MORE? <u>YES</u>

        STOCK RECORDS

PLEASE PUT THE RECORD DISK IN DRIVE #2

DO YOU WISH TO:

    'C'HANGE THE RECORD
    'R'ECORD DIVIDEND PAYMENTS, OR
    'P'RINT THE FILE

? <u>CHANGE</u>

DO YOU WANT TO:

    'ADD'   -   ADD A STOCK TO THE RECORD
    'SELL' - REPORT A STOCK SALE
    'REMOVE' - REMOVE A STOCK FROM RECORD

? <u>SELL</u>
WHICH STOCK DID YOU SELL? <u>GARLIC TIRES</u>
DATE SOLD (DD MMM YY)? <u>27 MAR 84</u>
AMOUNT RECEIVED? <u>4560</u>
MORE? <u>YES</u>

264

STOCK RECORDS

PLEASE PUT THE RECORD DISK IN DRIVE #2

DO YOU WISH TO:

    'C'HANGE THE RECORD
    'R'ECORD DIVIDEND PAYMENTS, OR
    'P'RINT THE FILE

? <u>RECORD</u>
DIVIDENDS RECEIVED ON GARLIC TIRES   ? <u>NO</u>
DIVIDENDS RECEIVED ON LITTLE COMPUTERS   ? <u>NO</u>
DIVIDENDS RECEIVED ON ORANGE SPROUTS   ? <u>YES</u>
FIRST PAYMENT OF YEAR? <u>YES</u>
AMOUNT OF DIVIDEND PAYMENT? <u>45</u>

MORE? <u>YES</u>

         STOCK RECORDS

PLEASE PUT THE RECORD DISK IN DRIVE #2

DO YOU WISH TO:

    'C'HANGE THE RECORD
    'R'ECORD DIVIDEND PAYMENTS, OR
    'P'RINT THE FILE

? <u>PRINT</u>

DO YOU WANT A:

    'D'IVIDEND RECORD
    'S'ALES RECORD
    'P'ORTFOLIO LIST

? <u>PORTFOLIO</u>
WHAT OUTPUT PORT? <u>2</u>
MORE? <u>YES</u>

```
                STOCK RECORDS
PLEASE PUT THE RECORD DISK IN DRIVE #2

DO YOU WISH TO:

    'C'HANGE THE RECORD
    'R'ECORD DIVIDEND PAYMENTS, OR
    'P'RINT THE FILE

? PRINT

DO YOU WANT A:

    'D'IVIDEND RECORD
    'S'ALES RECORD
    'P'ORTFOLIO LIST

? SALES
WHAT OUTPUT PORT? 2
MORE? YUP

                STOCK RECORDS
PLEASE PUT THE RECORD DISK IN DRIVE #2

DO YOU WISH TO:

    'C'HANGE THE RECORD
    'R'ECORD DIVIDEND PAYMENTS, OR
    'P'RINT THE FILE

? PRINT

DO YOU WANT A:

    'D'IVIDEND RECORD
    'S'ALES RECORD
    'P'ORTFOLIO LIST

? DIVIDEND
WHAT OUTPUT PORT? 2
MORE? YES
```

266

```
            STOCK RECORDS

PLEASE PUT THE RECORD DISK IN DRIVE #2

DO YOU WISH TO:

    'C'HANGE THE RECORD
    'R'ECORD DIVIDEND PAYMENTS, OR
    'P'RINT THE FILE

? CHANGE

DO YOU WANT TO:

    'ADD'    -   ADD A STOCK TO THE RECORD
    'SELL'   -   REPORT A STOCK SALE
    'REMOVE' -   REMOVE A STOCK FROM RECORD

? REMOVE
WHICH STOCK DO  YOU WANT TO DELETE? GARLIC TIRES
MORE?  YES

            STOCK RECORDS

PLEASE PUT THE RECORD DISK IN DRIVE #2

DO YOU WISH TO:

    'C'HANGE THE RECORD
    'R'ECORD DIVIDEND PAYMENTS, OR
    'P'RINT THE FILE

? PRINT

DO YOU WANT A:

    'D'IVIDEND RECORD
    'S'ALES RECORD
    'P'ORTFOLIO LIST

? PORTFOLIO
WHAT OUTPUT PORT? 2
MORE? NO

READY
#
```

SAMPLE OUTPUTS - STOCK RECORDS

STOCK PORTFOLIO

STOCK	NR OF SHARES	COST
GARLIC TIRES	100	4050.00
LITTLE COMPUTERS	500	522.00
ORANGE SPROUTS	200	2200.00

RECORD OF SALES

STOCK	BOUGHT		SOLD	
	DATE	AMOUNT	DATE	AMOUNT
GARLIC TIRES	13 MAR 82	4050.00	27 MAR 84	4560.00

DIVIDEND RECORD

STOCK	NR SHARES	DIVIDENDS
GARLIC TIRES	100	0.00
LITTLE COMPUTERS	500	0.00
ORANGE SPROUTS	200	45.00

TOTAL DIVIDENDS FOR YEAR ARE $45.00

STOCK PORTFOLIO

STOCK	NR OF SHARES	COST
LITTLE COMPUTERS	500	522.00
ORANGE SPROUTS	200	2200.00

268

```
0010 REM ********************************
0020 REM *           STOCK RECORD           *
0030 REM ********************************
0040 REM ********* VERSION 10 *********
0050 LINE= 0
0100 PRINT :PRINT:PRINT
0110 PRINT TAB(10);"STOCK RECORDS"
0120 PRINT
0130 PRINT "Please put the record disk in Drive #2"
0140 OPEN #10,2001
0150 PRINT
0160 PRINT "DO YOU WISH TO:"
0170 PRINT
0180 PRINT "    'C'HANGE THE RECORD"
0190 PRINT "    'R'ECORD DIVIDEND PAYMENTS, or"
0200 PRINT "    'P'RINT THE FILE"
0210 PRINT
0220 INPUT Z$
0230 IF LEFT$(Z$,1)="C" THEN 300
0240 IF LEFT$(Z$,1)="R" THEN 1000
0250 IF LEFT$(Z$,1)="P" THEN 1200
0260 IF LEFT$(Z$,1)="I" THEN 530
0270 PRINT "Sorry, I don't understand your answer of '";Z$;"',"
0280 PRINT "Please try again."
0290 GOTO 150
0300 REM ****** CHANGE THE RECORD ******
0310 PRINT
0320 PRINT "DO YOU WANT TO:"
0330 PRINT
0340 PRINT "    'ADD'    -   ADD A STOCK TO THE RECORD"
0350 PRINT "    'SELL'   -  REPORT A STOCK SALE"
0360 PRINT "    'REMOVE' -  REMOVE A STOCK FROM RECORD"
0370 PRINT
0380 INPUT Z$
0390 IF LEFT$(Z$,1)="A" THEN 500
0400 IF LEFT$(Z$,1)="S" THEN 600
0410 IF LEFT$(Z$,1)="R" THEN 800
0420 PRINT "Sorry, I don't understand '";Z$;"'.  Try again."
0430 GOTO 310
0500 REM ******** ADD  ROUTINE ********
0510 READ #10,S$,N$,C$,D$,P$,R$,A$,B$\530
0520 GOTO 510
0530 GOSUB 9000
0540 INPUT "Any more",Z$
0550 IF LEFT$(Z$,1)="Y" THEN 530
0560 CLOSE #10
0570 GOTO 2300
0600 REM ******** SELL ROUTINE ********
0610 OPEN #11,2001
0620 INPUT "Which stock did you sell",Y$
0630 READ #10,S$,N$,C$,D$,P$,R$,A$,B$\740
0640 IF LEFT$(S$,LEN(Y$))=Y$ THEN 670
0650 PRINT #11,S$;N$;C$;D$;P$;R$;A$;B$
0660 GOTO 630
```

269

```
0670 INPUT "Date sold (DD MMM YY)",R$
0680  R$=LEFT$(R$+"              ",10)
0690 INPUT "Amount received",A
0700  A$=STR$(A)
0710  A$=LEFT$(A$+"           ",10)
0720 GOTO 650
0730 PRINT
0740 CLOSE #11
0750 CLOSE #10
0760 GOTO 2300
0800 REM ******** REMOVE ROUTINE ********
0810 OPEN #11,2001
0820 INPUT "Which stock do you want to delete",Y$
0830 READ #10,S$,N$,C$,D$,P$,R$,A$,B$\870
0840 IF LEFT$(S$,LEN(Y$))=Y$ THEN 860
0850 PRINT #11,S$;N$;C$;D$;P$;R$;A$;B$
0860 GOTO 830
0870 CLOSE #11
0880 CLOSE #10
0890 GOTO 2300
1000 REM ******* RECORD DIVIDENDS *******
1010 OPEN #11,2001
1020 READ #10,S$,N$,C$,D$,P$,R$,A$,B$\1170
1030 PRINT "Dividends received on ";
1040 PRINT S$;
1050 INPUT Z$
1060 IF LEFT$(Z$,1)="Y" THEN 1090
1070 PRINT #11,S$;N$;C$;D$;P$;R$;A$;B$
1080 GOTO 1020
1090 INPUT "First payment of year",Z$
1100  D=VAL(D$)
1110 IF LEFT$(Z$,1)="Y" THEN D=0
1120 INPUT "Amount of dividend payment",D1
1130  D=D+D1
1140  D$=STR$(D)
1150  D$=LEFT$(D$+"          ",9)
1160 GOTO 1070
1170 CLOSE #11
1180 CLOSE #10
1190 GOTO 2300
1200 REM ******** PRINT  ROUTINE ********
1210 PRINT
1220 PRINT "DO YOU WANT A:"
1230 PRINT
1240 PRINT "    'D'IVIDEND RECORD"
1250 PRINT "    'S'ALES RECORD"
1260 PRINT "    'P'ORTFOLIO LIST"
1270 PRINT
1280 INPUT Z$
1290 IF LEFT$(Z$,1)="D" THEN 1400
1300 IF LEFT$(Z$,1)="S" THEN 1700
```

```
1310 IF LEFT$(Z$,1)="P" THEN 2000
1320 PRINT "Sorry, I don't understand '";Z$;"'.  Try again."
1330 GOTO 1210


1400 REM ****** DIVIDEND  RECORD ******
1410 INPUT "What output port",P
1420 PRINT #P:PRINT#P
1430 PRINT #P,TAB(32);"DIVIDEND RECORD"
1440 PRINT #P
1450 PRINT #P,"Stock";
1460 PRINT #P,TAB(35);"Nr Shares";
1470 PRINT #P,TAB(60);"Dividends"
1480 PRINT #P:PRINT#P
1490 READ #10,S$,N$,C$,D$,P$,R$,A$,B$\1600
1500  N=VAL(N$)
1510  D=VAL(D$)
1520 PRINT #P,S$;
1530 DIGITS= 0
1540 PRINT #P,TAB(42-LEN(STR$(N)));N;
1550 DIGITS= 2
1560 PRINT #P,TAB(66-LEN(STR$(D)));D
1570  T=T+D
1580 PRINT #P
1590 GOTO 1490
1600 PRINT #P
1610 PRINT #P,TAB(10);"Total dividends for year are  $";T
1620 PRINT #P,CHR$(12)
1630 CLOSE #10
1640 GOTO 2300
1700 REM ****** RECORD OF SALES ********
1710 INPUT "What output port",P
1720 PRINT #P:PRINT#P
1730 PRINT #P,TAB(32);"RECORD OF SALES"
1740 PRINT #P
1750 PRINT #P,"Stock";
1760 PRINT #P,TAB(40);"Bought";
1770 PRINT #P,TAB(63);"Sold"
1780 PRINT #P,TAB(35);"Date";
1790 PRINT #P,TAB(47);"Amount";
1800 PRINT #P,TAB(58);"Date";
1810 PRINT #P,TAB(68);"Amount":PRINT#P
1820 READ #10,S$,N$,C$,D$,P$,R$,A$,B$\1940
1830  C=VAL(C$)
1840  A=VAL(A$)
1850 DIGITS= 2
1860 IF LEFT$(R$,1)="" THEN 1820
1870 PRINT #P,S$;
1880 PRINT #P,TAB(32);P$;
1890 PRINT #P,TAB(53-LEN(STR$(C)));C;
1900 PRINT #P,TAB(56);R$;
```

```
1910 PRINT #P,TAB(75-LEN(STR$(A)));A
1920 PRINT #P
1930 GOTO 1820
1940 PRINT #P,CHR$(12)
1950 CLOSE #10
1960 GOTO 2300
2000 REM ****** PORTFOLIO  LISTING ******
2010 INPUT "What output port",P
2020 PRINT #P:PRINT#P
2030 PRINT #P,TAB(32);"STOCK PORTFOLIO"
2040 PRINT #P
2050 PRINT #P,"Stock";
2060 PRINT #P,TAB(40);"Nr of Shares";
2070 PRINT #P,TAB(60);"Cost"
2080 PRINT #P
2090 READ #10,S$,N$,C$,D$,P$,R$,A$,B$\2190
2100  N=VAL(N$)
2110  C=VAL(C$)
2120 PRINT #P,S$;
2130 DIGITS= 0
2140 PRINT #P,TAB(49-LEN(STR$(N)));N;
2150 DIGITS= 2
2160 PRINT #P,TAB(65-LEN(STR$(C)));C
2170 PRINT #P
2180 GOTO 2090
2190 PRINT #P,CHR$(12)
2200 CLOSE #10
2300 REM ******** PROGRAM  END ********
2310 INPUT "More",Z$
2320 IF LEFT$(Z$,1)="Y" THEN RUN
2330 END
9000 REM ****** INPUT SUBROUTINE ******
9010  X$="                               ": REM - 31 SPACES
9020 INPUT "Name of Stock",S$
9030  S$=LEFT$(S$+X$,31)
9040 INPUT "Number of Shares",N
9050  N$=STR$(N)
9060  N$=LEFT$(N$+X$,9)
9070 INPUT "Net Cost of Shares",C
9080  C$=STR$(C)
9090  C$=LEFT$(C$+X$,10)
9100 INPUT "Dividends received this year",D
9110  D$=STR$(D)
9120  D$=LEFT$(D$+X$,9)
9130 INPUT "Date Purchased (DD MMM YY)",P$
9140  P$=LEFT$(P$+X$,10)
9150 INPUT "Date Sold (DD MMM YY)",R$
9160  R$=LEFT$(R$+X$,10)
```

```
9170 INPUT "Amount Received from Sale",A
9180  A$=STR$(A)
9190  A$=LEFT$(A$+X$,10)
9200 INPUT "Broker",B$
9210  B$=LEFT$(B$+X$,31)
9220 PRINT
9230 PRINT #10,S$;N$;C$;D$;P$;R$;A$;B$
9240 RETURN
```

33
RENTAL UNIT

If you want a more active investment package, you might wish to try rental property. You'll spend more time managing a cabin, house, or apartment building than you'd spend collecting interest or cashing dividend checks. Your potential gain is a bit better, though. In addition to the current income from rents, you stand to make a nice profit on the sale of the property later. (Of course, if the real estate market goes sour, you risk a loss on the sale.)

A rental is a business venture. You need to consider rental expenses as well as income when you analyze the potential of such an investment. Rental Unit will help you investigate a possible property purchase and aid your management of the rental when you become a rental magnate. The program will calculate the gain or loss on your unit each year, and compute building depreciation in the bargain. It will let you know how profitable your investment is, and provide a report that can be used as an attachment to your yearly income tax returns.

BACKGROUND

No exotic mathematics routines are used in Rental Unit. The program collects income and expense data, sums the categories, and calculates the bottom line by adding and subtracting. The depreciation computation deserves a word or two, however.

Depreciation is the periodic decline in value of an asset. In accounting applications, depreciation is a method of estimating the annual wear and tear. There are a number of standard depreciation methods. The one used here is called "straight-line depreciation." Straight-line depreciation is the most commonly used method for real estate (in fact, it is the only approved method for most rentals). It estimates that the loss in value occurs uniformly with time. The building will depreciate as much in the first year of use as the last. Only buildings depreciate, by the way; land is not used up by being employed as a building site. We must also take into account the actual number of months in the year in which the building serves as a rental. Our depreciation formula is:

$$D = \frac{M}{12} * \frac{B - V}{L}$$

Where M is the number of months the asset is used during the current year, B is the building and land cost, V is the land value, and L is the estimated life of the building in years.

OPERATING NOTES

Our sample run illustrates a mythical single-family dwelling rental. The input task is spelled out in fair detail by the prompt messages. There are three fields that deserve special comment: The prompts for other income, repairs, and miscellaneous expenses permit the user to enter the type of income or expense as well as the amount. If you have few user-defined entries, type a comma and a zero to end each of these sequences. (The sample input illustrates this feature.)

The sample output shows that your rental-income report could be an attachment to your income tax return or bank-loan application. Note that the input categories for which a zero was entered are not included in the output. The zero suppression provides a neater output statement than one in which every entry is printed.

PROGRAMMING NOTES

Rental Unit will probably take a couple of evening sessions to keypunch and debug. It's not complex, but the length will mean a lot of keys to press. Otherwise, there's not much new in the routines.

The income-routine part of the input segment is housed in lines 200 through 290. Line 260 is the key that unlocks the FOR...NEXT loop when the user is through entering data. We use variable I(9) as the upper limit for the printing loop, so it must be set to the number of other-income entries.

A similar set of input statements is used for the expense-gathering statements of lines 300 to 620. The initial commands take care of the depreciation calculation. If you wish to mechanize a method other than straight-line depreciation, change line 350 for the appropriate formula.

The output report starts with line 700 and extends to line 1420. Every other line from 880 to 1140 is a zero suppressor. Line 1170, 1200, and 1230 perform the same function.

Lines 1330 to 1410 report the bottom line. Line 1340 steers the program flow to properly tag the result as a profit or loss. If your rental investment has produced a current-period loss, line 1350 converts the negative number to a positive one so that line 1370 can put brackets around it (the accounting designation for a negative quantity).

You can use Rental Unit as an estimator before you invest in a piece of property and as a management tool when you've selected the right rental for your portfolio.

RENTAL UNIT

RENTS RECEIVED? <u>6000</u>
ENTER OTHER INCOME BY TYPING
SOURCE <COMMA> AMOUNT
? <u>CLEANING DEPOSIT,250</u>
? <u>,0</u>
COST OR OTHER BASIS OF PROPERTY? <u>120000</u>
LAND VALUE? <u>20000</u>
LIFE (IN YEARS)? <u>25</u>
MONTHS IN USE THIS YEAR? <u>12</u>

ENTER TOTAL EXPENSES FOR:

ADVERTISING? <u>50</u>
CLEANING? <u>300</u>
COMMISSIONS? <u>0</u>
GARDENING/GROUNDS CARE? <u>1200</u>
INSURANCE? <u>450</u>
MORTGAGE INTEREST? <u>4523,18</u>
JANITOR/HEATING? <u>0</u>
LEGAL/ACCOUNTING? <u>75</u>
SUPPLIES? <u>125.50</u>
TAXES/LICENSES? <u>1200</u>
TELEPHONE/TELEGRAPH? <u>51.38</u>
TRAVEL EXPENSE/AUTO EXPENSE? <u>231.10</u>
UTILITIES? <u>0</u>
LIST REPAIRS BY TYPE <COMMA> AMOUNT
? <u>PLUMBING,265</u>
? <u>PAINTING,107</u>
? <u>,0</u>
LIST MISCELLANEOUS EXPENSES BY TYPE <COMMA> AMOUNT
? <u>TERMITE INSPECTION,133,50</u>
? <u>RECEIPT BOOK,2,50</u>
? <u>,0</u>

WHAT OUTPUT PORT? <u>2</u>
ANOTHER COPY? <u>NO</u>

READY
#

SAMPLE OUTPUT - RENTAL INCOME

                    INCOME

RENT RECEIVED $ 6000.00
CLEANING DEPOSIT   250.00

GROSS INCOME $ 6250.00

                    EXPENSES

MORTGAGE INTEREST $ 4523.18
ADVERTISING   50.00
CLEANING   300.00
DEPRECIATION   4000.00
GARDENING/GROUNDS CARE   1200.00
INSURANCE   450.00
LEGAL/ACCOUNTING   75.00
SUPPLIES   125.50
TAXES/LICENSES   1200.00
TELEPHONE/TELEGRAPH   51.38
TRAVEL/AUTO EXPENSES   231.10
REPAIRS:
     PLUMBING   265.00
     PAINTING   107.00
MISCELLANEOUS EXPENSES:
     TERMITE INSPECTION   133.50
     RECEIPT BOOK   2.50

TOTAL EXPENSES   12714.16

NET RENTAL LOSS $(6464.16)
                                                  ===========

```
0010 REM *********************************
0020 REM *        RENTAL  UNIT          *
0030 REM *********************************
0040 REM ********* VERSION 10 *********
0050 DIM R$(20),E(34)
0060 DEF FNX(A)=65-LEN(STR$(A))
0070 DEF FNY(B)=75-LEN(STR$(B))
0080 LINE= 0
0090 DIGITS= 2
0100 PRINT :PRINT:PRINT
0110 PRINT TAB(12);"RENTAL UNIT"
0120 PRINT
0200 REM *********** INCOME ***********
0210 INPUT "Rents Received",I(8)
0220 PRINT "Enter other income by typing"
0230 PRINT "SOURCE <COMMA> AMOUNT"
0240 FOR X=1 TO 7
0250 INPUT I$(X),I(X)
0260 IF I(X)=0 THEN I(9)=(X-1):X=7
0270 NEXT X
0280 IF I(7)<>0 THEN I(9)=7
0290   I=I(1)+I(2)+I(3)+I(4)+I(5)+I(6)+I(7)+I(8)
0300 REM *********** EXPENSES ***********
0310 INPUT "Cost or other Basis of Property",B
0320 INPUT "Land Value",V
0330 INPUT "Life (in years)",L
0340 INPUT "Months in use this year",M
0350   E(4)=(M/12)*(B-V)/L
0360 PRINT
0370 PRINT "Enter Total Expenses for:"
0380 PRINT
0390 INPUT "Advertising",E(1)
0400 INPUT "Cleaning",E(2)
0410 INPUT "Commissions",E(3)
0420 INPUT "Gardening/Grounds Care",E(5)
0430 INPUT "Insurance",E(6)
0440 INPUT "Mortgage Interest",E(7)
0450 INPUT "Janitor/Heating",E(8)
0460 INPUT "Legal/Accounting",E(9)
0470 INPUT "Supplies",E(10)
0480 INPUT "Taxes/Licenses",E(11)
0490 INPUT "Telephone/Telegraph",E(12)
0500 INPUT "Travel Expense/Auto Expense",E(13)
0510 INPUT "Utilities",E(14)
0520 PRINT "List Repairs by TYPE <COMMA> AMOUNT"
0530 FOR J=1 TO 10
0540 INPUT R$(J),E(14+J)
0550 IF E(14+J)=0 THEN J=10
0560 NEXT J
0570 PRINT "List Miscellaneous Expenses by TYPE <COMMA> AMOUNT"
0580 FOR J=11 TO 20
0590 INPUT R$(J),E(14+J)
0600 IF E(14+J)=0 THEN J=20
0610 NEXT J
```

```
0620 PRINT
0700 REM ******* OUTPUT ROUTINE *******
0710 INPUT "What output port";P
0720 FOR X=1 TO 4
0730 PRINT #P
0740 NEXT X
0750 PRINT #P,TAB(10);"INCOME"
0760 PRINT #P
0770 PRINT #P,"RENT RECEIVED";TAB(63-LEN(STR$(I(8))));"$ ";I(8)
0780 IF I(9)=0 THEN 820
0790 FOR X=1 TO I(9)
0800 PRINT #P,I$(X);TAB(FNX(I(X)));I(X)
0810 NEXT X
0820 PRINT #P,TAB(55);"----------"
0830 PRINT #P,"GROSS INCOME";TAB(73-LEN(STR$(I)));"$ ";I
0840 PRINT #P
0850 PRINT #P,TAB(10);"EXPENSES"
0860 PRINT #P
0870 PRINT #P,"MORTGAGE INTEREST";TAB(63-LEN(STR$(E(7))));"$ ";E(7)
0880 IF E(1)=0 THEN 900
0890 PRINT #P,"ADVERTISING";TAB(FNX(E(1)));E(1)
0900 IF E(2)=0 THEN 920
0910 PRINT #P,"CLEANING";TAB(FNX(E(2)));E(2)
0920 IF E(3)=0 THEN 940
0930 PRINT #P,"COMMISSIONS";TAB(FNX(E(3)));E(3)
0940 IF E(4)=0 THEN 960
0950 PRINT #P,"DEPRECIATION";TAB(FNX(E(4)));E(4)
0960 IF E(5)=0 THEN 980
0970 PRINT #P,"GARDENING/GROUNDS CARE";TAB(FNX(E(5)));E(5)
0980 IF E(6)=0 THEN 1000
0990 PRINT #P,"INSURANCE";TAB(FNX(E(6)));E(6)
1000 IF E(8)=0 THEN 1020
1010 PRINT #P,"JANITOR/HEATING";TAB(FNX(E(8)));E(8)
1020 IF E(9)=0 THEN 1040
1030 PRINT #P,"LEGAL/ACCOUNTING";TAB(FNX(E(9)));E(9)
1040 IF E(10)=0 THEN 1060
1050 PRINT #P,"SUPPLIES";TAB(FNX(E(10)));E(10)
1060 IF E(11)=0 THEN 1080
1070 PRINT #P,"TAXES/LICENSES";TAB(FNX(E(11)));E(11)
1080 IF E(12)=0 THEN 1100
1090 PRINT #P,"TELEPHONE/TELEGRAPH";TAB(FNX(E(12)));E(12)
1100 IF E(13)=0 THEN 1120
1110 PRINT #P,"TRAVEL/AUTO EXPENSES";TAB(FNX(E(13)));E(13)
1120 IF E(14)=0 THEN 1140
1130 PRINT #P,"UTILITIES";TAB(FNX(E(14)));E(14)
1140 IF E(15)=0 THEN 1200
1150 PRINT #P,"REPAIRS:"
1160 FOR J=1 TO 10
1170 IF E(14+J)=0 THEN 1190
1180 PRINT #P,TAB(5);R$(J);TAB(FNX(E(14+J)));E(14+J)
1190 NEXT J
1200 IF E(25)=0 THEN 1260
1210 PRINT #P,"MISCELLANEOUS EXPENSES:"
1220 FOR J=11 TO 20
1230 IF E(14+J)=0 THEN 1250
```

```
1240 PRINT #P,TAB(5);R$(J);TAB(FNX(E(14+J)));E(14+J)
1250 NEXT J
1260 PRINT #P,TAB(55);"----------"
1270  E=0
1280 FOR X=1 TO 34
1290  E=E+E(X)
1300 NEXT X
1310 PRINT #P,"TOTAL EXPENSES";TAB(FNY(E));E
1320 PRINT #P,TAB(65);"----------"
1330  C=I-E
1340 IF C>0 THEN 1390
1350  C=-C
1360 PRINT #P,"NET RENTAL LOSS";
1370 PRINT #P,TAB((FNY(C))-2);"$(";C;")"
1380 GOTO 1410
1390 PRINT #P,"NET RENTAL INCOME";
1400 PRINT #P,TAB((FNY(C))-2);"$ ";C
1410 PRINT #P,TAB(65);"=========="
1420 PRINT #P,CHR$(12)
1430 INPUT "Another copy",Z$
1440 IF LEFT$(Z$,1)="Y" THEN 700
1450 END
```

34
RENTAL BOOKKEEPING

Whether you own one or a hundred rentals, you need to keep income and expense records. Rental Bookkeeping will save your pencil and provide the inputs necessary for Rental Unit to give you the profit or loss report for each property. The program can handle up to 255 separate units on a single diskette. Add rental income and expense data on a daily, weekly, or monthly basis, and Rental Bookkeeping will record the facts faithfully to hand you a report of totals for each rental. With just a bit of extra effort, you can modify the program to be your record keeper for any business or personal venture.

The program is mechanized to use disk-memory storage, but you could implement it with tape cassettes. The tape version may run significantly slower, but it will serve your bookkeeping needs. No special mathematics routines are used, and the disk-read and disk-write segments are similar to those we've used previously.

OPERATING NOTES

Two sample runs are included to illustrate the initialization task and one update operation. The program prompts operator input of income and expense categories for each property. The output report is automatic with each program operation, and shows totals for each category. As with Rental Unit, expense categories with no entry are suppressed in the printout. The second output example illustrates the totalling function of the program, as the second entries are added to the first before the report is written.

You'll note that depreciation is not considered in the record-keeping routine, so the bottom line is cash flow, not profit or loss. This feature will give you a running tally of the effect of your rental investment on your bank balance. Depreciation is important at tax time, but it doesn't take cash out of your pocket.

This should be an interesting program, because there are several spots that just beg to be modified and personalized. You should have Rental Bookkeeping up and running in a couple of evenings.

Normally, the operator will elect to read the disk, so the program flows directly from line 140 to the disk-read segment of lines 200 through 370. Initialization adds a user input of the number of units and a DIMension of variables (line 170). With initialization, the sequence skips over the disk-reading code to the data-input routine.

Because the FOR...NEXT loops govern the disk reading, we will sense an end-of-data mark only with the wrong disk in the drive. Lines 240, 270, and 310 use the end-of-data vector to select the error sequence at lines 400 to 440.

Lines 620, 650, and 660 use the DATA statements (lines 1500 through 1540) to hold expense-category names. By leaving the titles in DATA statements, we can change them easily. As the program is written, there are 15 expense categories. Remember to change lines 0300, 0640, 0890, and 1210 if you alter the number of expense titles. The output routine will pick up the same category names.

Since our program is designed as a bookkeeper, there is no user option for disk storage. Program flow progresses from data input to storage. FOR...NEXT loops are used again to control the disk-data format. We've used only one disk file in the program because all data on the disk will be put into active memory for access, then written back to the disk in one operation.

The printing routine is standard. The expense categories are pulled from the DATA statements and printed in lines 1190, 1220, and 1240. Line 1230 is our zero suppressor. If you'd like to produce a separate page report for each property, change line 1360 to a form-feed command and delete the form-feed command in line 1380.

To really flex your programming muscles, go back to Rental Unit and adapt it to pick up the disk data recorded by this program. (Hint: Look at the Electronic Checkbook and Bookkeeping Worksheet programs for some sample techniques.) Rental Bookkeeping can serve your financial management system in many ways.

RENTAL BOOKKEEPING

DO YOU WISH TO READ A DISK? <u>NO</u>

HOW MANY RENTAL UNITS? <u>2</u>

RENTAL INCOME

FOR UNIT #1
RENTAL INCOME? <u>195</u>
OTHER INCOME? <u>5</u>

FOR UNIT #2
RENTAL INCOME? <u>600</u>
OTHER INCOME? <u>0</u>

RENTAL EXPENSES

FOR UNIT #1
ADVERTISING? <u>25</u>
CLEANING? <u>0</u>
COMMISSIONS? <u>0</u>
GARDENING? <u>0</u>
INSURANCE? <u>0</u>
MORTGAGE INTEREST? <u>0</u>
JANITOR/HEATING? <u>0</u>
LEGAL/ACCOUNTING? <u>50</u>
REPAIRS? <u>0</u>
SUPPLIES? <u>0</u>
TAXES/LICENSES? <u>50</u>
TELEPHONE/TELEGRAPH? <u>0</u>
TRAVEL/TRANSPORTATION? <u>0</u>
UTILITIES? <u>0</u>
MISCELLANEOUS/OTHER? <u>0</u>

FOR UNIT #2
ADVERTISING? <u>0</u>
CLEANING? <u>0</u>
COMMISSIONS? <u>0</u>
GARDENING? <u>100</u>
INSURANCE? <u>0</u>
MORTGAGE INTEREST? <u>378.12</u>
JANITOR/HEATING? <u>0</u>
LEGAL/ACCOUNTING? <u>0</u>
REPAIRS? <u>0</u>
SUPPLIES? <u>0</u>
TAXES/LICENSES? <u>100</u>
TELEPHONE/TELEGRAPH? <u>0</u>

```
TRAVEL/TRANSPORTATION? 13.25
UTILITIES? 0
MISCELLANEOUS/OTHER? 0

WHAT DISK DRIVE/SECTOR? 2100

WHAT PORT FOR OUTPUT? 2
ANOTHER COPY? NO

READY
#
```

SAMPLE OUTPUT #1

RENTAL INCOME AND EXPENSES

FOR UNIT NUMBER 1

RENTAL INCOME	195.00	
OTHER INCOME	5.00	
TOTAL INCOME		200.00
EXPENSES		
ADVERTISING	25.00	
LEGAL/ACCOUNTING	50.00	
TAXES/LICENSES	50.00	
TOTAL EXPENSES		125.00

CASH FLOW		75.00
		========

FOR UNIT NUMBER 2

RENTAL INCOME	600.00	
OTHER INCOME	0.00	
TOTAL INCOME		600.00
EXPENSES		
GARDENING	100.00	
MORTGAGE INTEREST	378.12	
TAXES/LICENSES	100.00	
TRAVEL/TRANSPORTATION	13.25	
TOTAL EXPENSES		591.37

CASH FLOW		8.63
		========

RENTAL BOOKKEEPING

DO YOU WISH TO READ A DISK? <u>YES</u>
WHAT IS DRIVE/SECTOR? <u>2100</u>

DO YOU WISH TO INPUT DATA? <u>YES</u>
RENTAL INCOME

FOR UNIT #1
RENTAL INCOME? <u>195</u>
OTHER INCOME? <u>0</u>

FOR UNIT #2
RENTAL INCOME? <u>600</u>
OTHER INCOME? <u>0</u>

RENTAL EXPENSES

FOR UNIT #1
ADVERTISING? <u>0</u>
CLEANING? <u>0</u>
COMMISSIONS? <u>0</u>
GARDENING? <u>0</u>
INSURANCE? <u>125</u>
MORTGAGE INTEREST? <u>0</u>
JANITOR/HEATING? <u>0</u>
LEGAL/ACCOUNTING? <u>0</u>
REPAIRS? <u>0</u>
SUPPLIES? <u>0</u>
TAXES/LICENSES? <u>50</u>
TELEPHONE/TELEGRAPH? <u>12</u>
TRAVEL/TRANSPORTATION? <u>0</u>
UTILITIES? <u>0</u>
MISCELLANEOUS/OTHER? <u>0</u>

FOR UNIT #2
ADVERTISING? <u>0</u>
CLEANING? <u>0</u>
COMMISSIONS? <u>0</u>
GARDENING? <u>100</u>
INSURANCE? <u>0</u>
MORTGAGE INTEREST? <u>377.86</u>
JANITOR/HEATING? <u>0</u>
LEGAL/ACCOUNTING? <u>0</u>
REPAIRS? <u>0</u>
SUPPLIES? <u>0</u>
TAXES/LICENSES? <u>100</u>
TELEPHONE/TELEGRAPH? <u>0</u>
TRAVEL/TRANSPORTATION? <u>0</u>
UTILITIES? <u>0</u>
MISCELLANEOUS/OTHER? <u>0</u>

```
WHAT DISK DRIVE/SECTOR? 2100

WHAT PORT FOR OUTPUT? 2
ANOTHER COPY? NO

READY
#
   SAMPLE OUTPUT #2



              RENTAL INCOME AND EXPENSES

         FOR UNIT NUMBER 1

RENTAL INCOME                           390.00
OTHER INCOME                              5.00

TOTAL INCOME                                        395.00

EXPENSES

ADVERTISING                              25.00
INSURANCE                               125.00
LEGAL/ACCOUNTING                         50.00
TAXES/LICENSES                          100.00
TELEPHONE/TELEGRAPH                       12.00

TOTAL EXPENSES                                      312.00
                                                  --------
CASH FLOW                                            83.00
                                                  ========

         FOR UNIT NUMBER 2

RENTAL INCOME                          1200.00
OTHER INCOME                              0.00

TOTAL INCOME                                       1200.00

EXPENSES

GARDENING                               200.00
MORTGAGE INTEREST                       755.98
TAXES/LICENSES                          200.00
TRAVEL/TRANSPORTATION                     13.25

TOTAL EXPENSES                                     1169.23
                                                  ---------
CASH FLOW                                            30.77
                                                  ========
```

287

```
0010 REM ***********************************
0020 REM *      RENTAL BOOKKEEPING       *
0030 REM ***********************************
0040 REM ********* VERSION -- *********
0050 LINE= 0
0100 PRINT :PRINT:PRINT
0110 PRINT TAB(10);"RENTAL BOOKKEEPING"
0120 PRINT
0130 INPUT "Do you wish to read a disk",Z$
0140 IF LEFT$(Z$,1)="Y" THEN 200
0150 PRINT
0160 INPUT "How many rental units",U
0170 DIM E(U,15),I(U,2)
0180 PRINT
0190 GOTO 500
0200 REM ********* READ  DISK *********
0210 INPUT "What is Drive/Sector",S
0220 OPEN #10,S
0230 PRINT
0240 READ #10,U\400
0250 DIM E(U,15),I(U,2)
0260 FOR X=1 TO U
0270 READ #10,I(X,1),I(X,2)\400
0280 NEXT X
0290 FOR X=1 TO U
0300 FOR Y=1 TO 15
0310 READ #10,E(X,Y)\400
0320 NEXT Y
0330 NEXT X
0340 PRINT
0345 CLOSE #10
0350 INPUT "Do you wish to input data",Z$
0360 IF LEFT$(Z$,1)="Y" THEN 500
0370 GOTO 1000
0400 PRINT "****** GOT A PROBLEM ******"
0410 PRINT "I'm getting a disk read error.  Please check"
0420 PRINT "to see if the proper disk is in the drive."
0430 PRINT
0440 GOTO 100
0500 REM ********* INPUT DATA *********
0510 PRINT "RENTAL INCOME":PRINT
0520 FOR X=1 TO U
0530 PRINT "For unit #";X
0540 INPUT "Rental Income",I
0550  I(X,1)=I(X,1)+I
0560 INPUT "Other Income",I
0570  I(X,2)=I(X,2)+I
0580 PRINT
0590 NEXT X
0600 PRINT "RENTAL EXPENSES":PRINT
0610 FOR X=1 TO U
0620 RESTORE
0630 PRINT "For unit #";X
0640 FOR Y=1 TO 15
```

```
0650 READ A$
0660 PRINT A$;
0670 INPUT E
0680   E(X,Y)=E(X,Y)+E
0690 NEXT Y
0700 PRINT
0710 NEXT X
0720 PRINT
0800 REM ******** WRITE A DISK ********
0810 INPUT "What disk Drive/Sector",S
0820 OPEN #10,S
0830 PRINT
0840 PRINT #10,U
0850 FOR X=1 TO U
0860 PRINT #10,I(X,1);I(X,2)
0870 NEXT X
0880 FOR X=1 TO U
0890 FOR Y=1 TO 15
0900 PRINT #10,E(X,Y)
0910 NEXT Y
0920 NEXT X
0930 CLOSE #10
1000 REM ******** PRINT  ROUTINE ********
1010 PRINT
1020 INPUT "What port for output",P
1030 PRINT #P:PRINT#P
1040 PRINT #P,TAB(27);"RENTAL INCOME AND EXPENSES"
1050 PRINT #P
1060 FOR X=1 TO U
1070 PRINT #P,TAB(10);"For Unit Number ";X
1080 PRINT #P
1090 DIGITS= 2
1100 PRINT #P,"Rental Income";
1110 PRINT #P,TAB(60-LEN(STR$(I(X,1))));I(X,1)
1120 PRINT #P,"Other Income";
1130 PRINT #P,TAB(60-LEN(STR$(I(X,2))));I(X,2)
1140   I=I(X,1)+I(X,2)
1150 PRINT #P:PRINT#P,"TOTAL INCOME";
1160 PRINT #P,TAB(70-LEN(STR$(I)));I
1170 PRINT #P
1180 PRINT #P,"EXPENSES":PRINT#P
1190 RESTORE
1200   E=0
1210 FOR Y=1 TO 15
1220 READ A$
1230 IF E(X,Y)=0 THEN 1270
1240 PRINT #P,A$;
1250 PRINT #P,TAB(60-LEN(STR$(E(X,Y))));E(X,Y)
1260   E=E+E(X,Y)
1270 NEXT Y
1280 PRINT #P:PRINT#P,"TOTAL EXPENSES";
1290 PRINT #P,TAB(70-LEN(STR$(E)));E
1300 PRINT #P,TAB(60);"-----------"
```

```
1310 PRINT #P,"CASH FLOW";
1320  C=I-E
1330 PRINT #P,TAB(70-LEN(STR$(C)));C
1340 PRINT #P,TAB(60);"=========="
1350 DIGITS= 0
1360 PRINT #P
1370 NEXT X
1380 PRINT #P,CHR$(12)
1390 INPUT "Another copy",Z$
1400 IF LEFT$(Z$,1)="Y" THEN 1000
1410 END


1500 DATA "Advertising","Cleaning","Commissions","Gardening"
1510 DATA "Insurance","Mortgage Interest","Janitor/Heating"
1520 DATA "Legal/Accounting","Repairs","Supplies","Taxes/Licenses"
1530 DATA "Telephone/Telegraph","Travel/Transportation","Utilities"
1540 DATA "Miscellaneous/Other"
```

V
WRAPPING IT UP

35
FILE MANAGER

What do you give someone who has everything? Other than
more of the same, how about a container for all those
possessions. What do you give a computer user with a
30-plus program system? A routine that will control
everything. We've produced a financial-management system
in this book. Our final program is the File Manager that
will allow you to summon any routine you want with only a
few keystrokes of entry.

When you keypunch your financial-management system,
you will modify and improve many of the programs. Some
will lengthen; some will shrink; some will disappear. All
of the programs in this book fit on one minidiskette--as
written. After modification, you may need more than one
diskette. In either event, File Manager can control the
system.

OPERATING NOTES

The sample run illustrates File Manager operation. After
a menu of the programs available in your financial management system has been presented, the routine asks which you
wish to run. Simply type the name and press the "RETURN"
key. File Manager will fetch the proper routine and start
it running. As the example shows, there is an error trap
to recycle the menu if you enter a nonexistent program name.
At the completion of each financial-management program run,
control returns to the File Manager for another menu. When
you've had enough, type "QUIT" and the management routine
will wrap things up for you. You don't need to type the
complete name of the program you wish to run, either. The
first few letters will suffice if they provide a unique
program name.

Keypunching File Manager will be a short, easy task. What will cost more time is modification of the END statements in all the other separate program routines. You'll need to perform that chore in a couple of steps, since the address of each financial-management program becomes a part of the code for File Manager.

The control routine should be the first one on the diskette. Since you can't complete the File Manager program until the rest of the disk is loaded, keypunch some dummy addresses for system programs the first time through. When everything else is loaded, you can go back and update File Manager to incorporate the proper numbers.

Let's look at the last part of the listing first. Lines 320 through 610 are DATA statements that hold the names and disk addresses of all programs in the book version of our financial-management system. (In the DOS on my computer, the program address consists of a four-digit number. The first digit specifies the drive; the next three specify the disk sector where the program starts. Since all addresses use drive 1, my disk will only operate in the first drive slot.) You can pick any names that you desire for the various programs. The titles used here are slightly different from the program titles; you may want to abbreviate the names even more. A separate DATA statement is used for each program to ease the task of changing the code.

Now, let's look at the operating code. Lines 90 through 170 print the menu and solicit user input of the desired program. The FOR...NEXT loop of lines 120 through 150 READs the program names and addresses into variables A\$, A, B\$, and B. If your financial-management system doesn't have an even number of programs, enter a null DATA item at the end of the listing for balance:

```
0620 DATA "", 0
```

should do the trick. Otherwise you'll get a BASIC READ error at run time. The numeric addresses are ignored by the PRINT command of line 140, so you can debug your menu display before you enter the proper program addresses.

The RESTORE of line 190 resets the DATA pointer before the FOR...NEXT loop of lines 220 to 270 checks program names against the operator entry; line 240 does the actual comparison. When a match is found, line 250 puts the program address into S. Line 260 terminates the loop, and line 280 calls the desired routine. (CHAIN is a multifunction command that calls for loading and running the program located at address S. If no match is found, lines 290, 300, and 310 send program flow back to the menu.

When you get the File Manager keypunched and loaded onto disk, note the starting and ending disk sectors. Your next program can be loaded after the ending address of the manager, after you change the END statement to a

CHAIN. The CHAIN should specify the start of File Manager.
(On my disk, File Manager starts at address 1001. The
END statement in every program in my version of this
financial-management system was eventually replaced with
CHAIN 1001.) Now, each program will direct computer operations back to the File Manager. This control routine will
be your most used program, so enter it carefully. When
you finish it, make at least one copy of your disk for
backup.

```
READY
# RUN
```

FINANCIAL MANAGEMENT

CHECKBOOK	TRADE STUDY
BOOKKEEPING	LIFE CYCLE COSTING
CASH FLOW	HOME INVENTORY
INCOME TAX ESTIMATE	SAVINGS ANALYSIS
BUDGET ANALYSIS	SAVINGS ACCOUNT RECORDS
CREDIT CARDS	RETIREMENT FUND
NET WORTH	BOND INVESTMENTS
CAR LOAN ANALYSIS	RETURN ON INVESTMENT
CONSUMER LOAN ANALYSIS	NET PRESENT VALUE
R.E. LOAN ANALYSIS	STOCK ANALYSIS
REAL ESTATE LOAN STATUS	10 DAY AVERAGE
LOAN RECORDS	PLOT STOCKS
LOAN PAYMENT	STOCK RECORDS
AUTO EXPENSE RECORDS	RENTAL UNIT
LEASE/BUY	RENTAL BOOKKEEPER

WHICH PROGRAM DO YOU WISH TO RUN? <u>SOLVE IT</u>

SORRY, I DON'T UNDERSTANT 'SOLVE IT' -- PLEASE TRY AGAIN.

FINANCIAL MANAGEMENT

CHECKBOOK	TRADE STUDY
BOOKKEEPING	LIFE CYCLE COSTING
CASH FLOW	HOME INVENTORY
INCOME TAX ESTIMATE	SAVINGS ANALYSIS
BUDGET ANALYSIS	SAVINGS ACCOUNT RECORDS
CREDIT CARDS	RETIREMENT FUND
NET WORTH	BOND INVESTMENTS
CAR LOAN ANALYSIS	RETURN ON INVESTMENT
CONSUMER LOAN ANALYSIS	NET PRESENT VALUE
R.E. LOAN ANALYSIS	STOCK ANALYSIS
REAL ESTATE LOAN STATUS	10 DAY AVERAGE
LOAN RECORDS	PLOT STOCKS
LOAN PAYMENT	STOCK RECORDS
AUTO EXPENSE RECORDS	RENTAL UNIT
LEASE/BUY	RENTAL BOOKKEEPER

WHICH PROGRAM DO YOU WISH TO RUN? <u>TRADE STUDY</u>

```
        TRADE STUDY
HOW MANY CANDIDATES? 3
HOW MANY FACTORS WILL YO
```

```
0010 REM *******************************
0020 REM *        FILE MANAGER         *
0030 REM *******************************
0040 REM ********* VERSION 30 *********
0050 LINE= 0
0090 PRINT :PRINT:PRINT
0100 PRINT TAB(23);"FINANCIAL MANAGEMENT"
0110 PRINT :PRINT
0120 FOR J=1 TO 15
0130 READ A$,A,B$,B
0140 PRINT A$;TAB(40);B$
0150 NEXT J
0160 PRINT :PRINT
0170 INPUT "Which program do you wish to run",P$
0180 IF P$="QUIT" THEN END
0190 RESTORE
0200  S=0
0210 PRINT
0220 FOR J=1 TO 30
0230 READ A$,A
0240 IF LEFT$(A$,LEN(P$))<>P$ THEN 270
0250  S=A
0260  J=30
0270 NEXT J
0280 IF S>1000 THEN CHAIN S
0290 PRINT "Sorry, I don't understand '";P$;"' -- Please try again."
0300 RESTORE
0310 GOTO 90
0320 DATA "CHECKBOOK",1007
0330 DATA "TRADE STUDY",1208
0340 DATA "BOOKKEEPING",1039
0350 DATA "LIFE CYCLE COSTING",1221
0360 DATA "CASH FLOW",1053
0370 DATA "HOME INVENTORY",1230
0380 DATA "INCOME TAX ESTIMATE",1063
0390 DATA "SAVINGS ANALYSIS",1239
0400 DATA "BUDGET ANALYSIS",1077
0410 DATA "SAVINGS ACCOUNT RECORDS",1247
0420 DATA "CREDIT CARDS",1099
0430 DATA "RETIREMENT FUND",1261
0440 DATA "NET WORTH",1111
0450 DATA "BOND INVESTMENTS",1267
0460 DATA "CAR LOAN ANALYSIS",1134
0470 DATA "RETURN ON INVESTMENT",1273
0480 DATA "CONSUMER LOAN ANALYSIS",1141
0490 DATA "NET PRESENT VALUE",1278
0500 DATA "R.E. LOAN ANALYSIS",1146
0510 DATA "STOCK ANALYSIS",1286
0520 DATA "REAL ESTATE LOAN STATUS",1156
0530 DATA "10 DAY AVERAGE",1293
0540 DATA "LOAN RECORDS",1161
0550 DATA "PLOT STOCKS",1301
0560 DATA "LOAN PAYMENT",1176
```

```
0570 DATA "STOCK RECORDS",1306
0580 DATA "AUTO EXPENSE RECORDS",1182
0590 DATA "RENTAL UNIT",1325
0600 DATA "LEASE/BUY",1196
0610 DATA "RENTAL BOOKKEEPER",1339
```

36
SUMMARY

Now that we've explored the four major areas of money management, credit control, major asset management, and investment factors, and you've seen all the programs, you may already have picked the programs that will make up your personal financial-management system. You certainly should have answers to the query, "What can you do with a home computer?"

You can use some of the programs without change, modify a few, combine others into different routines, and ignore the rest. When you finish, you'll have a fine financial-management system, one that reflects your own personality and needs. Any combination of programs that satisfies your needs is your system--programmed by you. Be proud of it!

You get more than a financial-control system, of course. As you adapt program ideas, you acquire a better knowledge of your BASIC. The keypunching and debugging effort will stretch your creative programming skills. You will also learn a bit more about accounting techniques. And any programs you decide not to use initially will wait on your bookshelf until you want them.

Your computerized system of financial management will be useful for years. You can stop with a baseline system and reap the benefits of your labor, or you can accept the challenge of our changing world and continue to write programs. Many of the monthly computer magazines provide ideas and listings along similar lines. Your own home needs will prompt program ideas, also. As you flex your programming muscle, look around your home and office to see where your computer can ease your burdens. You can program your digital servant to solve all manner of problems. It can be an electronic data bank, a game arena, and a mathematics whiz. If repetitive data storage or calculation will help, your computer is a natural ally.

And even though we're almost at the end of our book, this is only the beginning of a new computer power for you.

VI
APPENDIXES

APPENDIX A:
BASIC SUMMARY

Many different versions of BASIC language are available for computers. Every type of personal computer uses a BASIC that is slightly different from all others. You probably were furnished one version of BASIC with your computer. You can buy other versions to obtain faster operation, extra features, or greater standardization with other BASICs.

The BASIC language used to develop all of the programs in the book has been modified many times. It reflects the same commands used in most other BASICs now on the market. You may need to alter a few lines of your version of these programs to make the BASICs agree. The disk-operating system (DOS) in my computer is accessed by a modification called PERCOM BASIC BAND-AID (a trademark of Percom Data Company, 211 N. Kirby, Garland, Texas 75042). The rest of this appendix is a listing of the BASIC commands used in these programs. Each command is listed alphabetically, indexed by chapter, and explained briefly.

ABS The absolute value of a numeric expression. This function is used to strip the positive or negative sign from a number. (Chapters 9 and 28)

CHAIN A composite command combining the features of LOAD and RUN. It causes a program on the disk to be loaded into active computer memory and initiates program operation. (Chapter 35)

CLOSE A command for the termination of a disk file operation. It ensures that all data remaining in a disk file buffer will be recorded on the disk. (Chapters 5, 6, 16, 18, 22, 24, 30, 32, and 34)

DATA A label for program data lines, which permit storage of data within the routine. DATA statements are not executed by the program, but elements on a DATA line may be read by the program and used in PRINT commands or calculations. (Chapters 7, 10, 17, 34, and 35)

DEF An abbreviation for DEFine; this label allows special combinations of mathematical expressions to be inserted by the programmer as functions (FN). Certain computations can be performed by means of a function instead of a subroutine. DEFine is used in our programs for TAB calculations to provide a shorthand notation and save keypunch time. (Chapters 3, 5, 19, 28, 30, and 33)

DIGITS An indicator that specifies the number of digits to be printed to the right of the decimal point for numeric variables. If DIGITS=0 is set, BASIC will print nothing after the decimal point for integers and the number of digits needed for fractions. _(Chapters 3 to 9, 11 to 31, 33, and 34)

DIM An abbreviation for DIMension; this indicator is used to determine how many memory locations are to be reserved for each matrix variable. It is assumed in BASIC that each matrix variable requires 10 locations. DIMensioning to fewer than 10 will save memory space; DIMensioning to more than 10 (when necessary) will save a BASIC error message. (Chapters 3, 7, 9, 11, 16, 17, 20, 23, 24, 28 to 31, 33, and 34)

END The final statement in each program. (Chapters 3 to 35)

FOR...NEXT Indicator used to set up a program loop in which the statements between FOR and NEXT are executed a predetermined number of times. (Chapters 3, 5, 7, 9 to 12, 16, 17, 19 to 21, 23, 24, 27 to 31, and 33 to 35)

GOSUB...RETURN A command to call out a subroutine within the program. A subroutine is a sequence of instructions that is set apart in the program. Each subroutine must be terminated with a RETURN command to direct program flow back to the main routine that called the subroutine. (Chapters 5, 6, 9, 10, 16 to 18, 22, 24, and 32)

GOTO A command that causes an unconditional program jump to to the line number specified. (Chapters 3, 5 to 9, 13, 14, 16 to 20, 22 to 28, 30, and 32 to 35)

IF...THEN A conditional command that provides control of program flow during operation. When the IF condition is satisfied, the program will perform the action specified by the THEN expression. Should THEN be followed by a line number, program control will be transferred to that line when the IF condition is met. (Chapters 3 through 35)

INPUT An indicator that allows operator entry of data during program operation. (Chapters 3 through 35)

INT An abbreviation for INTeger; it provides the integer value of a mathematical expression. (Chapters 8, 9, 11, 13, 18, 22, and 31)

LEFT$ An instruction that specifies the elements of a character string variable upon which manipulations are made. The elements include the leftmost symbol and continue to the limit specified in the LEFT$(A$,n) statement. (Chapters 3 to 18, 20 to 30, and 32 to 35)

304

LEN An instruction that provides the number of characters included in a character string variable. Used most often in these programs to set a TAB function for printing. (Chapters 5 to 12, 17 to 19, 21, 23, 24, 26, and 28 to 35)

LINE An instruction to specify the line length to be recognized by the program. BASIC will transmit a carriage-return and line-feed when a space is printed within the last 25 percent of a line. To defeat this automatic feature, the programmer may enter a "LINE=0" command. (Chapters 3 to 6, 8 to 26, and 28 to 35)

LOAD A command that causes a program to be transferred from diskette (or cassette) storage into computer memory. (Not used for the programs in this book)

LOG An instruction to calculate the natural logarithm of the numeric variable specified. (Chapter 14).

MID$ An instruction that specifies the elements of a character string variable upon which manipulations will be made. The characters are designated by the MID$(A$, m,n) statement, and start with the mth character from the left and continue for n characters. (Chapters 5, 6, 18, and 24)

ON...GOTO A conditional command that transfers program flow to a line number determined by a calculated expression or a user entry. (Chapter 5)

OPEN A command used to initiate disk files. The OPEN command initializes all disk pointers and assigns a memory buffer to the disk file. (Chapters 5, 6, 16, 18, 22, 24, 30, 32, and 34)

PORT A label that defines the input/output port of the computer which will serve as the control. (Chapters 7, 9, and 11)

PRINT A command that directs BASIC to output values, defined text strings, or blanks to the terminal. Also used to write data into disk files. (Chapters 3 through 35)

READ A command used to access data in disk files or within DATA statements. (Chapters 7, 10, 16 to 18, 22, 30, 32, 34, and 35)

REM An abbreviation for REMark, a statement used to include nonexecutable comments in a program listing. (Chapters 3 through 35)

RESTORE A command to reset pointers to allow a file to be accessed anew. (Chapters 5 to 7, 10, 24, 34, and 35)

RUN A command that initiates program execution. Normally a user command, RUN may be included in a program to restart the operational sequence and initialize variables and pointers. (Chapter 32)

STR$ An instruction used to convert numeric variables to character string representation--usually for disk-storage file space management. (Chapters 5 to 9, 11, 12, 17 to 19, 21, 23, 24, 26, 28 to 30, and 32 to 34)

TAB An instruction that specifies the next PRINT position on an output device. (Chapters 3 to 13, 15 to 26, and 28 to 35)

VAL The inverse of the STR$ instruction. It provides the numeric value equivalent to a specified character string variable. (Chapters 5, 6, 14, 22, 24, and 32)

APPENDIX B:
HARDWARE

The purchase price of your computer is really only a down payment. Manufacturers are continually introducing new accessories that can make your machine more capable and useful. Fortunately, you can live without many of these advances for a while and let your computer evolve into the "ultimate" assistant. In case you'd like to profit from my experiences, I'll describe the system on which the programs in this book were developed and share my suggestions on an evolution plan for your own computer system.

MY PERSONAL SYSTEM

My personal system has evolved over about 4 years. There have been some additions, some replacements, and some soldering-iron modifications. Each month, I scan the advertisements in the various computer magazines to see if another "ultimate" accessory has hit the market. Here is my present configuration:

COMPUTER The black box that serves as the heart of my system has a 1-megahertz (approximately) microcomputer central processor unit (CPU), 36 kilobytes (K) of random-access memory (RAM), and five input/output (I/O) ports. About 10K of the memory is taken up by BASIC, and another 4K is dedicated to the disk-operating system (DOS). The I/O ports are devoted to the following tasks:

Port 0 - Tape-cassette data storage

Port 1 - Video-terminal control port

Port 2 - Dot matrix printer

Port 3 - Printing terminal (alternate control port)

Port 7 - Music generator (home-brew sound maker)

Ports 4 through 6 are not used.

DISK SYSTEM Most off-line storage is handled by a dual-drive mini-floppy disk system. The system will store 89,600 bytes of information on one side of a standard 5¼-inch minidiskette.

CASSETTE INTERFACE The tape-cassette system will read or store data on standard audio cassettes using the "Kansas City" hobbyist standard (300-baud transmission rate). Originally, tape was my only off-line storage method. Since the disk has become a part of the system, the tape interface rests on a closet shelf. It is connected only when a tape input is required.

VIDEO TERMINAL A 24-line, 80-character-per-line video terminal is the main operator interface. The terminal features a full ASCII character set and can communicate with the CPU at 9,600 baud.

PRINTING TERMINAL My printing terminal is a 72-character-per-line communications device that chugs along at 110 baud (about 10 characters per second). Although it was once the system printer, it serves as a backup terminal and I/O printer now.

DOT MATRIX PRINTER The primary-system output printer is a dot matrix impact device that will receive data at 1,200 baud and produce up to four carbon copies of output forms.

SUGGESTIONS FOR YOUR SYSTEM

How far you wish to go with your computer system will depend on your binary budget. You'll generally save a few dollars when your system is purchased in one trip to the store. You may be ahead of the game, however, if you pick up a piece at a time and master each new acquisition at your leisure.

INITIAL CONFIGURATION Your first bite of computer power should include a CPU with a minimum of 16K of user memory. The longest program in this book occupies about 12K, so the 16K in your computer provides a cushion. If you have to spend RAM for BASIC, add enough memory to have the 16K open for applications programs.

A video interface will probably come with your computer, but if you have a choice pick a printing terminal. The terminal can serve as your system printer until the right printer comes along at the right price.

Cassette storage is adequate for most of our programs. While the cassette is slower than a disk, I'd rather compute with a slow data-storage device than wait until I could afford a disk to get my computer.

ADDITIONS If you don't have a printing terminal, a printer should be <u>first</u> on your list of additions. The printer can provide your program listings for trouble-shooting as well as output reports.

After the printer, a disk system takes high priority. If you've been operating with a cassette data storage, the speed and convenience of disk will give you a rosy glow for weeks. I'd recommend that you plan on purchasing a dual-drive disk. The second drive gives you the capability to copy disks for back-up purposes and provides a hardware backup in case of mechanical breakdown of the primary drive.

If you've been using a printing terminal as your system output, a good-quality printer should be next on your priority list. Study your needs carefully before you invest in that printer. A dot matrix machine is less expensive than one of the "letter-quality" units, but don't substitute if you <u>need</u> typewriter-quality print. You may be able to get by with a thermal- or electrosensitive-paper machine, but consider the amount of printing you'll do. If you plan to output many pages per week, the money you saved on the special-paper printer may be spent on the special paper.

Other additions depend on your personal preference. A communication modulator-demodulator (modem) will be needed if you plan to join a time-sharing or electronic bulletin board service. Music, graphics, and voice capability are great if you want them. Let memory additions wait until you need them. There's no point in having a million bytes of on-line memory using up your power supply if your longest program takes only 10,000 bytes.

TAKING CARE OF BUSINESS Modern electronics technology has achieved a high level of reliability. The hardware is so reliable that we forget it can fail. A good practice is to acquire a set of diagnostic programs that will check the health of your computer electronics and run the diagnostics once a week or so. When a program stops running properly, the problem is probably in your hardware. The weekly diagnostic session is an investment in peace of mind.

APPENDIX C: MATHEMATICAL MANIPULATIONS

High on my list of "things I don't like" are books that show the first and last steps of a formula derivation and leave the rest "as an exercise for the reader." That's not my idea of exercise! This appendix answers "What happened between the first and last step?" or "How'd the author get there from here?"

INTEREST APPROXIMATION

In <u>Consumer Loan Analysis</u>, we use a formula for the first approximation of loan interest. The formula was derived from the compound interest equation:

$$P = M * \frac{1 - (1 + i)^{-n}}{i}$$

where P is the principal amount, M is monthly payment amount, n is the number of payments, and i is the interest per period. In an attempt to simplify the expression, we turn to the binomial-expansion form (see your favorite book of mathematical constants and formulae):

$$(1 + i)^{-n} = 1 - n*i + \frac{n*(n+1)*i^2}{2}$$

$$- \frac{n*(n+1)*(n+2)*i^3}{3} + \cdots$$

where 3! is 3-factorial (3 * 2 * 1). We can stand on i^2 term in our derivation, but the i^3 confuses the issue. We'll take the easy road and substitute the first three terms of the expansion into our original formula in place of $(1 + i)^{-n}$.

With the binomial-expansion substitution, the compound interest approximation equation becomes:

$$P = M * \frac{1 - 1 + n * i - \frac{n * (n + 1) * i^2}{2}}{i}$$

Since 1 - 1 = 0, these terms cancel out and disappear. We can simplify an i out of the numerator and denominator of the fraction to get:

$$P = M * (n - \frac{n * (n + 1) * i}{2})$$

If we then multiply both sides of the equation by 2 and divide by M, we have:

$$\frac{2P}{M} = 2n - n * (n + 1) * i$$

Next, we'll subtract a 2n term from both sides of the equation and multiply by -1 (to straighten up the signs):

$$2n - \frac{2P}{M} = n * (n + 1) * i$$

When we simplify the left term a bit, we're almost home:

$$2 * (n - \frac{P}{M}) = n * (n + 1) * i$$

Finally, we divide both sides by n * (n + 1) and transpose:

$$i = \frac{2 * (n - \frac{P}{M})}{n * (n + 1)}$$

which is the equation we'll use for our first approximation.

PRESENT-VALUE CALCULATION

In our <u>Real</u> <u>Estate</u> <u>Loan</u> <u>Analysis</u> program, we mechanize the calculation of loan principal value or present value by applying the compound-interest equation "straight."

CALCULATION OF PERIODIC PAYMENT

The formula manipulation to reconfigure our equation for calculation of monthly-payment amount is fairly easy. Starting with our compound-interest formula:

$$P = M * \frac{1 - (1 + i)^{-n}}{i}$$

we'll multiply both sides of the equation by the interest variable:

$$P * i = M * [1 - (1 + i)^{-n}]$$

and then divide by everything in brackets:

$$\frac{P * i}{1 - (1 + i)^{-n}} = M$$

311

Transpose to get the M on the left side where we're accustomed to seeing it, and you have the formula used in <u>Real</u> <u>Estate</u> <u>Analysis</u>.

NUMBER OF PAYMENTS

Since the number of payments is in the exponential term, we'll need to do a little special maneuvering. Starting with our compound-interest formula, we'll divide both sides by i/M:

$$\frac{i * P}{M} = 1 - (1 + i)^{-n}$$

When we subtract 1 from each side and multiply both sides by -1 to clean up the signs, we're left with:

$$1 - \frac{i * P}{M} = (1 + i)^{-n}$$

Remember that:

$$x^{-n} = \frac{1}{x^n}$$

Then let's multiply both sides of the equation by $(1 + i)^n$ and divide each side by the left-hand term:

$$1 - \frac{i * P}{M}$$

Our equation now is:

$$(1 + i)^n = \frac{1}{1 - \frac{i * P}{M}}$$

We can take the natural logarithm of both sides of the equation to pull n down out of the exponent:

$$n * \log (1 + i) = \log \left(\frac{1}{1 - \frac{i*P}{M}}\right)$$

Remember from that old algebra class that:

$$\log(x^n) = n * \log X$$

If we now divide both sides of the equation by the LOG (1 + i) term, we have a useful formula that will solve our number of payments problem:

$$n = \frac{\log \left(\frac{1}{1 - \frac{i * P}{M}}\right)}{\log (1 + i)}$$

312

In <u>Real Estate Loan Status</u>, we implement a calculation of total interest paid over a loan period. We'll back into this derivation a little. Your actual payments are M, the payment amount, times n_x, the number of payments made. This total represents interest paid and principal reduction. If we subtract the principal reduction from the total amount paid, we know how much your interest expense has been. With the payment amount and interest rate held constant, we can calculate the principal reduction by determining the remaining balance and subtracting from the original balance. To get the remaining balance, we'll again use our compound-interest formula:

$$P = M * \frac{1 - (1 + i)^{(n_x-n)}}{i}$$

By adding the number of the most recent payment n_x to the exponent, we reflect the reduction in total payments. Principal reduction is revealed by:

$$R = M * \frac{1 - (1 + i)^{-n} - 1 + (1 + i)^{(n_x-n)}}{i}$$

We can simplify the equation a little by combining terms (the ones cancel each other):

$$R_x = M * \frac{(1 + i)^{(n_x-n)} - (1 + i)^{(-n)}}{i}$$

To get the total interest paid from the beginning of the loan until payment x, we need to subtract the principal reduction from the total payments:

$$I_x = M * n_x - R_x$$

To calculate interest between any two payments, we need to compute the remaining balance at payment L (the later payment) and subtract it from the balance at payment E (the earlier payment). This principal reduction between the two payments can be used to find interest paid during the same period by subtracting the reduction from the amount paid between payment E and payment L. Our formula has three major elements. First:

$$\text{Amount paid} = M * (n_L - n_E) \tag{1}$$

Second, the principal reduction at earlier payment:

$$R_E = M * \frac{(1 + i)^{(n_E-n)} - (1 + i)^{(-n)}}{i} \tag{2}$$

Third, the principal reduction at later payment:

$$R_L = M * \frac{(1 + i)^{(n_L-n)} - (1 + i)^{(-n)}}{i} \tag{3}$$

If we subtract equation 3 from equation 2, we get:

$$R = M * \frac{(1 + i)^{(n_E - n)} - (1 + i)^{(n_L - n)}}{i} \qquad (4)$$

And then we combine equation 4 with equation 1 to get our desired answer:

$$I = M * (n_L - n_E + \frac{(1 + i)^{(n_E - n)} - (1 + i)^{(n_L - n)}}{i})$$